"Reading books like this one on [...]
ing of scriptural truths and their [...]
pecially when—I discover that I disagree fundamentally with certain presuppositions, arguments, or conclusions their subjects advance. Such is the case here. Gary Steward has done a remarkable job providing a clear and sympathetic explanation of Alexander's views on a wide array of important and relevant issues central to society and culture. I heartily commend a careful reading of this book."

Gregory A. Wills, Research Professor of Church History, Southwestern Baptist Theological Seminary

"In the past few years there has been something of a renaissance in the study of Old Princeton. Much of the attention has been on the central figures of the school such as Charles Hodge, Benjamin B. Warfield and J. Gresham Machen. Few of the lesser known figures have yet been touched. In this study we have one of the few scholarly efforts that goes beyond mere biographical detail of one of these figures, namely James W. Alexander. Working largely from Alexander's personal letters, Gary Steward presents a picture not only of a person, but of a place and an age: the northeastern United States at the height of the antebellum era. Moving beyond the immediate theological and ministerial concerns which one would expect to find in someone like Alexander, we learn about his views on slavery, democratic populism, trade unionism and education. Steward gives us an Old Princetonian who, while still sharing in the same theological mindset of his cohorts, is dealing with the "on the ground" social and political issues of his day. In this he shows us an example of Old Princeton theology in practical application. While many may not agree with Alexander's assessment or approach to these issues (some of which linger on in our own contemporary political currents), Steward provides the reader with helpful context and sympathetic consideration. Above all, this book gives us a fascinating study of one evangelical voice speaking out against the advent of a new and rising secularized American culture, a culture we still very much continue to inhabit."

Michael J. Plato, Assistant Professor of Intellectual History and Christian Thought, Colorado Christian University

"In Philippians 3:17 Paul instructs the church to 'keep your eyes on those who walk according to the example you have in us.' There seems to be an encouragement here for believers to read biographies of those who have gone before them in the Lord; and certainly Gary Steward's treatment of J.W. Alexander's life and thought falls within such criteria. Alexander was a 19th-century pastor and teacher whose life reflects how seriously he thought about the Scriptures, society, and the people of God. His genuine conviction was that the Scriptures possessed all the answers to man's problems and that they alone hold true hope for social reform in any era. I commend Steward's book to any Christian who desires to stretch his or her thinking on engaging society today."

Allen S. Nelson IV, Pastor, Perryville Second Baptist Church;
Author, *From Death to Life* and *Before the Throne*

"Christians haven't always responded well when it comes to addressing social issues. On the one end are those who capitulate to secular demands for a religionless compassion; on the other are those who overlook human suffering in the name of upholding the soul's preeminence. In *Reforming Culture*, Gary Stewart has done a masterful job uncovering the life of forgotten Princetonian James W. Alexander—a man who stalwartly resisted both ditches. For Alexander, just as it was impossible to address social reform without clear gospel reference, so it was impossible to claim personal transformation by the gospel without a resulting concern for society. In an increasingly polarized culture, I am convinced that Alexander's love for people, and his aversion to shallow solutions must become our own."

Benjamin Inglis, Editor, www.benjamininglis.ca;
Elder, Hill City Baptist Church, Peterborough

"In the current cultural milieu, where social reform is all the rage, we are in desperate need of theological conversation partners from times past to aid us in our present pursuit of following Christ in all aspects of life. Gary Steward offers us such a partner in Princetonian J.W. Alexander. Steward lets Alexander speak for himself, warts and all, which is part of what makes this work so valuable for Christians thinking about their own prejudices as it concerns cultural reform. Though Alexander's personal views on various issues may frustrate some people, moments like these create room for examining our own cultural blind spots. We need thinkers like Alexander to awaken our hearts and minds. May this be the beginning of a Christian historical retrieval of long-buried thoughts on government, economics, education, and race!"

Jordan L. Steffaniak, Co-host and Producer, The London Lyceum podcast

"James W. Alexander's approach to social reform in the first half of the nineteenth century is proof of the biblical dictum, 'What has been is what will be, and what has been done is what will be done, and there is nothing new under the sun' (Ecclesiastes 1:9). The same challenges that faced Alexander are the very same ones the church is contending with today: secular humanism, the degradation of the family unit, gender identity confusion, liberal theology, the social gospel, and the supposed utopian world promised by socialism. Alexander understood that the problems in his day grew out of a fundamental rejection of God—a worldview that has always had serious social consequences on any society where it has taken root. Alexander was also a great advocate of social order and believed the church had neglected its role in caring for the poor, much as it has done in the contemporary church. Though some of Alexander's views may seem controversial, especially his view of the abolitionist movement, it should be remembered that he was a man of his time and so should be judged accordingly. Through Alexander's life, Steward reminds us that if we fail to learn from the past, we will be condemned to repeat it."

Tony Costa, Ph.D., Professor of Islam and Apologetics,
Toronto Baptist Seminary

"The great hope for society today is an increasing number of individual Christians. Let the Church of God concentrate on that and not waste her time and energy on matters outside her province."

—Martyn Lloyd-Jones, *Studies in the Sermon the Mount*

Reforming Culture

ENG.^D BY JOHN SARTAIN FROM MURRAY PHOTOGRAPH.

REV. JAMES W. ALEXANDER, D.D.

Eng^d for the Estate

GARY STEWARD

REFORMING CULTURE

J.W. ALEXANDER'S CHRISTIAN APPROACH TO SOCIAL REFORM

FOREWORD BY **MATTHEW BARRETT**

joshua
press
AN IMPRINT OF
H&E *Publishing*

Reforming Culture: J.W. Alexander's Christian Approach to Social Reform

Copyright © 2020 Gary L. Steward

Published by: Joshua Press, Peterborough, Ontario
www.joshuapress.com

Cover design by Kseniia Piddubna
Cover image: Rocky Mountain Landscape by Albert Bierstadt, 1870
Interior font: Equity
First Edition, 2020

Paperback ISBN: 978-1-989174-45-6
Hardcover ISBN: 978-1-989174-58-6
eBook ISBN: 978-1-989174-46-3

Contents

Acknowledgements

Old Princeton is "an undiscovered country" for most. My entrance into the world of Old Princeton was through books and reprints published by the Banner of Truth Trust, some of which are referenced in this work. I am deeply thankful for the work of Iain Murray and others connected with Banner of Truth for first bringing the world of Old Princeton to my attention. I am especially grateful for David Calhoun's two-volume history of Princeton Seminary, which powerfully stirred in me over twenty years ago a desire to discover more about the greats who once taught there.

Those wanting to research Old Princeton now have access to a large amount of primary source material, thanks to the staff of the Special Collections division at the Princeton Seminary library. They have done an invaluable service in digitizing many of the books and journals connected with their institution. I am personally thankful for the hospitality and helpfulness shown to me during my visit to Princeton in November 2009 by the Special Collections staff, especially Kenneth Henke, Clifford Anderson, and Sarah Seraphin. The staff of the Special Collections department at the Princeton University's Firestone Library was courteous and helpful as well. Many others helped me in tracking down material related to J. W. Alexander, including Dale W. Hansen, church archivist at the Fifth Avenue Presbyterian Church in New York City, Pastor John Allan and Maria Newman of the First Presbyterian Church of Trenton, New Jersey, and the staff of the Newark Public Library's microfilm room. It was in this last location that I was able to locate Alexander's newspaper articles on trade unions, reproduced in Appendix 1.

This book originally began as a master's thesis written in 2010 as the culmination of a course of study at Westminster Theological

Seminary in Philadelphia under the auspices of the John Owen Centre for Theological Study, now called the Pastors Academy, at the London Theological Seminary, now called London Seminary. I am grateful for the friendship and hospitality of Philip and Jenny Eveson and the staff of LTS for their assistance in helping me through this program. Steve Nichols is also to be thanked for his support and helpful suggestions for this project. I was able to write the original work while serving as the pastor of Calvary Baptist Church in St. John's, Newfoundland, Canada, and I continue to be thankful for the ongoing friendship and support of the members of Calvary who allowed me to pursue this program of study alongside of my service to the church. Derek Butler, along with my mother-in-law Sally Michael and my brother Brian Steward, were supportive with their careful proofreading. As always, my wife Amy and our children Anna, Katie, and Joshua, continue to be a constant source of joy and encouragement.

I am grateful to P&R Publishing for giving me permission to reuse some of the material which lies behind this book. Portions of this work have been previously published in my introductory book on Old Princeton, entitled *Princeton Seminary (1812–1929): Its Leaders' Lives and Works* (Phillipsburg, NJ: P&R, 2014). Some material found in this current work originally appeared in chapters 8 and 9 of *Princeton Seminary*. Readers are encouraged to see this book for a broader exploration of Princeton Seminary's other leading theologians.

Finally, I'm thankful to Chance Faulkner and the staff of Joshua Press for their encouragement to publish this material in a revised form. While almost a decade has elapsed since this project began, it now seems timelier than ever, given the variety of views on social issues and social justice pressing upon the church today.

Gary L. Steward
Arvada, Colorado
January 20, 2020

Foreword

James W. Alexander has been forgotten. When Old Princeton resurfaces today, most remember B. B. Warfield or Charles Hodge. That is understandable: Warfield and Hodge were the theological stewards of their day; their tomes helped the church and academy alike maintain Reformed doctrine in an era of liberalism. But it was Alexander who, perhaps more than most, wrestled with challenges from the culture. Unfortunately, many assume such cultural challenges are now remnants of a bygone era, no longer relevant to the hurdles Christians face today. That assumption could not be more mistaken. The past has a way of repeating itself, or at least reincarnating itself. The culture has certainly evolved since Alexander's day—and perhaps in ways he could not have anticipated—but Alexander remains a lasting example of an evangelical attempting to live out his convictions in a world at odds. And Gary Steward, one of the premier historians of Old Princeton, is just the right person to reintroduce Alexander to contemporary evangelical Christians.

I admire Steward's courage in doing so, a historical boldness that is rare these days. Alexander will be a shock to evangelicals today, though it might just be the type of jolt evangelicals need. Many evangelicals have been trained to be culture warriors, approaching every and any issue in the culture as if it's warfare. Not Alexander. He presents us with a far more mature model of social reform. "Instead of building the kingdom of Christ by polemics, Alexander believed the church would primarily advance in the world by engaging those outside of it with truth and action," says Steward. Many evangelicals are so zealous to run into this cultural battlefield waving the social justice flag that they, intentionally or unintentionally, have slipped into a social gospel. Not Alexander. "While committed to social reform, Alexander rejected 'social gospel' approaches that minimized the central issue of personal salvation through faith in Jesus Christ" and was "careful to not bring his political opinions into his ministry." Many evangelicals are more concerned with whether the person in political office is agreeable to their ideal evangelical identity or matches their moral compass exactly that they could not care less whether their decisions in the booth result in a subtle but constant shift towards socialism. Not Alexander. He was suspicious of "social egalitarianism" and "utopian socialism in antebellum America," perceiving an underlying "secularism" that threatened the fabric of American virtues and democracy.

That is not to say, however, that the reader should follow Alexander blindly. For example, as an adherent to a two-kingdom approach to Christianity and culture, I might push back on the variety of ways Alexander meshes church and society, as if it is the responsibility of the former to transform the latter. I want to arm wrestle Alexander when he assumes the best way to transform society is just to make more followers of Christ. While there is some truth to that optimism, it assumes there is *the* Christian way to accomplish social reform. Not always, but Alexander may overlook God's common grace, collapsing God's sovereign reign over the natural order through ordinary means and institutions with his reign as Redeemer over his church through his special grace (the gospel). I can't help but wonder whether Alexander's approach to social reform might have been all the more effective if he had adopted a more nuanced approach to Christ and culture.

I also anticipate that readers will squirm at Alexander's solution to slavery. On the one hand, Alexander is a man ahead of his time, doing what many other Christians in his day refused to do: condemn slavery. "Slavery appalls me," Alexander once said. "I abhor slavery, and think the public mind should be enlightened, and every lawful means immediately taken for an eventual and speedy abolition." On the other hand, Alexander worried that instant liberation might create social chaos and even harm slaves and their families, leaving them destitute. Alexander also sympathized with slaveholders who provided for their slaves. Ultimately, Alexander could not support the abolitionist party; he grew frustrated with the political agenda lurking behind some of their politicians, believing they did not really care about putting to death racism as did Alexander. Christians today will likely have mixed feelings about Alexander on this issue, celebrating his condemnation of slavery and racism, but nevertheless irritated by his post-millennial optimism which led him to prioritize the slave's spiritual bondage over his physical bondage.

But the point of historical retrieval is not wholesale repristination, as if we can only appreciate or recover insight from historical figures that meet our modern standards. Not only does such an approach cultivate anachronistic history, failing to understand someone like Alexander within his own (very complicated) cultural context, but it reeks of what C. S. Lewis called chronological snobbery. All too often, evangelicals take their evolved moral outlook—which they assume is superior in every way to everyone who lived before them—and impose that standard back onto their Christian forefathers. In the name of social justice, it has even become acceptable to question whether the stalwarts of church history could be true Christians at all. If the reader brings such historical hubris to Alexander, he or she will conclude the man had no Holy Ghost in him at all. I would hate to see how Christians a century or two from now will judge our blind spots. We live in an age that worships tolerance all the while intolerant of anyone who disagrees. Are we no better, incapable of sitting at the feet of giants without stomping out of their classrooms the minute their evaluations do not live up to our own?

For that reason alone, Gary Steward's treatment of Alexander deserves to be read and re-read, consumed and absorbed. Not only does Steward model historical scholarship, but most importantly historical humility. If we cannot learn from someone like Alexander—warts and all as they say—then perhaps we can learn from no one at all.

Matthew Barrett
Associate Professor of Christian Theology,
Midwestern Baptist Theological Seminary;
Executive Editor, *Credo Magazine*

Introduction

Many Christians today are wrestling with questions of cultural reform, "social justice," and the social witness of the church. Those so engaged need the insights of history and the perspective of other believers who have addressed similar issues in the past. The socio-political questions facing believers today are nothing new. In fact, the theological leaders at Princeton Seminary wrestled with questions of social, racial, and economic disparities at great length. While we might not approach all of these questions in exactly the same way, it is important to listen to their thoughts and see what insights might be retrieved and wisely applied in the present.

The theological seminary established in 1812 at Princeton, New Jersey, had a significant impact upon the culture of antebellum America.[1] Its predecessor, the College of New Jersey, also helped shape American culture, with ministers Jonathan Dickinson, Aaron Burr, Sr., Jonathan Edwards, Samuel Davies, and John Witherspoon serving as some of its early presidents.[2] The cultural and religious significance of

---

[1] The seminary is now called Princeton Theological Seminary. It was originally referred to as the Theological Seminary of the Presbyterian Church in the United States of America, although the town's name quickly attached itself to the seminary. See *A Brief History of the Theological Seminary of the Presbyterian Church at Princeton, New Jersey* (Princeton: John Bogart, 1838), 10. For more on the religious and cultural impact of Princeton Seminary, see Mark A. Noll, ed., *The Princeton Theology, 1812–1921* (Grand Rapids: Baker Book House, 1983), 12–24.

[2] The College of New Jersey was the third institution of its kind established in America, preceded only by Harvard and Yale. Beginning in 1746 in Elizabethtown and relocating to Trenton in 1747, the college was moved to Princeton in 1756. It was long known as Princeton College, but it now bears

these institutions notwithstanding, few historical studies have been done on "Old Princeton" and its response to American culture.[3] Daryl Hart once observed that "the work on the Princeton theology has rarely moved beyond questions about Common Sense Philosophy and biblical inerrancy. Fuller treatments of Northern Presbyterian thought and culture have not been attempted."[4] It is a curious thing that a group so regarded as spiritual and theological leaders would be so widely ignored when it comes to social, political, and cultural issues.

Many of those who have written on Old Princeton have criticized the Princetonians' interaction with their surrounding culture. Mark Noll leaves the impression that the Princetonians unwittingly and uncritically adopted much of their overall outlook from the culture around them, stating that to a great extent the Princetonians "sailed along with the American intellectual mainstream."[5] Even Andrew Hoffecker, a

---

the name of Princeton University. For biographical sketches of hundreds of those who trained at Princeton in the eighteenth century, see Samuel Davies Alexander, *Princeton College During the Eighteenth Century* (New York: Anson D. F. Randolph, 1872). For more on the College of New Jersey, see Mark A. Noll, *Princeton and the Republic, 1768-1822* (Vancouver: Regent College Publishing, 1989).

[3] "Old Princeton" is commonly used to refer to Princeton Seminary as it existed from its beginning in 1812 to its reorganization in 1929. For a brief introduction to some of the leading figures of Old Princeton and their thought, see Gary Steward, *Princeton Seminary (1812-1929): Its Leaders' Lives and Works* (Phillipsburg, NJ: P&R, 2014). See also David B. Calhoun, *Princeton Seminary*, 2 vols. (Edinburgh: Banner of Truth, 1994–1996).

[4] Daryl G. Hart, *Defending the Faith: J. Gresham Machen and the Crisis of Conservative Protestantism in Modern America* (Philipsburg, NJ: Presbyterian and Reformed, 2003), 213.

[5] Noll, *The Princeton Theology*, 35. Noll views much of the theology in antebellum America as "Americanized" and heavily influenced by an uncritical accommodation to American political theory. See Mark A. Noll, *America's God: From Jonathan Edwards to Abraham Lincoln* (New York: Oxford University Press, 2000). Dissenting from Noll, Brooks Holifield understands antebellum American theologians to be "absorbed in European conversations" and more heavily influenced by "denominational competition" than by their broader American culture. See E. Brooks Holifield, "Republican Dialect or European Accent? The Sound of American Theology," *Church History* 72

great admirer of Old Princeton, once suggested that the Princetonians were culturally naïve and unable to intellectually relate their theology to their culture in a satisfactory manner, saying that "they displayed little sensitivity to historical conditions shaping doctrines and to the necessity of contextualizing faith for each generation."[6] If these things are true, then there perhaps is no reason to hear what they might have to say about social and cultural issues. Critics notwithstanding, the notion that the Princetonians were culturally uncritical and unreflective does not bear up when taking into account the whole scope of their writings. Where the Princetonians commented on social issues, one finds them biblically-informed, thoughtful, and discerning in their interaction with contemporary American culture.

Of all the Princeton theologians, James W. Alexander's comments on social reform are the most extensive and interesting. On social and cultural issues, instead of seeing a figure who "sailed along with the American intellectual mainstream," one sees a thoughtful Christian who "sailed against" many of the various strands of popular American thought with counter-cultural positions taken on a number of issues. He advocated a distinctly Christ-centered approach to social reform in contrast with a number of other secular reform movements and trends that were popular in the nineteenth century.

The following work examines James W. Alexander's approach to social reform in its antebellum American context. Chapter 1 gives an overview of Alexander's life and work, paying special attention to his interest in social reform as a Christian pastor and culturally-engaged intellectual. Chapter 2 analyzes his political views and his understanding of how a society should best be structured and governed. Chapters 3–5 analyze his interaction with four forms of social reform he rejected

---

(2003): 627. For Holifield's evaluation of Old Princeton, see E. Brooks Holifield, *Theology in America: Christian Thought from the Age of the Puritans to the Civil War* (New Haven: Yale University Press, 2003), 370–389.

[6] W. Andrew Hoffecker, "Princeton Theology" in *Dictionary of Christianity in America*, ed. Daniel G. Reid (Downers Grove, IL: InterVarsity Press, 1990), 941.

as fundamentally deficient: utopian socialism, trade unionism, abolitionism, and the "common school" movement. Chapter 6 describes his
own views and efforts for social reform, efforts which centered on the
spread of Christianity.

This examination of Alexander's views seeks to present his position largely in his own words, with minimal criticism. As such, this
work will largely be a restatement of how one committed follower of
Christ interacted with antebellum American culture and its varied social issues. Readers may be startled or surprised by some of his perspectives and choice of language, and yet this kind of historical study can
help us see our own assumptions and concerns in a new light. While
readers today may choose to take different positions than Alexander,
we should respect the fact that he was attempting to faithfully work out
his evangelical and Christian convictions in his own particular context.
The attempt to apply biblical truth to contemporary issues is a practice
we must do afresh in every generation. We cannot apply Alexander's
views uncritically to today's problems, but listening to his perspective
can help us avoid the uncritical adoption of views and trends today that
are merely faddish and not adequately Christian.

Chapter 1

J. W. Alexander:
Pastor and Social Reformer

James Waddel Alexander is not well known today. Scholars have published works on some of the theologians of Old Princeton, but little analysis has been done on the life and thought of Alexander.[1] Recognizing this oversight, historian John W. Stewart has written that "very little has been published about Archibald Alexander's two sons [James Waddel and Joseph Addison], who were extraordinary scholars in their own rights."[2] Only one doctoral dissertation has been produced on James W. Alexander, and this deals primarily with Alexander's rhetorical style and practice.[3] James Garretson has recently published an

---

[1] For studies on other leading figures at Old Princeton, in addition to those mention in the introduction, see: Lefferts A. Loetscher, *Facing the Enlightenment and Pietism: Archibald Alexander and the Founding of Princeton Theological Seminary* (Westport, CN: Greenwood Press, 1983), John W. Stewart and James H. Moorehead, eds., *Charles Hodge Revisited: A Critical Appraisal of His Life and Work* (Grand Rapids: William B. Eerdmans, 2002), James M. Garretson, *Princeton and Preaching: Archibald Alexander and the Christian Ministry* (Edinburgh: Banner of Truth, 2005), Gary L. W. Johnson, ed., *B. B. Warfield: Essays on His Life and Thought* (Phillipsburg, NJ: Presbyterian and Reformed, 2007), Paul Kjoss Helseth, *"Right Reason" and the Princeton Mind: An Unorthodox Proposal* (Phillipsburg, NJ: Presbyterian and Reformed, 2010), Fred G. Zaspel, *The Theology of B. B. Warfield* (Wheaton: Crossway, 2010), and James M. Garretson, *An Able and Faithful Ministry: Samuel Miller and the Pastoral Office* (Grand Rapids: Reformation Heritage, 2014).

[2] John W. Stewart, "Introducing Charles Hodge to Postmoderns," in Stewart and Morehead, *Charles Hodge Revisited*, 9.

[3] Gregory Martin Anderson, "The Religious Rhetoric of James W. Alexander: Texts and Contexts of an Antebellum Rhetorical Tradition" (PhD diss., University of Minnesota, 1994). Anderson doesn't deal with the broad

overview of Alexander's life that emphasizes his views on preaching and pastoral ministry.[4] Apart from this, however, no other substantial work on Alexander has appeared.

Alexander left an enormous amount of material behind for scholars to examine. He published over thirty popular books for the American Sunday School Union and over one hundred articles for the *Biblical Repertory and Princeton Review*.[5] A volume of sermons, a full biography of his father, and numerous other works are also readily available today.[6] Apart from his own published articles and books, much of what we know about Alexander is contained in a unique collection of regular letters sent over a forty-year period of time to his one regular correspondent, John Hall, a boyhood acquaintance who also became a Presbyterian minister.[7] Upon Alexander's death, Hall edited and published this series of letters in a two-volume work entitled *Forty Years' Familiar Letters of James W. Alexander, D. D.*[8] These letters contain a wealth of historical information about antebellum American culture from a

scope of Alexander's thought, and he unhelpfully asserts that the theological and intellectual views of Alexander and the Princetonians have been sufficiently studied (Anderson, "Religious Rhetoric of James W. Alexander," 2, cf. 5).

[4] James M. Garretson, *Thoughts on Preaching & Pastoral Ministry: Lessons from the Life and Writings of James W. Alexander* (Grand Rapids: Reformation Heritage, 2015).

[5] The most complete listing of Alexander's writings is contained in *The Biblical Repertory and Princeton Review: The Index Volume, 1825-1868* (Philadelphia: Peter Walker, 1871), 67–82. For more on the *Index Volume*, see "Notices of Recent Publications," *Biblical Repertory and Princeton Review* 42 (1870): 338–339.

[6] James W. Alexander, *Discourses on Common Topics of Christian Faith and Practice* (New York: Charles Scribner, 1858; repr., *A Shepherd's Heart: Sermons from the Pastoral Ministry of J. W. Alexander*, Birmingham, AL: Solid Ground Christian Books, 2004); James W. Alexander, *The Life of Archibald Alexander, D. D.* (New York: Charles Scribner, 1854; repr., Harrisonburg, VA: Sprinkle Publications, 1991).

[7] See *The Biblical Repertory and Princeton Review: Index Volume*, 189–190.

[8] James W. Alexander, *Forty Years' Familiar Letters of James W. Alexander, D. D.*, ed. John Hall, 2 vols. (New York: Charles Scribner, 1860).

Princetonian's candid perspective. Shortly after Alexander's death, Hall published these letters at the instigation of Charles Hodge, the leading Old Princeton theologian in antebellum America.[9] In a letter to Hall, Hodge encouraged him to make Alexander's letters public, stating: "This would be a unique work. It would be a literary, a theological, a religious and a conversational history of the past forty years."[10] Indeed, these letters are a unique and firsthand account of life in antebellum America. In a memorial address given in 1879, New York Presbyterian Theodore Cuyler lauded high praise on this published series of letters with these words:

> James Hamilton, of London, once said to me that a perusal of them [Alexander's letters] was the next best thing to a visit to America. The most brilliant Bishop in the Methodist Church also said to me that he regarded it as one of the dozen most remarkable works yet produced in this country! To the future historian it will be as valuable a picture of the times as Pepys' Diary and Burnet's Memoirs were to Lord Macaulay.[11]

Similarly, John W. Stewart has observed that these volumes of letters contain "a gold mine of insights about the Princeton theologians' participation in American culture."[12] While scholars have neglected these letters in historical studies of Old Princeton, they remain a major source for understanding Alexander's life, thought, and interaction with American culture.

---

[9] Archibald A. Hodge, *The Life of Charles Hodge, D.D., LL.D.* (London: T. Nelson and Sons, 1881), 436.

[10] Archibald Hodge, *Life of Charles Hodge*, 436.

[11] Theodore L. Cuyler, "Address on James Waddell Alexander, D.D." in *The Alexander Memorial* (New York: Anson D. F. Randolph, 1879), 23–24. Other reviewers of these volumes of letters also noted their uniqueness as a repository of historical information and commentary. See "Notices of Books," *New Englander and Yale Review* 18 (August 1860): 843.

[12] Stewart, "Introducing Charles Hodge to Postmoderns," 9.

Contemporaries of Alexander recognized him as a leading intellectual leader in the American Presbyterian church. Charles Hodge said of him in a memorial sermon given a few months after Alexander's death:

> Probably no minister in our Church was a more accomplished scholar. He was familiar with English literature in all periods of its history. He cultivated the Greek and Latin, French, German, Italian, and Spanish languages ... He was an erudite theologian. Few men were more conversant with the writings of the early fathers, or more familiar with Christian doctrine in all its phases.[13]

Hodge went on to eulogize Alexander's character, piety, philosophical acumen, literary abilities, and unique gifting as a preacher, concluding that he was "the first of preachers to sit under, month after month and year after year."[14] That such a significant and well-respected church leader is virtually unknown in our day requires that a general overview of Alexander's life be given before examining his views on social reform.

A Life between Princeton and the Pastorate

On March 13, 1804, James Waddel Alexander was born in Louisa County, Virginia.[15] The eldest of seven children, James was named

---

[13] Charles Hodge, "[Memorial] Sermon," in Charles Hodge and John Hall, *Sermons Preached Before the Congregation of the Presbyterian Church, Corner of Fifth Avenue and Nineteenth Street, at the "Memorial Services," October 9, 1859. Appointed in Reference to the Death of their Late Pastor, James Waddel Alexander, D. D.* (New York: Anson D. F. Randolph, 1859; repr., *Mourning a Beloved Shepherd: Memorial Sermons for James W. Alexander*, Birmingham, AL: Solid Ground Christian Books, 2004), 28.

[14] Charles Hodge, "[Memorial] Sermon," 33. For further assessment of Alexander as a preacher, see Anderson, "Religious Rhetoric of James W. Alexander," 5.

[15] There is some discrepancy as to the proper spelling of our subject's full name. Alexander's tombstone in the Princeton Cemetery spells his middle name as "Waddell," as do many of his children's gravestones. A genealogical

after his maternal grandfather, James Waddel, a blind Presbyterian minister known for his powerful preaching.[16] James grew up under the care and instruction of his father, Archibald Alexander, a Presbyterian minister and scholar noted for his wide range of learning, deep spirituality, and wise pastoral counsels. Archibald Alexander was the president of Hampden-Sydney College when James was born, and he went on to become the first professor at Princeton Seminary in 1812. After being instructed by a series of teachers and tutors, young Alexander entered the College of New Jersey at Princeton in 1817.[17] As a college student, he did not apply himself fully to his studies. In an early letter to Hall, Alexander stated:

> My time spent in college ran sadly to waste; indeed, I cannot look back upon the opportunities of acquiring useful knowledge which I then abused without shame and regret. Like most brainless and self-conceited boys, I undertook to determine that such and such studies were of no importance, and made this an excuse for neglecting them, although the wise of every age have united in declaring their utility. I was foolish enough to suffer almost all my previous knowledge of classical literature to leak out *e cerebro*, and consequently I found myself a much greater dolt when I was invested with the

---

record drawn up by William Alexander, James's son, also spells his name this way (William Alexander, "The Alexander Family — Virginia, Princeton, New York, Branch," 1920, Alexander Family Collection, 1:1, Department of Rare Books and Special Collections, Princeton University Library, Princeton, NJ). Alternatively, a cenotaph in Alexander's Fifth Avenue Presbyterian Church in New York City contains the variation "Waddel." While some printed publications contain the name "Waddell," the most common way of spelling out his middle name is "Waddel," and most material is to be found under this spelling.

[16] For more on James Waddel, see James W. Alexander, *Memoir of the Rev. James Waddel, D.D.* (n.p., 1880); and William Buell Sprague, *Annals of the American Pulpit*, 9 vols. (New York: Robert Carter and Brothers, 1857–1869), 3:235–242.

[17] For information on Alexander's early education, see John Hall, preface to James W. Alexander, *Forty Years' Letters*, 1:viii.

title and immunities of an A. B., than when I entered as a humble freshman.[18]

After graduating from Princeton College in 1820, he found it necessary to supplement his failed education with an almost two-year round of self-study in the classics. Through doing this, Alexander came to highly value the classical literature of ancient Greece and Rome, studying with the young Charles Hodge for "an hour each day...for eighteen months."[19]

As a teenager, Alexander entrusted his life to Christ and soon felt drawn toward pastoral ministry. Toward the end of his undergraduate studies, he confided to Hall that for the first time truly he "felt able to trust my whole hope and life upon the Lord."[20] A few months after this, he also came to the conclusion that "I never can, in conscience, embrace any other profession [i.e. vocation] but 'the gospel of Christ.'"[21] Despite having doubts about his natural abilities as a speaker, Alexander came to the conclusion that God might be able to at least make him "a useful preacher." He entered Princeton Seminary in 1822 and began his studies under the theological faculty of his father, Archibald Alexander, Samuel Miller, and Charles Hodge.[22] Through his entire career as a seminary student, Alexander flourished in the social atmosphere of learning, literature, and scholarship, and he took on his studies with new energy and devotion.[23] He completed his formal education in

---

[18] Alexander, *Forty Years' Letters*, 1:5.

[19] Alexander, *Forty Years' Letters*, 1:5, 7, 11.

[20] Alexander, *Forty Years' Letters*, 1:4.

[21] Alexander, *Forty Years' Letters*, 1:4.

[22] Alexander, *Forty Years' Letters*, 1:4.

[23] Alexander, *Forty Years' Letters*, 1:14–16, 41. In his memorial sermon, Hall stated: "The letters from his years in the Seminary are eloquent with descriptions of his enjoyments of the studies and of the companionship of the band of congenial minds, with whom the topics of the classroom were subjects of animated discussion in their more private and social encounters" (John Hall, "[Memorial] Sermon," in Charles Hodge and John Hall, *Sermons Preached Before the Congregation of the Presbyterian Church, Corner of Fifth Avenue and Nineteenth Street, at the "Memorial Services," October 9, 1859.*

1824, graduating from Princeton Seminary after two years of biblical and theological studies.

Alexander did not enter pastoral ministry right after seminary. Upon graduation, the trustees of Princeton College elected him to serve as a tutor in mathematics, much to his surprise.[24] While his "feelings instantly revolted" at the thought of tutoring, he accepted it after further consideration, concluding that "my mind needs maturing before taking upon me the character of a minister."[25] While he was tutor, he revealed to Hall his tendency toward "melancholy" and depression.[26] This would be a lifelong struggle for Alexander, as Hall later recounted:

> Even in that early period of his life, he was becoming acquainted with the violent and sudden alternations to which his delicate temperament continued subject, from the highest pitch of joyous excitement to the depths of melancholy and indescribable misery. ...Ascribe it to whatever cause we may, to delicate or disordered nerves, to morbid sensibilities, whether physical or moral, to excessive intellectual excitement, to preternatural susceptibility to the extremes of enjoyment and suffering, we know from the result, that this part of experience familiar to him in a greater or less measure from his youth to his last days, was the means sanctified to the production and maintenance of that depth, fullness, and richness of his spiritual traits.[27]

Appointed in Reference to the Death of their Late Pastor, James Waddel Alexander, D. D. (New York: Anson D. F. Randolph, 1859; repr., *Mourning a Beloved Shepherd: Memorial Sermons for James W. Alexander*, Birmingham, AL: Solid Ground Christian Books, 2004), 49.

[24] He was later charged with teaching the classics. See Alexander, *Forty Years' Letters*, 1:78.

[25] Alexander, *Forty Years' Letters*, 1:42.

[26] Alexander, *Forty Years' Letters*, 1:43–44, 49.

[27] Hall, "[Memorial] Sermon," 49–51.

Although Alexander gradually came to enjoy tutoring in Princeton, he decided to be licensed as a "probationer" for the ministry in the fall of 1825, taking up an itinerant ministry under the oversight of the Presbytery of New Brunswick in New Jersey.[28]

Alexander's first pastoral charge was in Virginia. After many months as a licentiate, he was called in 1827 to be a pastor in southern Virginia at Charlotte Court House in Louisa County, close to his family's roots. His father had once served in this church.[29] Alexander felt a strong familial attachment to Virginia, so he was happy to go there. While a seminary student, he had written to Hall:

> But all transmarine voyages apart, my wish to visit Virginia, the old dominion, the land of my fathers, my own natal soil,— to see the ruin (now a barn) in which my grandfather preached, the valley where I first saw the sun, the mountains where my father spent his boyhood, and where the Alexanders are "rife" even now; this wish I would not, and cannot repress.[30]

While in Virginia, Alexander enjoyed the opportunities a rural pastorate gave him for study, but he missed the mental stimulation he had enjoyed in Princeton: "I feel the need of some extrinsic excitement which might urge to continued exertion: the total absence of this, and the stagnation of mind consequent upon this want, convince me that I shall not lose by going forward a few steps nearer to the busy world."[31] For four years, Alexander remained in this pastorate until sickness made it necessary for him to resign and seek recovery before considering a pastorate in another church.[32]

---

[28] Alexander, *Forty Years' Letters*, 1:88.

[29] Charles Hodge, "[Memorial] Sermon," 25.

[30] Alexander, *Forty Years' Letters*, 1:33.

[31] Alexander, *Forty Years' Letters*, 1:115.

[32] Charles Hodge, "[Memorial] Sermon," 25. See also Hall, "[Memorial] Sermon," 56. Alexander blamed the southern climate for his episode of

Alexander's next church would be located in New Jersey, closer to his boyhood home in Princeton. In 1829 he accepted a call to serve as the pastor of First Presbyterian Church in Trenton—then the only Presbyterian congregation in the city.[33] At this same time, he became involved in writing and editing the *Biblical Repertory and Theological Review*.[34] While it is unclear how long Alexander filled the role of editor of this reputable journal, he continued to write regularly for it for the rest of his life.[35] Charles Hodge would state later in life: "To no one are the pages of this *Review* more indebted than to the late Dr. James W. Alexander. His communications were always numerous, varied, and instructive. The articles furnished by him were, for the most part, devoted to historical, literary, and practical subjects."[36] Alexander also began at this time to write regularly for the American Sunday School Union.[37] In this situation in Trenton, he seemed to thrive as a pastor.[38]

"bilious fever" (Alexander, *Forty Years' Letters*, 1:107). While convalescing in Princeton, Alexander stated: "I shall never seek a settlement south of the Potomac unless driven to it by necessity" (Alexander, *Forty Years' Letters*, 1:112).

[33] Hall, "[Memorial] Sermon," 57.

[34] Alexander, *Forty Years' Letters*, 1:137-138, 140. See also Hall, "[Memorial] Sermon," 57. This publication was started in 1825 by Charles Hodge as *The Biblical Repertory*. Its name changed to *The Biblical Repertory and Theological Review* in 1830 and *The Biblical Repertory and Princeton Review* in 1837.

[35] Archibald Hodge, *Life of Charles Hodge*, 436. See also *The Biblical Repertory and Princeton Review Index Volume*, 73.

[36] [Charles Hodge], "Retrospect of the History of the Princeton Review" in *The Biblical Repertory and Princeton Review Index Volume*, 2. Mark Noll says that Alexander "contributed more material to the *Biblical Repertory and Princeton Review* than anyone else except Charles Hodge" (Noll, *The Princeton Theology*, 16). For more on Alexander's contribution to the *Princeton Review*, see Mark Noll, "The *Princeton Review*," *Westminster Theological Journal* 50 (1988): 292-294.

[37] Hall, "[Memorial] Sermon," 57.

[38] Alexander was married to Elizabeth Cabell in 1830 (Alexander, *Forty Years' Letters*, 143). Together they would have seven children, only three of whom (Henry Carrington, James Waddell, Jr., and William) survived to adulthood. For genealogical information on Alexander's children, see William

After turning down a call to a church in Baltimore, Alexander wrote to Hall in 1832 of his satisfaction with his ministry in Trenton:

> If I am to be a pastor, and nothing but necessity could make me willing to be any thing else, I believe I have more openings to serve Christ here, than in any more laborious charge. ... Some of my most delightful hours have been spent in sick-rooms, by dying-beds, or among poor, unlettered believers, or especially in rejoicing with them that do rejoice for the first time in Christ.[39]

Alexander's failing health again disrupted his ministry and forced him to seek a change of pace.[40] After receiving invitations both from the American Sunday School Union and the proprietors of a periodical called the *Presbyterian*, Alexander resigned his ministry in Trenton and relocated in January 1833 to Philadelphia to serve as the editor of the *Presbyterian*.[41] He hoped that this position would afford him more rest.

Alexander's career as an editor in Philadelphia was short-lived, however. Before the year was out, he was appointed to serve as the Professor of Rhetoric and *Belles Lettres* at Princeton College. He accepted this position, believing, according to Hall, that "a less vexatious and more retired department would be better suited to his taste and circumstances."[42] He served in this role at Princeton for eleven years, and even as a professor he continued to preach regularly and write numerous books and articles for a popular audience.[43] While the halls of learning had their charms, the memory of full-time pastoral work continued

---

Alexander, "The Alexander Family," Department of Rare Books and Special Collections, Princeton University Library, Princeton, NJ.

[39] Alexander, *Forty Years' Letters*, 1:185.

[40] *The Biblical Repertory and Princeton Review Index Volume,* 72.

[41] Alexander, *Forty Years' Letters*, 1:197–198.

[42] Hall, "[Memorial] Sermon," 69.

[43] Hall, "[Memorial] Sermon," 69–72. During these years as a teacher, Alexander's preaching "averaged sixty times for each year" (*The Biblical Repertory and Princeton Review Index Volume,* 73).

to pull at him. While teaching oratory and classical literature in Princeton, he confided to Hall in 1839: "I sigh to be a pastor, instead of a professor."[44]

In 1844 Alexander was back in the pastorate, this time as the pastor of Duane Street Church in New York City. In this bustling metropolis, Alexander worked tirelessly for those under his charge, taking a special interest in his weekly catechism classes with a number of children of church-going families.[45] He continued to write prolifically while engaged in this busy urban setting. In spite of his preference for pastoral work, he was soon called back to the classroom in Princeton. In 1849 the General Assembly of the Presbyterian Church appointed him to be the Professor of Ecclesiastical History and Church Government at Princeton Seminary, thus filling the vacancy created by Samuel Miller's retirement. Upon hearing of the General Assembly's decision, Alexander was filled with sorrow:

> This thing gives me unspeakable pain. …any little unction of
> flattery in the appointment is instantly more than absorbed by
> the greatness of the question, and the anguish of a separation
> from my charge, if I accept. …to *know* that I might remain here
> would be a joy unspeakable. No dream of mine respecting the
> social happiness of the pastoral relation have failed to be real-
> ized: in this I compare it to marriage. I have tried academic
> and Princeton life, and was less happy.[46]

After dutifully yielding to this academic appointment, Alexander came to believe that the change was really for his own good: "I have seen as clearly that my powers were tasked to a tension which must soon be

---

[44] Alexander, *Forty Years' Letters*, 1:281.

[45] See James W. Alexander, "Pastoral Records of my Connexion with the Duane Street Church, New York," 1844–1848, Fifth Avenue Presbyterian Church Archives, 21:B2-3-1, Fifth Avenue Presbyterian Church, New York. He told Hall in 1844 that the weekly catechism class was "my pleasantest hour in the week" (Alexander, *Forty Years' Letters*, 2:12).

[46] Alexander, *Forty Years' Letters*, 2:97.

fatal; while, in the steadier routine of teaching, I might last a season, with ordinary favour of Providence."[47] His life as a professor, however, would not be one of leisure. While enjoying the closeness of friends and family at Princeton, Alexander's pace of activity did not relent: "I have preached as much as usual ever since I left New York, besides the tough work of getting ready for classes."[48] Before long, Alexander bemoaned his loss of a pastoral charge: "I did not leave pastoral life willingly; I foresaw the very evils I begin to feel; but they distress me more than I reckoned for. I miss my old women; and especially my weekly catechumens, my sick-rooms, my rapid walks, and my nights of right-down fatigue."[49] Alexander would only serve as a professor at Princeton Seminary for two years, as the Duane Street church in New York unexpectedly re-called him, promising to build a new church building in a better location for expanded ministry.[50] Greatly missing "pulpit and pastoral work" and feeling that his real talent was in preaching rather than teaching, Alexander left Princeton Seminary in 1851 for his old church, which now went by the name Fifth Avenue Church.[51]

Knowing his tendency to overwork, his old church in New York sought to ensure he would reenter the pastorate strengthened and refreshed. Before allowing him to return to ministry, the Fifth Avenue Church convinced Alexander to "first recruit his health by a voyage."[52]

---

[47] Alexander, *Forty Years' Letters*, 2:99.

[48] Alexander, *Forty Years' Letters*, 2:106.

[49] Alexander, *Forty Years' Letters*, 2:107.

[50] Alexander, *Forty Years' Letters*, 2:128. See *The Biblical Repertory and Princeton Review Index Volume*, 76. John Broadus writes of James P. Boyce's time at Princeton Seminary: "It was Boyce's singular good fortune to hear [J. W. Alexander's] only course of lectures on [the Composition of Delivery of Sermons],—the notes of which lectures the student always greatly valued" (John A. Broadus, *Memoir of James Petigru Boyce, D. D., LL.D.* [New York: A. C. Armstrong and Son, 1893; repr., *A Gentleman and a Scholar: A Memoir of James Petigru Boyce*, Vestavia Hills, AL: Solid Ground Christian Books, 2004], 69). Boyce went on to found the Southern Baptist seminary now in Louisville, Kentucky.

[51] Alexander, *Forty Years' Letters*, 2:128.

[52] *The Biblical Repertory and Princeton Review Index Volume*, 76.

This he did, taking five months abroad to tour Europe. He began his ministry at Fifth Street in November, 1851. His diligent labors in New York necessitated another extended visit to Europe in 1857.[53] When Alexander returned to New York from Europe this second time, he immediately found the city in a state of spiritual excitement and genuine revival. Writing to Hall in 1858, Alexander declared: "You may rest assured that there is a great awakening among us."[54] He immediately set up special prayer meetings and special sessions where he was available to advise those seeking counsel for their souls.[55] He also worked to publish a series of evangelistic addresses originally aimed at those being affected by the ongoing revival.[56]

The extra demands taken on by Alexander during this period of revival seem to have utterly broken his health. By the spring of 1859, Alexander was so weak and depleted that removal from the city of New York seemed necessary.[57] On his way to a place of recuperation and rest, Alexander contracted dysentery and died on July 31, 1859, in Red Sweet Springs, Virginia. Thus ended the career of a man who tirelessly labored for the cause of Christ for over thirty years between the classroom in Princeton and the pastorate.

---

[53] *The Biblical Repertory and Princeton Review Index Volume*, 78.

[54] Alexander, *Forty Years' Letters*, 2:277. For information on the New York City Revival of 1857–1858, see: Samuel Prime, *The Power of Prayer: Illustrated in the Wonderful Displays of Divine Grace at the Fulton Street and Other Meetings in New York* (Halifax: Milner, 1860); and T. W. Chambers, *The Noon Prayer Meeting* (New York: Board of Publication of the Protestant Dutch Church, 1858).

[55] Alexander, *Forty Years' Letters*, 2:276–279.

[56] These tracts were compiled and published together in a book called *The Revival and its Lessons: A Collection of Fugitive Papers, Having Reference to the Great Awakening, 1858* (New York: American Tract Society, 1858). For more on Alexander and the New York City Revival of 1857–1858, see Iain H. Murray, *Revival and Revivalism: The Making and Marring of American Evangelicalism, 1750–1858* (Edinburgh: Banner of Truth, 1994), 331–353.

[57] *The Biblical Repertory and Princeton Review Index Volume*, 79.

Alexander's Evangelical Calvinism

In surveying Alexander's multi-faceted career, his restless intellect and tireless activity stand out. Mark Noll once referred to him as a "general whirlwind of activity."[58] Behind this activity was a deep-seated adherence to the evangelical Calvinism of his Presbyterian denomination. Alexander's many efforts to actively bring good to others were not at odds with his Calvinistic understanding of God's absolute sovereignty. God's divine foreordination of all things did not negate the responsibility he felt to zealously obey all that God had commanded. Alexander was in fact a strong adherent to the "Old Calvinism" held historically by Francis Turretin, Herman Witsius, John Owen, and the Westminster Confession of Faith. He drew inspiration from Calvinists who were active as pastors, missionaries, and evangelists such as Robert Murray M'Cheyne, John Newton, Jonathan Edwards, Samuel Davies, Thomas Scott, and Henry Martyn.[59] He came to his Calvinistic conviction as a young man, writing to Hall in 1823, "I consider the system called Calvinistic as the only system founded on the obvious meaning of the Bible, the only system reconcilable to a sound philosophy, and the most consoling system to one who feels himself a lost sinner."[60]

While an adherent of historic Calvinism, Alexander abhorred a type of hyper-Calvinism which promoted fatalism or passivity among its followers: "I have heard horrid extremes of fatalism, under the notion of Calvinistic doctrine."[61] This he despised as worse than even Roman Catholicism:

---

[58] Noll, *The Princeton Theology*, 16.

[59] Alexander, *Forty Years' Letters*, 1:55, 56, 221; 2:11. Alexander's approval of Edwards' theology was not without qualification. In a discussion on the doctrine of imputation, Alexander states: "Edwards has never been regarded as an interpreter of our doctrines" (Alexander, *Forty Years' Letters*, 1:221). On the other hand, Alexander's appreciation for Henry Martyn was quite strong (Alexander, *Forty Years' Letters*, 50, 85). For Alexander's extended defenses of Calvinism to the young Hall, see Alexander, *Forty Years' Letters*, 1:53–56, 61–62.

[60] Alexander, *Forty Years' Letters*, 1:32.

[61] Alexander, *Forty Years' Letters*, 1:150.

The popish creed does contain, shrouded in great superstition, I confess—but still it does contain the great fundamental saving doctrines of the Bible. Better far would it be [instead of cursing Catholicism] to curse those doctrines which many our communion hold, to wit, that every thought of man is an immediate effect of God's efficiency; that every blasphemous thought is, as much as every pious thought, caused by God's immediate agency. From my soul I could curse such blasphemy as this.[62]

Alexander's favorite expositor of Calvinism was a Scottish minister named David Russell. He commended Russell's *Letters Practical and Consolatory* as coming closest to his own views: "Who this Russell is I know not, probably a Scotch Dissenter; but I have read no human production which comes nearer my views of Calvinism: it is theology without one shred of scholasticism; orthodoxy without one film of mystification; purity without one note of ecclesiastical harshness."[63] Assessing Alexander's theological convictions, Hodge stated in his memorial sermon that Alexander "embraced the faith of the Reformed Churches in its integrity with a strength of conviction which nothing but the accordance of that system with his religious experience could produce."[64]

---

[62] Alexander, *Forty Years' Letters*, 1:51.

[63] Alexander, *Forty Years' Letters*, 1:215.

[64] Hodge, "[Memorial] Sermon," 28. The consistency of Alexander's Calvinism has been called into question by Gregory Anderson, who, in examining Alexander's rhetoric during the New York prayer revivals, states that: "Alexander became one of the most fervent advocates of the awakening, to the point where his view of limited atonement collapsed. He, an Old School Calvinist Princeton Presbyterian proclaimed that any person could be saved who 'yielding to the moving of the gracious Spirit, takes God at His Word, and makes the universal offer his own particular salvation'" (Anderson, "The Religious Rhetoric of James W. Alexander," 73). Further, Anderson states that "Alexander found himself changing from an 'Old School' anti-revivalist into an ardent revivalist, with a resulting change from a view of limited to universal atonement in his theology, due to his rhetorical practice" (Anderson, "The Religious Rhetoric of James W. Alexander," 209). Despite these assertions,

While a committed Calvinist, Alexander was no fiery polemicist or narrow partisan. At certain times in his life he did express his appreciation for those who carried on the theological debates of his day:

> The most flourishing seasons for piety have been those of the most active debates: witness the days of Augustine, of Luther, of the English Nonconformists; that the conservative principle of Protestantism is discussion of all points; and that the friction of debate is temporary, while the gain on the side of truth is permanent. I am sure there has been no age in which controvertists have been more polite towards one another than the present.[65]

At other times he expressed exasperation over the narrow, party spirit of some which he observed in these controversies:

> O how much more is the presumption in favour of Catholic Christianity than of those who cry with every

---

Anderson fails to provide support for these surprising statements. Certainly, Alexander believed in the universal offer of the gospel and that all who hear the gospel have a warrant to believe and be saved (see Alexander, "Looking unto Jesus" in *The Revival and Its Lessons*, 10). Anderson's assessment fails to properly distinguish between the universal gospel offer and a doctrine of universal atonement. The universal gospel offer, as declared by Alexander, is part of historic Calvinism, and holding to it makes him faithful to evangelical Calvinism, versus the hyper-Calvinism he abhorred. The Old School Presbyterians of Princeton were generally very favorable to revivals (see Archibald Alexander, *Biographical Sketches of the Founder and Principal Alumni of the Log College* [Philadelphia: Presbyterian Board of Publication, 1851]). Anderson's failure to distinguish between revivals and revivalism also cause him to mischaracterize Alexander and the Princetonians' position on revival. It seems, instead, that the revivals reinforced Alexander in his Calvinistic views. In a local awakening that occurred under his preaching in 1837, Alexander stated that "the whole tenour of the revival has been very pleasing to me, as confirming that high Calvinistic view of the gratuity of salvation." (Alexander, *Forty Years' Letters*, 1:253). For Alexander's participation in the New York City Revival of 1857–1858, see Alexander, *Forty Years' Letters*, 2:276–279.

[65] Alexander, *Forty Years' Letters*, 1:254–255.

breath "the temple of the Lord, the temple of the Lord are *we*," whether Papists, Oxonians, Baptists, or Separatists! How much more exercise of Christian tempers with the former than the latter! I can get along with a Quaker, but not with a bigot.[66]

As the Presbyterians were factioning into what would become the Old School-New School split of 1837, Alexander would state: "I am almost converted to the extreme doctrine of 'no controversy.' We are too anxious lest God should not maintain his own truth. I know no cause why we may not devote ourselves to other work."[67] While personally shrinking back from this controversy, Alexander valued the work of those who strove for doctrinal precision, especially the Reformed polemicists in the past, believing that they shed a valuable light on the theological errors raised in the Old School-New School debate:

I have...been delving very doggedly at the controversial divinity of the 17th century. Truly I am astounded at the acumen and learning of the Reformed theologians; I mean those of whom a specimen appears at the Synod of Dort... The scholastic studies of the age, while they perhaps confined the mind to a narrow channel, increased the vigorous impetuosity of the torrent. I perceive no important point in the controversy

---

[66] Alexander, *Forty Years' Letters*, 1:320.

[67] Alexander, *Forty Years' Letters*, 1:225. While agreeing with the Old School leaders doctrinally, Alexander and Charles Hodge opposed some of the actions taken by the Old School leaders in the Old School-New School controversy (Archibald Hodge, *Life of Charles Hodge*, 303–320). Alexander stated: "The truth is, the Princetonians are as thoroughly old-school in their theology as Dr. [Ashbel] Green [leader of the Old School party] himself, but they are unable to see that it is the path of duty to denounce every dissentient individual." (Alexander, *Forty Years' Letters*, 1:177). For more on the Old School-New School split, see D. G. Hart and John R. Muether, *Seeking a Better Country: 300 Years of American Presbyterianism* (Phillipsburg, NJ: Presbyterian and Reformed Publishing, 2007), 121–127, 138–143.

actuellement agitated in America, which was not apprehended and brought out in full proportion and relief by the ancients.[68]

While appreciating the precision of the seventeenth century Reformed theologians, Alexander, according to Hall, held a higher estimation "of an experimental above a merely technical theology."[69] As such, Alexander possessed a strong spirit of evangelical catholicity. In 1858, he would write: "Weary, weary, am I of these [theological] controversies *de lana caprina* [literally, "concerning goat's wool," i.e., worthless matters]. I have a peculiar position; being in favour of strict subscription, but to a very short creed."[70] Wary of the "Fanaticism of the Symbol" within his own circles, as he called it, he showed appreciation for a wide variety of evangelical authors.[71] For example, in 1830 he stated: "I have read eight out of the ten volumes of Wesley's works, and esteem him one of the greatest and best men that ever lived."[72]

While catholic and broadly evangelical in his sentiments, Alexander was a committed Presbyterian, as well as a Calvinist.[73] He held that denominational or "sectarian" distinctives among church organizations were not to be minimized, suppressed, or abandoned for a generic organizational unity:

[T]he unity which is to arise from the compromise and suppression of every thing peculiar, I cannot understand; and if

---

[68] Alexander, *Forty Years' Letters*, 1:169.

[69] Hall, "[Memorial] Sermon," 61.

[70] Alexander, *Forty Years' Letters*, 2:281.

[71] Alexander, *Forty Years' Letters*, 1:226–227.

[72] Alexander, *Forty Years' Letters*, 1:167.

[73] Alexander, *Forty Years' Letters*, 1:223. Alexander was not a "divine right" Presbyterian. He once stated to Hall: "It seems to me, in looking over the history of the church, that the real progress of religion has been in a very small degree dependent on the spread of permanency of any external form of polity" (Alexander, *Forty Years' Letters*, 1:239). Alexander was uncomfortable with theological conflicts being decided by the Presbyterian General Assembly and seemed uncomfortable with the ecclesiastical structures beyond that of the Presbytery (see Alexander, *Forty Years' Letters*, 1:251; 2:288).

there were a society on the principle that no sectarian procliv-
ities of doctrine should be preached...I should abhor it little
less than I do the Pope's church. Indeed, it is only the liberty
of declaring within each separate pale the supposed truths of
the gospel, in their length and breadth, which for a moment
reconciles me to the compromise of the Sunday School Union, or the Tract Society.[74]

Only as a Calvinist and as a Presbyterian would Alexander involve himself in more "ecumenical" organizations, and only then because they
did not encourage him to compromise or suppress his denominational
distinctives. Alexander did indeed attach himself to broadly-evangelical
agencies like the American Sunday School Union, driven by his over-
whelming concern for the great numbers of poor and untaught who
stood in need of both spiritual and material help. Expressing his evangelical catholicity, Alexander stated: "I feel as if I could join with any
who would humbly unite in direct and kind efforts to save sinners and
relieve human misery."[75] Even so, he did not compromise his commitment to the robust doctrines of historic Protestantism and evangelical
Calvinism.

A Lifelong Commitment to Social Reform
Alexander developed a commitment to social reform that burned
stronger than his desire for theological precisionism. Instead of building
the kingdom of Christ by polemics, Alexander believed the church
would primarily advance in the world by engaging those outside of it
with truth and action. This comment to Hall is representative of his
sentiment:

If, instead of reviling the Catholics, we would surpass them in
schools, in personal charities, in persevering missions, and in
the preparation of our ministers, I believe we should make

---

[74] Alexander, *Forty Years' Letters*, 1:240.
[75] Alexander, *Forty Years' Letters*, 1:227.

more head against them. Every day I live I become more sick of controversy; I cannot persuade myself that the Church was meant to be kept always in hot water.[76]

Instead of being consumed with in-house controversies in the church, Alexander carefully followed the intellectual, religious, and cultural movements that were immediately impacting the culture of his day. He was more concerned about those not connected with the church and with the plight of the general population than he was with those in the church. This caused him to devote a large amount of his attention to the thought and lives of ordinary men and women in antebellum America.

Alexander would remain greatly concerned about the state of American society throughout his entire life. This was true of him even when he was a first-year seminary student. In one of his earliest seminary exercises he addressed the school's Theological Society, exhorting his hearers to labor in "the work of ameliorating society" in spreading "useful knowledge among the mass of society." In addressing his fellow students preparing for the ministry, he called them to "direct the stream of social conscience into a religious channel" and to labor for "a general reformation of society."[77] The passion Alexander expressed for social reform as a young seminary student did not lessen as he entered the ministry. As a pastor in Trenton, he would write to Hall in 1830:

I am very much impressed with a sentiment which I cannot express otherwise than thus: "It is the duty of some men to

---

[76] Alexander, *Forty Years' Letters*, 1:226.

[77] James W. Alexander, "Speech for the Theological Society," February 1823, The James Waddel Alexander Manuscript Collection, 1:11, Special Collections, Princeton Theological Seminary Library, Princeton, NJ. Alexander preserved this handwritten manuscript and handed it down to his son, Henry Carrington Alexander, who also became a Presbyterian minister. Written on the reverse is the note: "For H. C. A., I send you my earliest Seminary exercises; for your encouragement."

devote their attention to the relief of the temporal miseries of mankind." Let me explain. I do not exclude spiritual beneficence; I do not mean that a man should become a knight errant; but I verily think that Christians are not touched as they should be with human suffering, bodily suffering, privation, etc., etc. Now, if a few men would concentrate their thoughts upon this, write upon it, paragraph upon it, influence the press, talk upon it, in a word Clarksonize, I believe great things must be done. In reading the N.T. I have recently been much struck with the fact that *all* the miracles of our Saviour were acts of benevolence, and usually in *relief of human bodily distresses*. Now, the thought has powerfully come over me, Am I, and are Christians, acting in any degree like their master? I have recently preached upon the subject from Heb. xiii., 3. I have an idea that the amount of effort now put forth in Christendom would produce a hundred times as much real good, if it were systematized and properly directed. Perhaps this crude thought will not be lost upon you.[78]

Again, while serving as a pastor in Trenton, Alexander made Hall the recipient of this thought:

Do we not restrict our faith in prayer too much to *spiritual* blessings? I know these are infinitely the more important, and that our petitions for earthly good are to be under submission to the Divine will; but then how plain it is, that when Christ was on earth, he listened to the request of the sick and mourning, that he never chided any one who asked healing and deliverance, as asking amiss, and that he invariable heard the prayer of all such. How plain, but how much forgotten, that he is the same Saviour now, with just the same views of poor, suffering, and sinning men.[79]

---

[78] Alexander, *Forty Years' Letters*, 1:142. The word "Clarksonize" refers to Thomas Clarkson, the Anglican abolitionist whose publications and active campaigning helped reveal the horrors of the African Slave Trade to the people of Britain, who brought it to an end in 1807.

[79] Alexander, *Forty Years' Letters*, 1:173–174.

Although comfortably situated in society himself, Alexander shows in his letters to Hall that he was a man deeply concerned by the plight of the poor and lower classes of society. As a pastor in New York City, especially, he was deeply touched by the masses outside the circles of an active gospel witness. In 1851, Alexander would write to Hall:

> My mind works incessantly on such themes as these:—the abounding misery; the unreached masses; the waste of church energy on the rich; its small operation on the poor; emigrant wretchedness; our boy-population; our hopeless prostitutes; our 4,000 grog-shops; the absence of poor from Presbyterian churches; the farces of our church-alms; confinement of our church-efforts to pew-holders; the do-nothing life of our Christian professors, in regard to the masses; our copying the Priest and Levite in the parable; our need of a Christian Lord Bacon, to produce a Novum Organon of Philanthropy; our dread of innovation; our luxury and pride.[80]

Disappointed with how fellow Christians were neglecting the poor, Alexander devoted himself to helping the downtrodden and vulnerable in society, including children and youth.[81] This heart for the oppressed helps explain the great efforts this Princeton scholar expended in

---

[80] Alexander, *Forty Years' Letters*, 2:165.

[81] While in Trenton, Alexander stated: "If my life is spared...I will (D. V.) devote much of my time to babes' books" (Alexander, *Forty Years' Letters*, 1:195). Some of the books Alexander wrote for children include: *Letters to a Very Young Lady* (Philadelphia: American Sunday School Union, 1843); *Charles Clifford* (Philadelphia: American Sunday School Union, 1834); *My Brother's Keeper: Letters to a Younger Brother on the Virtues and Vices, Duties and Dangers of Youth* (Philadelphia: American Sunday School Union, 1838); and *School-Boy Heroes: The Story of Maurice Gray and Carl Adler* (London: T. Nelson and Sons, 1872). Alexander hoped that a book could be written for the many thousands of "Factory Children" who were "cut off from instruction and home influence and exposed to numberless corruptions" (Alexander, *Forty Years' Letters*, 1:225).

writing numerous popular books for the betterment of immigrants and the working-class.[82]

The Social Gospel Rejected

While committed to social reform, Alexander rejected "social gospel" approaches that minimized the central issue of personal salvation through faith in Jesus Christ. This rejection is seen in his interaction with the thought of Stephen Colwell. Colwell was a contemporary of Alexander who also wrote about social reform and social ethics.[83] Although not a clergyman, Colwell was heavily involved in the life of the Presbyterian Church, including as a trustee of Princeton Seminary itself.[84] For many years, Colwell worked to establish a chair of Christian ethics at Princeton, which was finally set up in 1871.[85] Colwell was an important thinker and writer on social reform, and his emphasis on social reform greatly impacted how the American Presbyterian church viewed their role in addressing the social ills of society.[86] Colwell wrote

[82] Books which Alexander wrote for immigrants and the working-class include: *Carl, The Young Emigrant* (Philadelphia: American Sunday School Union, 1851); *The American Mechanic and Working-Man*, 2 vols. (New York: William S. Martien, 1847); and *The Merchant's Clerk Cheered and Counselled* (New York: Anson D. F. Randolph, 1856).

[83] For more information on Colwell see Bruce Morgan, "Stephen Colwell (1800-1871): Social Prophet Before the Social Gospel" in *Sons of the Prophets: Leaders in Protestantism from Princeton Seminary*, ed. Hugh T. Kerr (Princeton: Princeton University Press, 1963), 123-147.

[84] Morgan, "Stephen Colwell," 124.

[85] Henry Charles Carey, *A Memoir of Stephen Colwell* (Philadelphia: Henry Carey Baird, 1872), 16. Colwell was heavily influenced by Carey, an economic protectionist and interventionist who served as a chief economic advisor to Abraham Lincoln. For more information on the relationship between Colwell and Carey, see Henry F. May, *Protestant Churches and the Industrial Revolution* (New York: Octagon Books, 1963), 17-20.

[86] Elwyn Allen Smith credits Colwell with contributing to the shift in American Presbyterianism away from a theologically-oriented ministry toward a "social ministry." See Elwyn Allen Smith, *The Presbyterian Ministry in American Culture: A Study in Changing Concepts, 1700-1900* (Philadelphia: Westminster Press, 1962), 235-237.

an article in the *Repertory* in 1841 on "The Poor and the Poor Laws of Great Britain," as well as many other books addressing social and economic issues.[87] His *New Themes for the Protestant Clergy* received the most attention. In it he caustically expressed outrage at the Church and the clergy for neglecting the poor and impoverished and for focusing too much on theology at the expense of charity.[88] This work was controversial and sparked a heated sequence of responses.[89] Colwell expressed many of the same themes which were popularized by later purveyors of "the social gospel," including an emphasis on "the Fatherhood of God and the brotherhood of man."[90] In fact, some have viewed his writings as the "earliest statement of a social gospel in the modern

---

[87] Stephen Colwell, "The Poor and Poor Laws of Great Britain," *Biblical Repertory and Princeton Review* 13 (1841): 99–131. Other examples of Colwell's work include: *New Themes for the Protestant Clergy: Creeds without Charity, Theology without Humanity, and Protestantism without Christianity* (Philadelphia: Lippincott, Grambo, 1852); *The Position of Christianity in the United States, in Its Relations with our Political Institutions, and Specially with Reference to Religious Instruction in the Public Schools* (Philadelphia: Lippincott, Grambo, 1854); and *The South: A Letter from a Friend in the North, with Special Reference to the Effects of Disunion upon Slavery* (Philadelphia: C. Sherman & Son, 1856).

[88] Smith states that "Colwell demanded that the church repudiate theology and give itself to ethics" (Smith, *Presbyterian Ministry in American Culture*, 235). This might be an overstatement of Colwell's position, but it captures his emphasis nonetheless.

[89] Samuel Austen Allibone, a Philadelphia banker, first replied to Colwell anonymously in *A Review by a Layman, of a Work Entitled, "New Themes for the Protestant Clergy: Creeds without Charity, Theology without Humanity, and Protestantism without Christianity"* (Philadelphia: Lippincott, Grambo, 1852). William Henry Ruffner, a Presbyterian minister of Philadelphia, replied with a moderate defense of Colwell's *New Themes*, entitled *Charity and the Clergy: Being a Review by a Protestant Clergyman of the "New Themes Controversy"* (Philadelphia: Lippincott, Grambo, 1853). This in turn produced another heated response by Allibone, entitled *New Themes Condemned: Or, Thirty Opinions upon "New Themes," and its "Reviewer"* (Philadelphia: Lippincott, Grambo, 1853). For more information on this controversy, see May, *Protestant Churches and the Industrial Revolution*, 19.

[90] Colwell, *New Themes for the Protestant Clergy*, 152, 182, 190, 243. See also Smith, *Presbyterian Ministry in American Culture*, 235.

sense."[91] While not a socialist, Colwell expressed a qualified appreciation for the socialists of his day, agreeing with their rejection of economic individualism and their elevation of labor over capital.[92]

Alexander was well aware of Colwell's work on social reform.
While he found it stimulating, he ultimately rejected its overall thrust.
After a quick scan of *New Themes for the Protestant Clergy* in 1851, Alexander gave Hall this terse review: "abuse of clergy; abuse of
churches; abuse of theology; everybody wrong but *moi*; sneers at societies, creeds, catechisms, etc, etc.; yet, after all, a book that no one can
read without deep and anxious reflection. The mixture of truth is great
and suggestive, and the style is tip-top, sometimes as keen as Pascal."[93]
A few days later, after further reading, Alexander wrote again to Hall,
saying: "Colwell, in his episcopo-mastix, ['New Themes,'] seems to
be in favour of a plan which shall dissolve all churches, charities, and
associations, and solve all great social problems by this formula, 'Let
every man be perfectly good.' This is the avowed conclusion of his
strange book."[94] In a later letter to Hall, Alexander criticized Colwell
for "sacrificing plain scripture to doubtful theories of economic science."[95]

Setting Colwell aside as an eccentric, Alexander did not work out
his ideas for social reform along the same lines as this controversial figure in Old Princeton's history. Alexander would offer his own assessment of American society and various approaches to social reform.[96]

---

[91] Charles Howard Hopkins, *The Rise of the Social Gospel in American Protestantism, 1865–1915* (New Haven: Yale University Press, 1940), 6.

[92] See the numerous quotations in Morgan, "Stephen Colwell," 128–
131. See also May, *Protestant Churches in Industrial America*, 18–20.

[93] Alexander, *Forty Years' Letters*, 2:165.

[94] Alexander, *Forty Years' Letters*, 2:166. The insertion in brackets is
made by Hall.

[95] Alexander, *Forty Years' Letters*, 2:275.

[96] Alexander's support and critique of the temperance movement are il-
lustrative of his independence of mind regarding social reform. Alexander was
concerned throughout his life about the destructive effects of alcohol on so
many in his day. While a pastor in Trenton, he told Hall: "Every day I am more

While Colwell promoted a kind of moralistic approach to social reform, one which would develop into a full-blown "social gospel" in American life, Alexander's thought on social reform did not move in that direction.[97] For him, the Christian gospel of individual salvation must not be set aside for "doubtful theories."

---

impressed with the importance of being zealous in the Temperance Reformation" (Alexander, *Forty Years' Letters*, 1:155). When asked to preach a sermon to the Temperance Society, Alexander complied, and his sermon was printed in 1831 as an article in the *Repertory* (James W. Alexander, "Suggestions in Vindication of the Temperance Society," *Biblical Repertory and Theological Review* 3 [1831]: 44–60; see Alexander, *Forty Years' Letters*, 1:150). Although this article was mistakenly attributed to Samuel Miller in *The Biblical Repertory and Princeton Review Index Volume*, Alexander was responsible for it, and it was immediately reprinted under Alexander's name in 1831 by Russell and Martin of Philadelphia. While an early advocate of the temperance movement, Alexander came to be critical of certain aspects of it. Although Alexander was practically a teetotaler himself, he came to question the rightness of calling people to a pledge of total abstinence (Alexander, *Forty Years' Letters*, 1:237, 243, 299). He certainly did not agree with individuals in the temperance movement like Moses Stuart who held that total abstinence from alcoholic beverages should be a requirement for church membership (see Moses Stuart, *Essay on the Prize-Question, Whether the Use of Distilled Liquors, or Traffic of them, is Compatible at the Present Time, with Making a Profession of Christianity?* [New York: John P. Haven, 1830]). Writing again to Hall, Alexander stated: "I am alarmed at the progress of the ultra-temperance doctrine; I mean that of Stuart's tract, that total abstinence ought to be made a term of church communion. It will undoubtedly produce great divisions in our church, if it receive any countenance" (Alexander, *Forty Years' Letters*, 1:157; cf. 1:229). Over time, Alexander gradually withdrew from the Temperance Society, even though he remained in agreement with their goal and purpose. Writing to Hall in 1842, Alexander stated: "I am no longer a member of any Temperance Society of any sort, except that which is 1,800 years ago" (Alexander, *Forty Years' Letters*, 1:358).

[97] The so-called "social gospel" movement developed in the late nineteenth century and become popular in the early twentieth century, with leading proponents including Washington Gladden and Walter Rauschenbusch. See Rauschenbusch's *Christianity and the Social Crisis* (New York: Macmillan, 1907) and *A Theology for the Social Gospel* (New York: Macmillan, 1917).

Conclusion

James W. Alexander lived out his life between Princeton and the pastorate. While a Princetonian by upbringing and education, Alexander was deeply concerned with the plight of the masses and the general state of American society outside of Princeton. Although he served as a professor at both Princeton College and at Princeton Seminary, his greatest love was for the pastorate. He was a committed Calvinist, yet he shied away from theological polemics and ecclesiastical disagreements. He was strongly committed to evangelical catholicity and was willing to work with a variety of evangelicals, especially when it came to alleviating the needs of the poor.

Like fellow Presbyterian Stephen Colwell, Alexander was concerned that Presbyterians were not doing enough to address the needs of the poor in antebellum America. While similarly burdened for the poor and oppressed, Alexander did not share Colwell's collectivist sympathies or his harsh repudiation of American churches and clergy. While Colwell's thought anticipated what would later become known as "the social gospel," Alexander did not develop his views on social reform along these lines. Social and economic theorizing would not supplant his commitment to the gospel of individual salvation and its importance in addressing the ills of society.

Chapter 2
Politics and the Structure of Society

Alexander's views on social reform were intertwined with his views on society in general and his vision of the ideal society and ideal political structures. His political views, then, are important for understanding his views on social reform. In his personal letters to John Hall, James W. Alexander wrote a great deal about the political affairs affecting America in the first half of the nineteenth century. From these letters one can reconstruct his political views, which are closely connected to his understanding of antebellum American society. A survey of Alexander's comments on political matters also illustrates how thoughtfully and critically he interacted with his contemporary American culture.

"An Adams Man" in a "Perverse and Jacksonian Generation"
In the "Age of Jackson," popular political sentiments moved strongly in a populist, democratic, and egalitarian direction.[1] Older ideas of societal stratification and of a distinct ruling class were in decline, and the electorate was being expanded as individual states began dropping their property requirements for voting.[2] While the clamour for a popular democracy was on the rise during the "Second Party Era" of American history, there was no universal American consensus on political

---

[1] See Howe, *What God Hath Wrought*, 328–366. See also Arthur M. Schlesinger, Jr., *The Age of Jackson* (Boston: Little, Brown, 1945) and John William Ward, *Andrew Jackson: Symbol for an Age* (New York: Oxford University Press, 1955).

[2] See Robert J. Steinfeld, "Property and Suffrage in the Early American Republic," *Stanford Law Review* 41 (1989): 335–376.

matters, and many individuals like Alexander disagreed with the Jacksonian vision of social equality and democratic populism.[3]

Alexander came to his political persuasions at a young age. As a twenty-year-old tutor at Princeton College, Alexander first raised the issue of politics with his friend Hall by commenting on the heated election of 1824 as follows: "What do you think of the presidential squabble? Jackson brightens wonderfully. His recent letters—I mean his recently published letters, set the man's character in a noble light, and command my highest respect."[4] Despite these initial comments, Alexander suddenly started expressing anti-Jacksonian sentiments to Hall and ended up supporting his rival in the election of 1824, John Quincy Adams.

John Quincy Adams was widely considered to be a devout, serious, and hard-working man of religious faith and deep integrity. As an intellectual and a scholar, however, Adams had extreme difficulty inspiring and connecting with the general public.[5] As the election of 1824 was about to be decided in the early days of 1825, Alexander lamented the almost certain defeat of his preferred candidate: "Appearances seem to indicate that all our fears are to be realized with regard to the election of General Jackson. I suppose, in that case, we must try how loyally we

---

[3] Daniel Walker Howe, *What Hath God Wrought: The Transformation of America, 1815–1848* (New York: Oxford University Press, 2007), 331. The diversity of religious, economic, political, and regional perspectives in antebellum America brought about a fragmented political landscape that has been interpreted in a variety of ways. For helpful analysis of the various political perspectives, see Noll, *America's God*, 209–224, 447–451; Daniel Walker Howe, "Religion and Politics in the Antebellum North," in *Religion and American Politics: From the Colonial Period to the 1980s*, ed. Mark A. Noll (New York: Oxford University Press, 1990), 121–145; and Richard J. Carwardine, *Evangelicals and Politics in Antebellum America* (New Haven: Yale University Press, 1993). It is beyond the scope of this work to attempt a full analysis of antebellum American politics. For a magisterial work on the "Second Party Era," see Michael F. Holt, *The Rise and Fall of the American Whig Party: Jacksonian Politics and the Onset of the Civil War* (New York: Oxford University Press, 1999).

[4] Alexander, *Forty Years' Letters*, 1:46.

[5] Howe, *What Hath God Wrought*, 245.

can support his administration."[6] Although Jackson would go on to receive a plurality of the popular and electoral votes in the election of 1824, no candidate received a majority, and the House of Representatives ended up electing Adams.[7] Alexander was elated: "The success of John Q. Adams has pleased me as much as it can have done you. ...My only fear is that the tranquil and equitable administration of our President will be somewhat *ennuyante* [boring]."[8] Alexander sardonically expressed what he knew to be true: the scholarly Adams was unable to generate the kind of popular excitement generated by the colorful Jackson.

As Alexander began his ministry in Charlotte County, Virginia, he immediately discovered how out-of-step his support of Adams was with his parishioners. In a letter written to Hall in May 1826, Alexander stated: "I have never yet met with a friend of Adams in this State."[9] Early next year, Alexander would further state: "I think that our friend John Q. [Adams] is gaining ground in Virginia, though not in this quarter. Everybody in these parts hates him, hates the Panama measures, hates Clay, hates roads and canals, hates internal improvements, and abominates the tariff."[10] While in southern Virginia, Adams eventually found one individual who shared his political views in the person of Edward C. Carrington. In the same letter just mentioned, Alexander informed Hall of his new-found friend: "General Edward Carrington is the only man who dares to lift up his voice here in favour of the Administration: he speaks at almost every assemblage of people, though

---

[6] Alexander, *Forty Years' Letters*, 1:73.

[7] Henry Clay, the Speaker of the House, had also been a candidate for the Presidency. Adams won in the House after Clay threw his support to Adams. Clay would go on to become Adam's Secretary of State, sparking outcries of corruption.

[8] Alexander, *Forty Years' Letters*, 1:73.

[9] Alexander, *Forty Years' Letters*, 1:95.

[10] Alexander, *Forty Years' Letters*, 1:96. Henry Clay's "America System" put in place a high protective tariff which largely helped New England to industrialize but also hurt the export market for the raw materials produced in the agrarian South. See Howe, *What Hath God Wrought*, 270–275.

without support, and without converts."[11] In the following month, Alexander would write: "Gen. Edward C. Carrington...is a scholar and a gentleman, and has large possessions. The information which he has acquired in his travels in Europe, renders his conversation highly interesting. He is bold enough to advocate the cause of Adams and patriotism in the midst of this perverse and Jacksonian generation."[12]

While Alexander disagreed strongly with the Jacksonian sentiments of his Southern parishioners, he was careful to not bring his political opinions into his ministry.[13] In the following month, Alexander would tell Hall:

> I do not think it by any means incumbent upon me as an Adams man, or consistent as a preacher, to talk much about politics, but I am sorely vexed from day to day at the enormities of the opposition. My ears are forever ringing with the cant which has become so current on this subject. There is some show of reason, I must confess, in the arguments of the politicians here. The tariff forces them to pay more for many articles, and repays them with no advantage.[14]

---

[11] Alexander, *Forty Years' Letters*, 1:96.

[12] Alexander, *Forty Years' Letters*, 1:97.

[13] This was Alexander's consistent practice. Toward the end of his life, Alexander bemoaned that "Politics, Abstinence, and Slavery usurp the 'sacred desk'" in New England (Alexander, *Forty Years' Letters*, 2:227).

[14] Alexander, *Forty Years' Letters*, 1:99. In a letter written just after this time, Alexander would express similar sentiments to Charles Hodge, who was then studying in Germany: "You wish to hear something of our politics, but where shall I begin? From the troubled ocean I might draw you many a bucketfull, did I know what to select. J. Q. Adams is perhaps as unpopular a man as ever held that office. Many of his old friends have deserted him, and the clamours in all the Southern states are most vehement. The odious measures amongst us are—the Tariff, the system of Internal Improvements, and especially the diplomatic measures with regard to the Colonial trade, which have issued in the total destruction of our commerce with the British West Indies. No man is in nomination except General Jackson, and I have no doubt he will be our next President. I have no love for him, and believe that he stands already pledged to support the same measures which render Adams unpopular..." (James W. Alexander to Charles Hodge, May 14, 1827, The James Waddel

Alexander's disagreement with the political sentiments popular in southern Virginia continued throughout the four years of the Adams administration. Writing to Hall on July 3, 1827, Alexander stated:

> I take a lively interest in the improvements of our country, notwithstanding my being hemmed in with political heretics... I take no trouble to conceal my sentiments, although I enter into no disputes. Although I hear incessant eulogies of General Jackson, yet I am utterly at a loss to discover among the wagon-loads of chaff which they pour forth about him one grain of real qualification for the Presidency.[15]

Continuing to resist the political opinions of his Virginia parishioners, Alexander wrote again to Hall in the summer of 1828, as the rematch between Adams and Jackson was underway:

> The cause of Mr. Adams is sustained, as I fully believe, by the great mass of enlightened and sober men. As for myself, I admire the man for that simple dignity which has marked all his proceedings. How pitiful are the Southern recalcitrations against the tariff! They remind one of the pet child who will not eat his dinner, because he is forbidden the use of certain articles.[16]

With a sober admiration for John Quincy Adams's "simple dignity," Alexander resisted the rising clamour and excitement which Jackson inspired, even among his own southern parishioners.

As the 1828 election grew near, Alexander understood how much his anti-Jacksonian views were in the minority, even amongst certain friends and family members at Princeton. Writing to Hall on October 4, 1828, Alexander expressed his fear:

Alexander Manuscript Collection, 3:3, Special Collections, Princeton Theological Seminary Library, Princeton, NJ).

[15] Alexander, *Forty Years' Letters*, 1:107.

[16] Alexander, *Forty Years' Letters*, 1:110–111.

> I suppose Archibald[17] in the plentitude of his Jacksonianism
> has informed you that Princeton is ornamented with a Hick-
> ory pole, in the most conspicuous part of the village. It is
> strange to see with what phrenetic zeal the Hickories are trav-
> ersing all the country. Invasion or civil war could scarcely pro-
> duce a greater fermentation among the populace. My fear is
> that New Jersey will give her vote for the Chieftain; and in-
> deed, further, that he will be our President.[18]

As the election of 1828 grew near, Alexander's Virginia parishioners were optimistic that their candidate would this time prevail. Writing to Hall on November 16, 1828, Alexander stated: "On my return to Virginia, I found the whole population in a ferment upon the subject of the Presidential election. Jackson is carrying it with a high hand, and there seems little doubt among the politicians here as to his election."[19]

Jackson did prevail in the raucous election campaign of 1828, dominating in all but New England, New Jersey, Delaware, and parts of New York and Maryland.[20] In the course of the campaign, Adams's opponents successfully painted him as an aloof and aristocratic leader in a society which was becoming more and more populistic, democratic and egalitarian.[21] While a wide sweep of Americans were embracing

---

[17] This is a reference to Alexander's younger brother. Alexander also differed markedly with his other brother William Cowper Alexander, who was among "the first stump speakers" in New Jersey and who campaigned actively for Andrew Jackson in the 1828 election ("Biographical Sketch of Col. Alexander," 1856[?], Alexander Family Collection, 3:1, Department of Rare Books and Special Collections, Princeton University Library, Princeton, NJ). William was later elected to the New Jersey legislature as a Democrat (the party of Jackson), and ran unsuccessfully as the Democratic candidate for Governor of New Jersey. For more on William Cowper Alexander, see John Frelinghuysen Hageman, *History of Princeton and Its Institutions* (Philadelphia: J. B. Lippincott, 1878), 1:351–354.

[18] Alexander, *Forty Years' Letters*, 1:113.

[19] Alexander, *Forty Years' Letters*, 1:114.

[20] Howe, *What Hath God Wrought*, 281.

[21] Howe, *What Hath God Wrought*, 278.

Jacksonian notions of social equality and democratic populism, Alexander found his dissenting views to be in the minority.

Political Influences

Alexander's letters to Hall give us some indication as to who influenced him in his anti-Jacksonian views. While an "Adams man" in the 1824 and 1828 elections, Alexander seemed to identify most with the political views of John Quincy Adams' father, John Adams. John Adams (along with George Washington, Alexander Hamilton, and others) had given leadership to the Federalist Party, a political party which grew out of the ratification debates over the United States Constitution. The Federalists believed in a strong central government and a strong executive branch. They were pro-British in their sentiments and did not look favorably upon the French Revolution.[22] According to Richard Carwardine: "Guided by a vision of a hierarchical society, and shivering at the tremors of emerging democracy, Federalists valued religion, education, and the law as the means of maintaining a harmonious and controllable social order."[23] Although the Federalist Party had dissolved by the late 1820s, Alexander found the Federalist views expressed in the writings of John Adams to be compelling. On April 8, 1829, Alexander wrote Hall:

> I have been reading John Adams's Defence [sic] of the American Constitution, and have found it a very interesting work. I am especially pleased with his abstract of the history of the Italian republic, which I have never found so clearly given in any other book. It has almost set me upon studying Italian, and reading Machiavel, Fuicciardini, Malavolti, etc., in the original. A general survey of all history, with reference to the principles of our constitution, would be a great and useful work. It

---

[22] For more on the Federalist Party and the period of its predominance, see Stanley Elkins and Eric McKitrick, *The Age of Federalism* (Oxford: Oxford University Press, 1993).

[23] Richard J. Carwardine, "The Politics of Charles Hodge," in Stewart and Morehead, *Charles Hodge Revisited*, 257.

seems to me that our Colleges ought to have lectures upon that very subject. The simple principles assumed as fundamental by Adams, have really cast a new light upon all the history I have read. The annals of all nations seem to be a commentary upon the doctrine that the three primary forms of government [monarchy, aristocracy, democracy] must be so tempered and balanced in every government, as to check the extravagance of each.[24]

Alexander found Adams's views of a "balanced" government to be more satisfying than the "extravagance" of Jeffersonian democracy. By mid-1829, then, Alexander's political views had shifted from a mere personal attachment to John Quincy Adams to a full embrace, even "love," of the older Federalism of Adams.[25]

Alexander expressed appreciation for the social and political writings of others in America who held to politically "conservative" or federalist positions. One such writer was Robert Walsh Jr. Walsh was a highly-educated social and political commentator and the founding editor of both *The American Review of History and Politics* and *The National Gazette*. He eventually served as an American diplomat in Paris as well.[26] The most important of Walsh's political works were *An Appeal from the Judgments of Great Britain respecting the United States of America* and *A Letter on the Genius and Dispositions of the French Government*, an extended critique against the oppressive and anti-commercial

---

[24] Alexander, *Forty Years' Letters*, 1:125-126. For more on Adam's political philosophy, see Elkins and McKitrick, *The Age of Federalism*, 313–314.

[25] Alexander, *Forty Years' Letters*, 1:126. Alexander mentions in this letter that he had read a critique of John Quincy Adams made by Judge James Gould, which encouraged him all the more to embrace the older Federalism of John Adams. Gould's critique can be found in Henry Adams, ed., *Documents Relating to New-England Federalism* (Cambridge: John Wilson and Sons, 1887), 93–106.

[26] For more information on Walsh, see Mary Frederick Lochemes, *Robert Walsh: His Story* (New York: American-Irish Historical Society, 1941).

policies of Revolutionary France.[27] Walsh's writings reflected the views of the conservative, educated classes in America. Going against Jacksonian sentiments, Walsh defended the privileged classes in America and argued against universal suffrage.[28] With such views Alexander was in agreement.

As a young man, Alexander developed a life-long affection for the writings of Walsh. Referring to him as "the modern [Samuel] Johnson," Alexander stated as a pastor in Trenton that "there are few men in our country whose acquaintance would be a greater prize."[29] His letters to Hall are filled with references to Walsh and his writings. After Walsh died in 1859, Alexander stated toward the end of his own life: "I really miss Walsh, and few perhaps do. ...He had noble, rare moral traits; his patriotism seemed never chilled by expatriation; he was always the American, and of an old time type."[30] Alexander admired Walsh and his literary style so much that he seems to have adopted aspects of it as his own.[31] When Alexander and his brothers Addison and William started a short-lived periodical of social commentary called *The Princeton Magazine* in 1851, Walsh voiced his approval of their

---

[27] Robert Walsh Jr., *An Appeal from the Judgments of Great Britain respecting the United States of America* (Philadelphia: Mitchell, Ames, and White, 1819); Robert Walsh Jr., *A Letter on the Genius and Dispositions of the French Government* (Baltimore: P. H. Nicklin, 1810).

[28] Robert Walsh, *Didactics: Social, Literary, Political*, 2 vols. (Philadelphia: Carey, Lea, & Blanchard, 1836), 1:171–175; 2:27–34, 124–125.

[29] Alexander, *Forty Years' Letters*, 1:126. James W. Alexander's son, Henry Carrington Alexander, lavished high praise on Walsh in his biography of J. Addison Alexander, stating: "It is a sad commentary on the evanescence of fame that the name of such a man...should now be strange to many who think themselves versed in the literature of the day. Mr. Robert Walsh may be said to have been at one time the prince of elegant letters in this country" (Henry Carrington Alexander, *The Life of Joseph Addison Alexander, D.D.*, 2 vols. [New York: Charles Scribner, 1870], 1:203–204).

[30] Alexander, *Forty Years' Letters*, 2:285. For more on Alexander's appreciation of Walsh, see Alexander, *Forty Years' Letters*, 1:310, 322, 401.

[31] Alexander, *Forty Years' Letters*, 2:285.

work in a letter to the editor.[32] This must have thrilled Alexander. He (and his brother Addison) also wrote a few pieces for Walsh's *National Gazette*, and their frequent collaboration underscores their shared interest and outlook in literary, intellectual, and political matters.[33]

In addition to Adams and Walsh, Alexander admired the political writings of British conservatives like Edmund Burke. Burke was an eighteenth-century British statements and political theorist who wrote a strong critique of the French Revolution in his *Reflections on the Revolution in France.*[34] Regarding Burke's work, Alexander wrote in 1827:

> I have been looking over Burke's works again and especially his Reflections on the French Revolution. Surely he is the prince of English writers. ...the profundity of his reasoning, the political sagacity of his views, the rich contexture of his language, all render him the most fascinating and commanding of writers on Government.[35]

Burke believed in "the sacredness of property" and that one of government's primary purposes was to protect the property rights of its citizens.[36] According to Burke, the natural inequality in talents and property distribution led to a naturally stratified society, and the existence of different classes of people was to be accepted as natural.[37] Writing

---

[32] Alexander, *Forty Years' Letters*, 2:112.

[33] Alexander, *Forty Years' Letters*, 1:135. For more on Walsh's impact upon both James and Addison Alexander, see Henry Alexander, *Life of Joseph Addison Alexander*, 1:203–211.

[34] Edmund Burke, *Reflections on the Revolution in France*, ed. Frank M. Turner (London: J. Dodsley, 1790; repr., New Haven, Yale University Press, 2003). This critique provoked Thomas Paine to write a reply entitled *The Rights of Man* (London: J. S. Jordan, 1791), a work defending the French Revolution along Enlightenment lines.

[35] Alexander, *Forty Years' Letters*, 1:103.

[36] Frank M. Turner, "Edmund Burke: The Political Actor Thinking," introduction to Burke, *Reflections on the Revolution in France*, xxxi.

[37] Turner, "Edmund Burke," xxxix-xl. Turner notes that this was a similar position taken by John Locke.

along similar lines as John Adams, Burke believed that all societies naturally have a "regal, aristocratic, and popular" element which must be harmonized into "an intricate machine."[38] Burke also believed that this harmony of diverse elements could only be brought about by religion, and that "religion was the ultimate foundation of good government, and the bedrock of civil society."[39] Since a false theology and a false political philosophy often went hand-in-hand, Burke believed that "those who undermined faith in the living Christian God also undermined faith in the natural social order."[40]

Alexander also expressed appreciation for the political writings of Hannah More, a British evangelical and social reformer. Hannah More was a friend of Edmund Burke, as well as of a circle of evangelicals known as the Clapham Sect. This group consisted of Christian leaders like Henry Venn and William Wilberforce, and they advocated for social reform in Britain from an evangelical perspective.[41] In 1828 Alexander would write: "I have been reading Miss Hannah More's works. There is an unaccountable prejudice against that good and useful woman. I esteem her to be the best of female writers."[42] In 1834, Alexander would write again to his friend: "I am deep in [Hannah] More's

---

[38] Edmund Burke, *Vindication of Natural Society*, in *The Works of the Right Honourable Edmund Burke* (Boston: Wells and Lilly, 1826), 1:54. For the relationship between the political thought of John Adams and Edmund Burke, see Elkins and McKitrick, *The Age of Federalism*, 313–314.

[39] Darrin M. McMahon, "Edmund Burke and the Literary Cabal: A Tale of Two Enlightenments," afterward in Burke, *Reflections on the Revolution in France*, 234.

[40] McMahon, "Edmund Burke and the Literary Cabal," 234–235.

[41] For more on Hannah More and the Clapham Sect, see Karen Swallow Prior, *Hannah More: The Extraordinary Life of Hannah More: Poet, Reformer, Abolitionist* (Nashville: Thomas Nelson, 2014), Anne Stott, *Hannah More: The First Victorian* (New York: Oxford University Press, 2003); Ernest Marshall Howse, *Saints in Politics: "Clapham Sect" and the Growth of Freedom* (London: Allen & Unwin, 1953).

[42] Alexander, *Forty Years' Letters*, 1:117.

life; a lovely book, from which I augur great things for evangelical religion."[43]

Alexander was especially appreciative of More's *Village Politics*, a pamphlet which expressed her rejection of the French Revolution and the political views of Thomas Paine.[44] Later in 1836, Alexander made this comment about Hannah More, showing how he understood the aristocratic classes of Britain and America, as well as his own position in American society:

> Reperusing the life of Hannah More; with more admiration and instruction than before. Truly the circle in which she moved was brilliant and great, beyond compare; but look ye, when you or I talk of emigrating to England, let us never forget that we could never gain access to that aristocratic class. The caste would forever exclude us, and our Americanism would be semi-barbarism. And therefore I should prefer the upper circle here, to the English middlings, who cringe and truckle with servility which no American could endure.[45]

Alexander understood both British and American society to be stratified into certain "circles," of which he (due to the privileges of education and status as a clergyman) was in "the upper circle," at least in America society. Hannah More shared these views of social stratification and wrote favorably of a stratified and hierarchical society, even as an abolitionist.[46] This vision of society, along with More's evangelical beliefs, her heart for social reform, and her political conservatism all resonated with Alexander.

---

[43] Alexander, *Forty Years' Letters*, 1:220.

[44] Will Chip [Hannah More], *Village Politics: Addresses to All the Mechanics, Journeymen, and Day-Labourers in Great Britain* (York: G. Walker, 1793), 4–5, 9–11.

[45] Alexander, *Forty Years' Letters*, 1:240.

[46] See Stott, *Hannah More*, 142.

The French Revolution and American "Ultra-Democracy"

American and British conservatives like Adams, Walsh, Burke, and More developed their political views against the backdrop of the French Revolution, a traumatic event that shocked and horrified many in Britain and America for its violence and godlessness.[47] Alexander's antipathy to the French Revolution grew over time. In 1827 Alexander expressed a partial admiration for the leaders of the French Revolution upon reading a biography of Napoleon:

> Never has such a spectacle been set before the world, as in the convulsive efforts of the French nation to put an end to tyranny. Never has there been exhibited such a union of physical and intellectual greatness, with the lowest and most debasing passion. The leaders of the Revolution fascinate us into admiration at their energy and daring, while their atrocity fills us with contempt and abhorrence. Danton, Mirabeau, Marat, Robespierre, Hebert, Clootz; such were the comets which first astonished, and then consumed the nation. The *Liberty* whom they adored, would have her emblem in a gigantic goddess, whose brow and glance are fired with the enthusiasm of genius, while the lower visage is that of the brute, the satyr, the fiend.[48]

The French Revolution grew more and more distasteful to Alexander as the Revolutionary spirit produced further waves of violence and social upheaval in France. After hearing of the so-called "July Revolution" of 1830, Alexander expressed his hopes that France might follow the course taken by England in 1688: "My sanguine hope is...that the French will settle down upon a limited monarchy, with a liberal charter, annual parliaments, just representation, and universal liberty of

---

[47] See More, *Village Politics*, 15–17; John Forsyth, "Alison's History of Europe," *Biblical Repertory and Princeton Review* 15 (1843): 256; and Rachel Hope Cleves, *The Reign of Terror in America: Visions of Violence from Anti-Jacobinism to Antislavery* (New York: Cambridge University Press, 2009).

[48] Alexander, *Forty Years' Letters*, 1:105.

conscience. France would then be a glorious land."[49] As civil unrest continued in France, Alexander would write on November 27, 1830: "My enthusiasm about the French Revolution has come down to zero. We may well fear a repetition of former enormities in Paris."[50] Finally, as the revolutionary spirit in France spilled over into the Belgian Revolution of 1831, Alexander would write in November of that year: "I am sick of imbecile revolutions in Europe…"[51] Alexander became so disgusted by the French revolts and rebellions that he would express a strong dislike of the French as a people. In 1840, he would write privately to Hall: "…I confess to a violent antipathy to the great nation [of France]. Except from necessity, they seem to me to be the same people they were during the Revolution. What a blessing it is to belong to the Teutonic race! The more I see of the black-eyed races of the South of Europe, the less I respect them."[52]

As a political conservative, Alexander viewed the purveyors of the French Revolution and supporters of an excessive democracy in America alike with great concern. Furthermore, he saw a connection between the populist ferment produced by Jacksonian democracy in America and the mobs that clamoured in the streets of revolutionary Paris.[53] Both proceeded from a principle of rebellion, discontentment, godlessness, and unbelief, and both were to be equally rejected.[54] After reading

---

[49] Alexander, *Forty Years' Letters*, 1:147.

[50] Alexander, *Forty Years' Letters*, 1:154.

[51] Alexander, *Forty Years' Letters*, 1:180.

[52] Alexander, *Forty Years' Letters*, 1:306–307. Alexander would later express admiration for the city of Paris upon his visit there in 1851, and yet he continued to note the godlessness among the people of Paris, as well as the "revolutionary atheism" and "French infidel democracy" that marked the land. See Alexander, *Forty Years' Letters*, 2:144–145, 147–148.

[53] Rev. Charles Nisbet, president of Dickinson College, also saw a link between the "enormities of French anarchy" and "the real anomalies and excesses of American democracy" (Samuel Miller, *Memoir of Rev. Charles Nisbet, D.D.* [New York: Robert Carter, 1840], 252; cf. 247–281).

[54] The religious views of Thomas Jefferson and Thomas Paine, both supporters of the French Revolution, likely affected the assessment of many like Alexander. Alexander referred to Jefferson as an "infidel" (Alexander, *Forty*

Basil Hall's *Travels in North America in the Years 1827 and 1828*, a British work critical of some aspects of American society, Alexander commented in 1829 that "I accede to many of his political doctrines and join in his abomination of absolute democracy."[55] Preferring a government which balanced the sentiments of the different social classes, Alexander would say in 1836: "Democracy and I are less and less friends every day I live."[56] Again, in 1843 he would write: "I am opposed to all ultra-democracy, of which the very extreme, I take it, is to make our tribute of respect dependent on mere popular like or dislike."[57] Ultra-democracy easily turned into "mob rule," something Alexander feared: "In the progress of mobs, I see everything portentous."[58] The prevalence of unruly mobs in American cities in the 1830s only confirmed these fears.[59]

Alexander also believed that the emotional rallying and stirring up of popular sentiments in the "Age of Jackson" was harmful to peace and order, and he disliked the way frenzied political campaigns went to great lengths to stir up support for particular candidates.[60] In 1844, Alexander stated:

> The agitation of the public mind at our election-crises is a very injurious paroxysm. Democracy must be a cornucopia, to balance such evils; processions, rallies, torch-bearings, "yaller-kiver" minstrelsy, poles, coons, banners, lies, idle days and weeks, gaping for office by ten for one who gets it, rotation, absorption of mind in matters too high for such minds, endless

---

Years' Letters, 2:279) and had a similar appraisal of Thomas Paine. Alexander referred to a birthday celebration for Paine held by the Society of Free Inquirers as "a horrible outrage upon the moral and religious public" (Alexander, *Forty Years' Letters*, 1:122).

[55] Alexander, *Forty Years' Letters*, 1:134.

[56] Alexander, *Forty Years' Letters*, 1:239.

[57] Alexander, *Forty Years' Letters*, 1:374.

[58] Alexander, *Forty Years' Letters*, 1:234.

[59] On the prevalence of mobs and riots in the mid-1830s, see Howe, *What Hath God Wrought*, 430-439.

[60] Alexander, *Forty Years' Letters*, 1:314.

restlessness, sacrifice of regular trades, etc., for temporary office, loquacity and debate, ending in alienation, disappointment, chagrin, and disaffection to lawful authorities. Such are the heads of my next political brochure.[61]

While preferring government to be established on a more dignified and balanced foundation, Alexander understood that a popular democracy was the only viable option for America. He stated with resignation: "...nothing else [but democracy] would do for a country like ours. It must be several ages yet before we have a noblesse, or a literary caste; and until we have, nominal aristocracy would be as ridiculous as the "Duc de Limonade," etc., of St. Domingo."[62]

The Root of "Infidel Politics"

Alexander was alarmed by the spirit of "ultra-democracy" because he believed it was connected with secularism and atheism, which were quickly gaining ground in the Western world and causing much unrest around the globe.[63] Alexander commented to Hall in 1835: "I am almost a convert to the German notion of a Spirit of the Age, independent of communication, breaking forth in simultaneous manifestation. Look at the reigning *mobs*; convent-burnings in Spain, and commotions even in quiet Berlin."[64] Alexander frequently noted that atheism was on the rise, and he believed that this global trend was at the root of much of the world's political unrest.[65]

Antebellum America was not immune to the global trend toward secularism and atheistic thought. After a visit to New York in 1830, Alexander noted: "The signs of increasing infidelity and atheism

---

[61] Alexander, *Forty Years' Letters*, 1:401.

[62] Alexander, *Forty Years' Letters*, 1:239.

[63] Alexander, *Forty Years' Letters*, 1:321.

[64] Alexander, *Forty Years' Letters*, 1:232.

[65] For his account of atheism in Germany, see Alexander, *Forty Years' Letters*, 2:319; cf. 2:150. For his thoughts on the looming specter of "revolutionary atheism" in France in 1851, see Alexander, *Forty Years' Letters*, 2:147.

greatly alarmed me."[66] In 1840, Alexander would note that "The German atheism (pantheism or Emersonism or Carlyle-ism) makes fearful progress in Boston...."[67] When President Jackson refused a proposal made by the New York City clergy for a national day of fasting at the beginning of a cholera outbreak in 1832, Alexander said to his friend Hall:

> Pray put this thought into shape, and publish it in the daily papers, viz.: "the affectation of courage or indifference, or fool-hardiness, on the approach of such a pestilence, is a contempt of God; a Pharaoh-like hardening of the heart: like Nineveh, we should all be in sackcloth. The question is not between evangelical and rational Christians, nor even between Christians and infidels, but between Theists and Atheists; for if there is a God and a controlling power, then it is wise to humble ourselves before him." ...we ought to be awake as we have never been before, in calling aloud upon sinners to save themselves from this untoward generation of practical atheism.[68]

Alexander was concerned about the effects of atheism upon America, holding that "true religion" lies at the foundation of a free society:

> The great and invaluable gift of freedom furnishes no safeguard here, unless it be coupled with true religion. Freedom is only a condition, under which men's principles act. If those principles are destructive, freedom is but an open door to ruin. The absolute freedom of a thoroughly immoral people, "hateful and hating one another," would be nothing short of hell. Indeed, the instinct of self-preservation does not allow men to

---

[66] Alexander, *Forty Years' Letters*, 1:149.

[67] Alexander, *Forty Years' Letters*, 1:290. Alexander is referring here to the Transcendentalist movement. For his extended critique of the Transcendentalists, see James W. Alexander and Albert Dod, "Transcendentalism," *Biblical Repertory and Princeton Review* 11 (1839): 37–101. The first half of this article was written by Alexander.

[68] Alexander, *Forty Years' Letters*, 1:191.

remain long in any state approaching this; for, in dread of one another, they are fain to take refuge under the protective shadow of military domination or imperial tyranny.[69]

Alexander believed that the tyranny of a godless democracy was just as cruel as the tyranny of a godless despot, and both forms of political oppression have their root in the denial of God. Alexander noted to Hall in 1834 his concurrence with this piece of writing by the Prussian judge and politician Ludwig von Gerlach:

> Liberalism and Absolutism, though seeming opposites, may be traced to a common trunk, viz., the severance of the State from God... God...is the sole source of all liberty. He is the sole, legitimate, supreme Sovereign. Therefore a prince who does not consider his lordship as God's loan, who does not limit it by God's law, and who places the highest source and principle of his rights, not in the divine will, but in some earthly end of state... or who does not accord to his subjects the sacred rights given them of God, is a true *Revolutionist*. And a popular association, however democratically constituted, which makes their own will, or the will of the sovereign multitude, the highest state-law, is truly *despotic*.[70]

Alexander also commended German Christians like Gerlach for their contentment and loyalty to the monarch over against the rebellious spirit of the Jacksonian democrats: "The Christians of Germany...are all (except Neander and his school) legitimatists, who regard the king as God's earthly image, and hold the twofold command, Fear God *and* honor the king, as indivisible. They cannot abstract democracy from infidelity. This loyalty, in some of them, is very lovely."[71]

---

[69] Alexander, *Discourses on Common Topics*, 29.

[70] Alexander, *Forty Years' Letters*, 1:223. Alexander refers to him as "Louis," the French variation of this name. Ernst Ludwig von Gerlach was a conservative political figure who would go on to oppose Otto von Bismarck's consolidation of Germany.

[71] Alexander, *Forty Years' Letters*, 1:222; cf. 2:93.

While commending the German Christians of the 1830s for their resistance to the revolutionary spirit, Alexander was pessimistic regarding the future of America: "Every thing nowadays seems to betoken the triumph, at least for a season, of ignorance, violence, agrarianism, and the canaille [unruly mobs]; and the worst is, that when a country comes out of this fit, it usually falls into that of despotism."[72] Years before a civil war actually broke out, Alexander saw enough cause for alarm in the religious and political spirit of the day. Writing in 1836, Alexander would say:

> I am alarmed at the unexampled audacity of the 19 Van Buren electors of Maryland. It seems to have come to this, that when the wagon of state goes in a road unpleasant to a minority of passengers, they may be allowed to remove all the linch-pins and cut the traces. Take this in connexion with Dallas's doctrine that conventions may annul compacts, and we have the spectre of anarchy and civil war before us. I fear things must be worst before they are better.[73]

As the forces of secularism were impacting and revolutionizing countries around the world, Alexander believed that Jacksonian America was not immune. It too was being shaped by a popular godlessness which took the form of "ultra-democracy" and "infidel politics."[74] With his conservative and Christian outlook, Alexander felt he was increasingly out of step with the prevailing American spirit of his day.

---

[72] Alexander, *Forty Years' Letters*, 1:237.

[73] Alexander, *Forty Years' Letters*, 1:243–244. For more on this incident, see *A Brief Outline of the Rise, Progress, and Failure of the Revolutionary Scheme of the Nineteen Van Buren Electors* (Baltimore: Sands & Neilson, 1837).

[74] Alexander, *Forty Years' Letters*, 1:311. This phrase "infidel politics" was used by Alexander in reference to Orestes Brownson's *Charles Ellwood* (London: Chapman Brothers, 1845). Brownson later converted to Roman Catholicism and repudiated the political views expressed in this book.

Politics and Princeton

Alexander's Federalist and conservative political views may have differed from the dominant Jacksonian sentiments of his day, but they
were not at all unusual for a Princetonian. While many connected to
Old Princeton were interested in political issues, Charles Hodge wrote
the most on this subject, even more than Alexander, especially as the
Civil War approached and brought a formal division among the Old
School Presbyterians.[75] Although a variety of views may have existed
among the Princetonians, the political perspective expressed by Hodge
was strikingly similar to the views expressed by Alexander.[76]

Hodge, like Alexander, disliked the party of Jackson and Van Buren and the populist egalitarianism it represented. Like Alexander, his
attachment to Federalist positions ran deep. According to Archibald
Alexander Hodge, Charles Hodge was "trained by his family in the
opinions of the old Federalist party of Washington, Hamilton, and
Madison... He had a poor opinion of President Jackson."[77] Hodge

---

[75] For a fuller discussion of Hodge's political views, see Carwardine,
"The Politics of Charles Hodge," 247-297; John W. Stewart, *Mediating the
Center: Charles Hodge on American Science, Language, Literature, and Politics*
(Princeton: Princeton Theological Seminary, 1995), 67-110; William S.
Barker, "The Social Views of Charles Hodge (1797-1878): A Study in 19th-
Century Calvinism and Conservatism," *Presbyterian* 1 (Spring 1975): 1-22.

[76] As a young man, Samuel Miller was greatly interested in political affairs as well and had at one time been a strong supporter of Thomas Jefferson,
taking a position against John Adams and the Federalist Party. He later regret-
ted his choice, and his son referred to his attachment to Jefferson as "a temporary hallucination" (Samuel Miller, Jr., *The Life of Samuel Miller, D.D.,
LL.D.,* 2 vols. [Philadelphia: Claxton, Remsen, and Haffelfinger, 1869], 1:129;
cf. 1:128-136). As a supporter of Jefferson, Miller had held a favorable view of
the French Revolution for longer than others, and he considered himself
throughout his life to be a "sincere and honest Republican" (Miller, *Life of
Samuel Miller*, 1:94-96, 133). Alexander's father, Archibald Alexander, was
not as interested in political matters as his son, and he only expressed his political views in private (Alexander, *Life of Archibald Alexander*, 379).

[77] Archibald Hodge, *Life of Charles Hodge*, 230.

stated in 1861: "We never had a blood relation in the world, so far as we know, who was not a federalist in the old sense of the word."[78]

Hodge's dislike of Jacksonianism is evident in his dislike of universal suffrage—a component of the "ultra-democracy" which Alexander disliked as well. In a letter to his brother Hugh, Hodge wrote disparagingly in 1837 of "the ascendancy of the rabble" and voiced his opposition to universal suffrage: "If we could have a Republic with the right of suffrage restricted to householders, who can read and write, and have been at least ten years in the country, we could get along grandly. But a democracy with universal suffrage will soon be worse than an aristocracy..."[79] As Jackson's successor, Martin Van Buren, was about to be elected, Hodge wrote again to his brother in 1837: "It seems that, notwithstanding all the country has suffered, the elections are going in favor of Van Buren, almost as much as ever. I do not believe we can stand it much longer. We must get rid of universal suffrage or we shall go to ruin."[80] Hodge, like Alexander, also understood that an egalitarian democracy had gained the ascendancy in America and little could be done about it. He bemoaned this fact in a letter to his brother, written in 1844: "In this country the Democratic party must always be the strongest, and it is only on extraordinary occasions, and for a short period, that the Whig, the Conservative, the Federal, or by whatever name the mass of the intelligence and property of the country may be called, can get the upper hand."[81] As committed Federalists, both Hodge and

---

[78] Charles Hodge, "The Church and the Country," *Biblical Repertory and Princeton Review* 33 (1861): 333.

[79] Archibald Hodge, *Life of Charles Hodge*, 233. Hodge was not alone among Presbyterians in his rejection of universal suffrage. According to Charles Nisbet: "the right of universal suffrage...is a nuisance and not a blessing, as it reduces elections to a mere lottery, in which demagogues have the disposal of the prizes, and ninety-nine parts in a hundred of the electors know nothing of either of the candidates, and often care as little" (Miller, *Life of Nisbet*, 263).

[80] Archibald Hodge, *Life of Charles Hodge*, 233.

[81] Archibald Hodge, *Life of Charles Hodge*, 346.

Alexander understood that their political views were inescapably in the minority in the "Age of Jackson."

Conclusion

James W. Alexander opposed the great societal forces of egalitarian populism and "ultra-democracy" that were sweeping America during the "Age of Jackson." As a political conservative of "Federalist" persuasions, Alexander preferred a more traditional social order and abhorred the revolutionary spirit percolating among the masses. In Alexander's mind, the political shift toward democratic egalitarianism was due to secular ideology and atheistic philosophies that were gaining ground in the minds of the general public.[82]

While differing politically from at least two of his brothers, Alexander's political views were not unusual for one attached to Princeton Seminary. Together with individuals like Charles Hodge, Alexander resisted the dominant political thought of his day and sought to conserve a social and political order that was more like the stratified society of England than the egalitarian vision of society promoted in revolutionary France. While Alexander and Hodge were not alone in their anti-Jacksonian views, they stood apart from what was a dominant force in antebellum American thought. Alexander recognized certain social inequalities that existed as natural and legitimate, and he would not strive to overthrow them.

Alexander's social reforms were not driven by a vision of absolute social equality. He simply did not think that Scripture supported the vision of political and social egalitarianism advanced by the supporters of Jefferson and Jackson. Not all social inequalities were regarded by Alexander as moral wrongs to be righted. Social theories which did not recognize the ultimate authority and sovereignty of God to establish

---

[82] This conclusion is similar to that expressed by Christian historian C. Gregg Singer. See C. Gregg Singer, *A Theological Interpretation of American History*, 3rd ed. (Greenville, SC: A Press, 1994), 24–91.

individuals in unequal stations in life were to be regarded as fundamentally godless and immoral.

Chapter 3
The Rejection of Economic Collectivism

As a conservative, Alexander rejected forms of economic collectivism which sought to overturn the social disparities rooted in the ownership of private property. Just as he rejected the political leveling, egalitarianism, and "ultra-democracy" of the Jacksonian era, he also rejected attempts to apply these principles to the economic sphere. Numerous social theorists in antebellum America advanced forms of economic collectivism as a key strategy for reforming society. Many were attracted to attempts to set up collectivist communities as a means of social reform in America. Some of these communities were secular in nature, held together by an optimistic philosophy of central planning, economic cooperation, and shared property. Later socialists would call the communalistic rejections of free-market capitalism in this period "utopian socialism."[1] Alongside the utopian socialist movement, trade unionism began to take root in antebellum America as well, holding out the promise of a better life to the working classes. Alexander rejected both of these approaches to social reform. In keeping with his more conservative set of social and economic principles, he labored to better the poor and working classes through more biblical and evangelical means.

The Utopian Socialists

Utopian socialism was brought to antebellum America by a group of innovators and social engineers who rejected traditional Christianity

---

[1] Frederick Engels, *Socialism: Utopian and Scientific* (Chicago: Charles H. Kerr, 1914), 51–75. See also J. F. C. Harrison, *Robert Owen and the Owenites in Britain and America: The Quest for the New Moral World* (London: Routledge and Kegan Paul, 1969), 46.

and held to an essentially secular and humanist philosophy. Most of these visionaries came to America from Europe, where class conflict between industrialists and factory workers was more severe.[2] One such innovator was Robert Owen. Owen had been a successful businessman in New Lanark, Scotland, where he creatively extended philanthropy among his textile workers to the level of complete social reorganization.[3] Being radically opposed to religion and traditional marriage, Owen wrote many pamphlets to express his social philosophy of secular communalism.[4] The founder of British socialism, Robert Owen worked to establish harmonious communities of laborers that would win the world to his social philosophy by their example.[5] Owen devised the plan of a self-governing, model community where five hundred to twenty-five hundred people would unite around an enlarged social unity, holding all their property in common. Many familial rights and duties would be reorganized so that family loyalties would not compete or interfere with the loyalty that was to be shown equally to the entire community.[6] Through "scientific" analysis and central planning, Owen believed

---

[2] Walter A. McDougall, *Throes of Democracy: The American Civil War Era* (New York: Harper Collins, 2008), 139.

[3] Harrison, *Robert Owen and the Owenites in Britain and America*, 11–42.

[4] Engels, *Socialism*, 72. For an anthology of Owen's social and political thought, see Robert Owen, *A New View of Society and Other Writings*, ed. Gregory Claeys (London: Penguin Books, 1991).

[5] Engels, *Socialism*, 73.

[6] Although Robert Owen was very critical of traditional marriage and the traditional family unit, the Owenites did not go as far in their restructuring of the family as John Humphrey Noyes's Oneida community. In Noyes's scheme, sexual expression was made communal, with no other family unit recognized but that of the community. See Harrison, *Robert Owen*, 59–62; Donald E. Pitzer, "The New Moral World of Robert Owen and New Harmony," in Donald E. Pitzer, ed., *America's Communal Utopias* (Chapel Hill, NC: University of North Carolina Press, 1997), 119; and Lawrence Foster, "Free Love and Community: John Humphrey Noyes and the Oneida Perfectionists," in Pitzer, *America's Communal Utopias*, 256–258.

that human happiness could be obtained and a harmonious, cooperative society established.[7]

When Owen first came to America in 1824, his views on marriage, family, and religion were not widely known.[8] Upon his arrival, he was received by a largely favorable press as a philanthropist, obtaining an audience with politicians at the highest levels, including President Monroe and former presidents Jefferson and Madison.[9] In 1825, President-elect John Quincy Adams gave Owen permission to deliver two special addresses in the Capitol building, which he himself attended.[10] As President, Adams even displayed in the White House a six-foot-square architectural model of a village designed by Owen to bring about his vision of a "New Moral World" in America.[11] In 1825 Owen established a collectivist community in New Harmony, Indiana, but this experiment failed after two years.[12] With many Owenite colonies attempted in Great Britain as well, at least eighteen others were attempted in antebellum America, all of which disbanded after a few years.[13]

Frances Wright, a follower of Owen and a part of the New Harmony commune, tried to carry out the Owenite vision, pressing social

---

[7] Pitzer, "New Moral World of Robert Owen," 100–101.

[8] In 1829, Owen publicly debated "the evidences of Christianity" with Alexander Campbell. These debates made Owen's unorthodox religious views known to the general population. See Robert Owen and Alexander Campbell, *Debate on the Evidences of Christianity* (Bethany, VA: Alexander Campbell, 1829).

[9] Howe, *What Hath God Wrought*, 293.

[10] Howe, *What Hath God Wrought*, 294.

[11] Pitzer, "The New Moral World of Robert Owen," 96–98.

[12] Harrison, *Robert Owen and the Owenites*, 164-165. The failure of this colony prompted Alexander to write later to Hall: "A grand book might be made (for the English market) out of a full and fair account of the New Harmony (Owenite) Institute in the West. Say and McCullough, and some other men, could tell some good stories of Socialism. It would sell in England and do much to cripple Owen" (Alexander, *Forty Years' Letters*, 1:297).

[13] Howe, *What Hath God Wrought*, 294. For a list of these communities, see the appendix in Pitzer, *America's Communal Utopias*, 481–482.

egalitarianism along even further. Like Owen's son Robert Dale Owen, Wright was an abolitionist, and she attempted to combine Owen's vision of a model community with abolitionism.[14] In 1826, Wright tried to organize an Owenite community of former slaves in Nashoba, Tennessee, in which she enjoyed the support of many prominent individuals, including Jefferson, Madison, Jackson, and the Marquis de Lafayette.[15] While her collectivist community in Nashoba ended after only four years, Wright's influence in antebellum America was secured by her bold advocacy of emancipation and women's rights.[16]

Another utopian socialist that generated an even broader following in America was Charles Fourier, a French social theorist. Fourier, like Owen, believed that society could be revolutionized through the example of planned, collectivist communities, which he called "phalanxes."[17] As an expression of social evolution, individuals in these communities would cooperate instead of compete and would work together for the common good of the commune.[18] Fourier's ideas were popularized and adapted for an American audience by Arthur Brisbane, and Fourierism quickly found adherents among such notables as Horace Greeley, William Henry Channing, and Parke Godwin.[19] Unlike the Owenites, the American Fourierites did not attack religion or marriage.

[14] Pitzer, "Robert Owen and New Harmony," 118. See also Robert Dale Owen, *The Wrong of Slavery, The Right of Emancipation, and the Future of the African Race in the United States* (Philadelphia: J. B. Lippincott, 1864).

[15] Howe, *What Hath God Wrought*, 309.

[16] Pitzer, "Robert Owen and New Harmony," 118. For more on Frances Wright, see Celia Morris, *Fanny Wright: Rebel in America* (Harvard: Harvard University Press, 1984).

[17] Howe, *What Hath God Wrought*, 295.

[18] Carl J. Guarneri, "Brook Farm and the Fourierist Phalanxes," in Pitzer, *America's Communal Utopias*, 162–163.

[19] Sydney E. Ahlstrom, *A Religious History of the American People*, 2nd ed. (New Haven: Yale University Press, 2004), 498. See also Carl J. Guarneri, *The Utopian Alternative: Fourierism in Nineteenth-Century America* (Ithaca, NY: Cornell University Press, 1991), 25–34. For the essence of Brisbane's thought, see Albert Brisbane, *Social Destiny of Man* (Philadelphia: C. F. Stollmeyer, 1840).

Instead, some of them presented the phalanxes as completely compatible with Christianity.[20] When the Transcendentalist community in Brook Farm, Massachusetts, adopted Fourierism in the late 1830s, Fourierism spread even further, attaching itself to the Transcendentalist movement as a whole.[21] Between 1843 and 1858, at least twenty-eight Fourierite "phalanxes" were established in America, directly involving at least 15,000 people.[22] While these experiments were entered into with great enthusiasm, most of them were abandoned before the outbreak of the Civil War.[23]

Many other social theorists besides Owen, Wright, and the Fourierites were also promoting forms of utopian socialism in antebellum America.[24] While utopian socialism may have existed only in pockets of antebellum American culture, the concern for social reform and the optimistic humanism that it embodied were widespread. According to Ralph Waldo Emerson, "We are all a little wild here with numberless projects of social reform. Not a reading man but has a draft of a new community in his waistcoat pocket."[25] Far from being a fringe

---

[20] Howe, *What Hath God Wrought*, 295. See also Guarneri, "Brook Farm and the Fourierist Phalanxes,"164.

[21] For more on the relation between Fourierism and Transcendentalism in antebellum America, see Guarneri, *The Utopian Alternative*, 44–59.

[22] Guarneri, "Brook Farm and the Fourierist Phalanxes," 167. For a list of Fourierite communities, see the appendix in Pitzer, *America's Communal Utopias*, 460–461.

[23] Howe, *What Hath God Wrought*, 296.

[24] There were many types of socialism and communalism present in antebellum America. Orestes Brownson, before his conversion, along with Étienne Cabet, also promoted forms of socialist thought in America through their writings and communal experiments. For information on Cabet, see Robert P. Sutton, "An American Elysium: The Icarian Communities" in Pitzer, *America's Communal Utopias*, 279–294. For information on Brownson, see Ahlstrom, *A Religious History of the American People*, 549–552. For a comparison of Owenism and Fourierism, see Philip S. Foner, *History of the Labor Movement in the United States*, 10 vols. (New York: International Publishers, 1947–1994), 1:170–178.

[25] Quoted in Ahlstrom, *Religious History of the American People*, 491.

movement, utopian socialism embodied the secular and egalitarian ideals that were increasingly popular in the "Age of Jackson."[26]

Alexander's Rejection of Utopian Socialism

Utopian socialism was not a distant phenomenon to Alexander and Old Princeton. Alexander wrote to Hall in 1844 that: "Brisbane, the Fourierist, and some aids, are looking out for a farm of a thousand acres in this neighbourhood [of Princeton], whereon to exemplify their socialism."[27] Albert Brisbane, one of the leading proponents of Fourier's views, was successful in his search. Along with Horace Greeley, he did in fact establish the "North American Phalanx" community in Monmouth County, New Jersey, not far from Princeton. It attracted many visitors and received a significant amount of attention in the press.[28] As Fourierism progressed, Alexander noted that even a number of Princeton alumni were being attracted to it. Writing to Hall that same year, Alexander stated: "Parke Godwin, the leading Fourierite, is an alumnus of the College and Seminary. Cooke represents the scheme as becoming formidable, from the numbers taken in."[29]

In spite of its appeal to many, even some connected with Princeton, Alexander categorically rejected utopian socialism as incompatible with biblical Christianity. He believed that the man-centered and materialistic approach of the utopian socialists set it apart from the spiritual solutions offered by biblical Christianity:

> The excesses [of social alteration] toward which infidelity drives [its followers], are counterfeits and caricatures of the very blessings which we owe to true religion. For, is not Christianity the religion of the poor and oppressed? Is it not the

---

[26] Howe, *What Hath God Wrought*, 292–293.

[27] Alexander, *Forty Years' Letters*, 1:375.

[28] Guarneri, "Brook Farm and Fourierist Phalanxes," 168.

[29] Alexander, *Forty Years' Letters*, 1:392. For more on Parke Godwin, see Carlos Baker, "Parke Godwin: Pathfinder in Politics and Journalism," in *The Lives of Eighteen from Princeton*, ed. William Thorp (Princeton: Princeton University Press, 1946), 212–231.

religion of philanthropy? Does it not teach the common origin and spiritual equality of all men, in the sight of God? Does it not seek, and at the safest moments procure, human freedom and social rights? Must it not be named pre-eminently the system of true progress? Yea, yea, in despite of Garrison and Proudhon, forever yea.[30]

Whereas utopian socialism seemed to elevate man, with its platitudes of equality and harmony, only Christianity provides the true solutions for the ills of mankind. It alone can answer man's problems. Since utopian socialism promoted an alternative assessment of human ills and an alternative solution to the woes of humanity, Alexander rejected it as a counterfeit competitor to Christianity.[31]

Alexander saw the utopian socialism of Owen, Wright, and Fourier as an expression of the contemporary unbelief threatening the fabric of American society. In a sermon entitled, "Our Modern Unbelief," Alexander analyzed the nature of unbelieving thought in his day, connecting experiments in "social progress" with the same secularism and godlessness that was behind the French Revolution:

> The Infidelity of our age connects itself with freedom and social progress. So far as the infidelity of France was a reaction against hierarchy and the pope, it had the same colours. Hence the very men who murdered priesthood in the September massacres, were loud in cries of liberty, equality, and fraternity. But this policy of modern unbelief is much more boldly marked. Hence the cry, on every side, that Christianity

---

[30] Alexander, *Discourses on Common Topics*, 24-25. Pierre-Joseph Proudhon was a French socialist and political philosopher. For more on Proudhon, see Henri de Lubac, *The un-Marxian Socialist: A Study of Proudhon*, trans. Canon R. E. Scantlebury (New York: Sheed & Ward, 1948).

[31] Alexander's friend and collaborator at the American Sunday School Union, Frederick Augustus Packard wrote a critical biography of Robert Owen, entitled *Life of Robert Owen* (Philadelphia: Ashmead & Evans, 1866). Packard shared Alexander's overall assessment of Owen and utopian socialism.

is a failure; that the Church has not made men happy... It is a part of this scheme to glory in humanity as such; to assert the independence and self-sufficiency of man; to deify the creature, and pushing the rights of man to a jacobinical and impracticable extreme.[32]

Alexander saw the "modern unbelief" expressed in social experiments like utopian socialism as having similar characteristics to the humanism and rationalism expressed in the philosophy behind the French Revolution. Each of these movements rejected Christianity and elevated human potential, reasoning, and autonomy to the extreme. Building on a foundation of human pride, the utopian socialists were spreading their destructive philosophies in antebellum America at an alarming rate. Alexander sketched out how harmful these philosophies were to American society:

There is something so attaching and gracious in the first aspect of a levelling system, that any scheme of this kind gains multitudes of converts among the oppressed, the suffering, the discontented, the aspiring, and the greedy. Even in our own free commonwealth, where every man who deserves to rise may succeed in it, so far as outward restrictions are concerned, there begins to be more and more every year, a half suppressed hum and murmur among certain large classes; as if all ranks must be brought to a common level; as if the capitalist and the transient worker must share alike; as if the accumulations of industry must become a spoil for the idlest; as if labour with the hands were the only title to enjoyment. This being openly and diametrically opposed to the letter of Scripture, these teachers...are pretty sure to end up discovering

---

[32] Alexander, *Discourses on Common Topics*, 23. In this sermon, Alexander noted many differences as well as similarities between eighteenth and nineteenth century unbelief, and his entire sermon is filled with a perceptive analysis of the history of ideas. For a helpful analysis of late eighteenth century unbelief, Alexander endorsed Robert Hall's *Modern Infidelity Considered with Respect to Its Influence upon Society* (Charlestown, SC: Samuel Etheridge, 1801).

that the Bible is false. Thus, strange as it may seem, philanthropy, unsanctified, may lead unsound minds to unbelief.
…with the unheard-of emigration from foreign countries, we
have imported infidel socialism and communism… I leave, as
not pertaining to the pulpit, the question how far this influx
from corrupt sources may be expected to modify our political
institutions.[33]

Alexander saw the social egalitarianism of Jacksonian democracy and
the economic egalitarianism of utopian socialism as both part of a "leveling system" of unscriptural thought that was coming to America from
Europe. Since these schemes of reform would actually bring harm to
the unique character of American society and its political institutions,
Alexander rejected them in all their varied expressions.

Another reason Alexander rejected utopian socialism was for its
assault upon marriage and the family. Utopian socialists like Owen recognized that not only did private property stand in the way of his societal vision, so also did the family unit. Differences in family and upbringing lie at the root of a large measure of social and economic inequalities. This is why it must be done away with. With utopian socialists
in mind, Alexander stated: "It is almost an unfailing index of the modern infidel, that he inveighs against the perpetuity and sanctity of marriage. By an easy process, the sanctions of property are worn away."[34]
In Henry A. Boardman's *The Bible in the Family*, which was bound together and sold with Alexander's *Thoughts on Family Worship* as early
as 1858, Boardman calls "socialism" (along with polygamy and "the
unrestrained power of divorce") one of the three "chief systems or
principles opposed to the family constitution."[35] Responding to the attack of Robert Dale Owen on "single-family arrangements," Boardman
describes Owen's system in connection with its position on the family:

---

[33] Alexander, *Discourses on Common Topics*, 23–24.

[34] Alexander, *Discourses on Common Topics*, 29.

[35] Henry A. Boardman, *The Bible in the Family*, in Henry A. Boardman
and James W. Alexander, *The Bible in the Family; and Thoughts on Family Worship* (London: T. Nelson, 1858), 11.

The two distinctive features of his scheme are—*first*, That marriage shall continue only during the pleasure of the parties; and, *secondly*, That in place of single families individuals shall live in communities, the property being held in common, and the children to be separated from their parents and trained together by nurses appointed for that purpose. It seems incredible that a system so monstrous and so absurd, should meet with the slightest countenance in any civilized country.[36]

Alexander made his agreement with Boardman explicit in his *Thoughts on Family Worship*, stating that "the empirical schemes of Godwin, St. Simon, Fourier, and Owen...tear the household elements asunder."[37] Elsewhere, Alexander stated: "These Fourier-systems would make every one live in public, and obliterate little family-circles, and all that we call Home."[38]

Alexander believed that strong families make for a strong society, in that it is strong families that are able to train children to be healthy, independent, responsible, and able to take care of themselves. Utopian socialists attacked the family, Alexander believed, because they wanted to encourage dependency and weakness amongst men and women instead of strength and independency. According to Alexander:

It is not more true that the infant brood grows to the power of caring for themselves in the nest, than that men are formed into the habits of life in the family. It is the earliest, cheapest, safest, and mightiest institution for this purpose. *Hence it is the*

---

[36] Boardman, *The Bible in the Family*, 12.

[37] James W. Alexander, *Thoughts on Family Worship* (Philadelphia: Presbyterian Board of Education, 1847), 103. Henri de Saint-Simon was an early French socialist, whose followers also interacted with Fourier (see Guarneri, *The Utopian Alternative*, 20-22). William Godwin was a British political philosopher who advocated an anarchist political philosophy. See Peter Marshall, *The Anarchist Writings of William Godwin* (London: Freedom Press, 1986).

[38] Alexander, *Forty Years' Letters*, 1:376.

especial object of assault from the gathering hordes of disorganizing reformers in our day. On every side, under the guidance of the St. Simons, Fouriers, and Owens, we hear the outcry against the domestic temple.[39]

Strong families produced strong individuals, and strong families make for a healthy society, since they are the fundamental unit of social government. Alexander continues: "As the family was the earliest community, so this is the earliest form of government; and, notwithstanding the dreams of Rousseau and his disciples, about a *social contract*, which never existed, here is the true origin of States."[40] Alexander believed that a great deal of the social evils in his day resulted from a breakdown in the traditional family. He stated: "The popular evils which threaten our country, arise in good measure from a spirit of insubordination, and this is caused by neglect of parental authority. He who has never learned to obey and honour his father and his mother, will never yield to magistracy and law. The evil is bold and increasing."[41] By wrongly diagnosing the cause of society's ills, utopian socialists were proposing solutions that were actually doing more harm to society than good:

> Ignorant of the true sources of pauperism and oppression, our ruling pseudo-philanthropists are in perpetual agitation about the wrongs of labour, the rights of women, and the reconstruction of society. "Association," such as they propose, would pluck away the hearthstone and break the marriage-ring. Forgetful of the homely sentence, that the largest house is not large enough for two families, they would take down all partitions, throw a whole community into one, cashier the natural guardians of infancy, and subject masses of youth, in phalanxes, to the regimental drill of newly-invented education. As bubble after bubble explodes, and successive prophets of socialism fall into deserved contempt, it is hoped that the world

---

[39] Alexander, *Thoughts on Family Worship*, 164 (emphasis mine).

[40] Alexander, *Thoughts on Family Worship*, 166.

[41] Alexander, *Thoughts on Family Worship*, 167.

will become satisfied with the constitution which dates back as far as Paradise.[42]

By making the family unit secondary to the broader community, utopian socialism weakened the family, the basic unit of society. Socialism's tendency to dislocate and destroy the family unit is a significant reason why Alexander opposed it.[43]

Alexander's Opposition to Trade Unionism

Another system promoting social and economic egalitarianism as a means of social reform in antebellum America was trade unionism. Like the utopian socialists, the trade unionists believed that the lives of laborers could be improved through unification and mutual cooperation. Some utopian socialists in the nineteenth century lent their support to trade unionism as well.[44] Instead of competing for employment, trade unions encouraged workers to unite together so that they might effectively demand increased wages and better working conditions from their employers. Although trade unions had only a limited presence in antebellum America, they too alarmed Alexander, who saw them

---

[42] Alexander, *Thoughts on Family Worship*, 165. Packard similarly concluded: "Whatever theory of social reform men may devise, and however flattering may be the temporary success of schemes for the alleviation of specific evils, the grand central point from which all must spring, and to which all must converge, is the *family*. The state and the church are but expansion of this original, divinely-constituted social organization..." (Packard, *Life of Robert Owen*, 212).

[43] For a discussion of family life in Fourierist communities, see Guarneri, *The Utopian Alternative*, 197-203.

[44] Robert Owen, for one, was a supporter of trade unionism as well as socialism (Engels, *Socialism*, 73). Most utopian socialists did not believe that trade unionism would be ultimately successful, given that it tried to work within the capitalistic system of "labor for wages" (Foner, *History of the Labor Movement*, 1:188-190).

closely linked to the socialist thought of Fourier and Owen.[45] Writing
to Hall in 1830, Alexander stated:

> The movements of the Jacobin party calling themselves...the
> "Working Men," give me unfeigned alarm, more than any
> threats of disunion, or violence of mere party rage. If we love
> our country, something must be done. It will not do to despise
> so formidable an array. They are indeed, with us, not the *dregs*,
> but in the exercise of their elective franchise, the *primum mo-*
> *bile* of this nation. The Godwinism, Owenism, *sans culottism*,
> (aut quocunque gaudent nomine,) [or whatever name they de-
> light in] which possesses them, may ruin us. Could not a series
> of "Letters to Working Men" be put in some popular journal
> commending honest labour, asserting the rights of mechanics,
> etc., but unveiling the naked deformity of this levelling sys-
> tem? Could not you serve your country, by doing something
> of the sort? It would be arduous, but by so doing, you would
> deserve well of posterity. No better work, I truly think, could
> just now engage any honest patriot. If I could, I would try, but
> I cannot.[46]

---

[45] Howe, *What Hath God Wrought*, 549. For more on trade unions in an-
tebellum America, see Howe, *What Hath God Wrought*, 546-552. Robert Lewis
Dabney also noted a close connection between trade unionism and socialism.
See Robert Lewis Dabney, "Labor Unions, the Strike and the Commune," in
Discussions, 5 vols. (Harrisonburg, VA: Sprinkle Publications, 1994-1999),
4:294-320.

[46] Alexander, *Forty Years' Letters*, 1:145-146. The words "Jacobin" and
"*sans culottism*" have reference to the revolutionary parties and ideology of
the French Revolution. For more on the "Working Men" political parties and
their connection with trades unions, see Howe, *What Hath God Wrought*, 539-
548; and Foner, *History of the Labor Movement*, 1:130-140. For an expression
of the Working Men's views, see Stephen Simpson, *The Working Man's Manual: A New Theory of Political Economy* (Philadelphia: Thomas L. Bonsal, 1831).

In 1836, Alexander continued to hope that someone might produce something in print to counter trade unionism among the working classes: "It occurs to me that a tract might be written in the dialogue form, after the model of [Hannah] More's *Village Politics*, against the trades unions; but how could it be circulated?"[47]

Over time, Alexander resolved himself to take up the task of writing a wide-ranging series of anonymous letters to the working classes to provide them with an alternative message. He did so under the pen-name "Charles Quill."[48] As Charles Quill, Alexander wrote numerous letters to the working classes in the *Newark Daily Advertiser*, some of which were bound together and printed in a volume entitled, *The American Mechanic*.[49] After this title went through multiple printings, Alexander decided to write a second book of Charles Quill letters. He mentioned his plan for a sequel to Hall in 1839, saying:

> I should like to advise with you a little about the sequel to the American Mechanic, which I have been preparing… The plan is just the same, but I have pitched the tone of it two or three degrees higher, as to style, allusion, etc. Still I wish it to be a book for the working classes. I feel encouraged to bestow such little labours as I may be able to put forth, more and more on the working classes, the rather because they are the great object of the infidels, socialists, agrarians, Owenites, Wrightites, and diabolians generally.[50]

---

[47] Alexander, *Forty Years' Letters*, 1:240.

[48] See Appendix 1 for the *Newark Daily Advertiser*'s description of Charles Quill to its readers.

[49] Charles Quill [James W. Alexander], *The American Mechanic* (Philadelphia: Henry Perkins, 1838).

[50] Alexander, *Forty Years' Letters*, 1:283. The "Agrarians," led by Thomas Skidmore and George Henry Evans, held that every man has a right to own enough land to till for his own subsistence. Skidmore believed that all property should be seized and equally redistributed, while Evans believed that the unsettled land in the west could be successfully divided up and given away, thus attracting excess labor westward and driving up the price of labor in eastern cities. Evans' National Reform Association was influential in the eventual formulation and passage of the Homestead Act of 1862 (Howe, *What Hath*

This book appeared in 1839 under the title *The Working-Man.*[51] It too went through numerous printings.

One series of Alexander's "Charles Quill" letters took up the issue of trade unionism directly. Writing to Hall in 1838, Alexander stated: "By recourse to the 'Newark Daily' you will see some able papers, by a great political economist [Charles Quill], on Trades Unions."[52] In these articles, Alexander made his case against allowing trade unionism to advance in America.[53] Alexander began these articles by stating: "In what is to be offered, I shall make little effort to be original, but rather attempt to abridge and popularize important views of this subject, which have been given in works not very accessible to the persons for whom I write."[54] After giving some historical background on trade unionism, Alexander recounted the workings of trade unions in Europe, quoting from a wide variety of sources.[55] The picture Alexander paints of trade unions in Europe is one of coercion, secrecy, and violence.[56] Because trades unions seek to raise and keep up wages "above their natural rate," they must work against nature and strive against employers and non-unionized workers by intimidation and oppression.[57] Alexander quoted Henry Vethake's *Principles of Political*

God Wrought, 540–541). For an expression of Skidmore's philosophy, see Thomas Skidmore, *The Rights of Man to Property!* (New York: Alexander Ming, 1829).

[51] Charles Quill [James W. Alexander], *The Working Man* (Philadelphia: Perkins, 1839).

[52] Alexander, *Forty Years' Letters*, 1:266.

[53] Alexander wrote a series of eight articles for the *Newark Daily Advertiser* on trade unions in the summer of 1838. Two of these were reprinted in *The Working Man* and the rest of them were never reprinted. For the complete text of the full series of these newspaper articles, see Appendix 2.

[54] Charles Quill [James W. Alexander], "Trades Unions, No. 1," *Newark Daily Advertiser*, June 30, 1838.

[55] Charles Quill [James W. Alexander], "Trades Unions, No. 2," *Newark Daily Advertiser*, July 3, 1838.

[56] Charles Quill [James W. Alexander], "Trades Unions, No. 7," *Newark Daily Advertiser*, July 21, 1838.

[57] Quill [Alexander], "Trades Unions, No. 1."

Economy at length in these articles to show that an artificial expansion of wages to the working class will ultimately result in increased inflation, decreased levels of employment, or an eventual contraction of wages back to their original level.[58] With earnestness and passion, Alexander closed this series of articles by pleading: "For virtue's sake, for our children's sake, for our country's sake, for God's sake, throw not the determination of our destiny into the hands of an organized conspiracy."[59] His opposition to trade unions could not have been stated more forcibly than in this series of articles.

Alexander's *The American Mechanic* and *The Working-Man*

In order to help the working classes better their condition, Alexander gave in his collection of Charles Quill letters an alternative message to those who were being drawn into trade unionism. Written in a simple and plain style, *The American Mechanic* and *The Working-Man* encouraged common laborers to better their own condition by legitimate means. Instead of looking to change society through organized coercion, the working classes should look to change and better themselves as individuals. While some of Alexander's "Charles Quill" letters contained advice relating to the Christian faith and the Bible, most of them were not of an overtly religious character. For example, Alexander encouraged the working classes to be content and to find pleasure in the

---

[58] Charles Quill [James W. Alexander], "Trades Unions, No. 3," *Newark Daily Advertiser*, July 7, 1838. See Henry Vethake, *Principles of Political Economy* (Philadelphia: P. H. Nicklin & T. Johnson, 1838), 329. Henry Vethake belonged to a group of conservative, *laissez faire* economists in antebellum America who wrote against labor unions. For standard works by this group of economists, see John McVickar, *Outlines of Political Economy* (New York: Wilder & Campbell, 1825); Francis Wayland, *The Elements of Political Economy*, 4th ed. (Boston: Gould & Lincoln, 1841); and Alonzo Potter, *Political Economy* (New York: Harper & Brothers, 1840). For more on these economists and their thought, see May, *Protestant Churches and Industrial America*, 14–16.

[59] Charles Quill [James W. Alexander], "Trades Unions, No. 8," *Newark Daily Advertiser*, July 24, 1838.

simple things of life: nature, music, home, friendship, and family.[60] Alexander also commended wholesome activities such as gardening as a pleasurable way of unwinding from one's work and of enjoying what God has made: "I entreat my friends of the labouring classes to cultivate the earth. I entreat them to take advantage of every little nook of the ground about their dwellings."[61] As happiness is not to be found in one's possessions or money, the working man must learn to enjoy and find contentment in the gifts that God has given to all, irrespective of one's wealth or position.[62]

One of the greatest pleasures that God has given to all, according to Alexander, is the pleasure of learning.[63] Regarding this, Alexander stated:

> My desire is to impress on the mind of every young mechanic, that a little increase of learning will give him a great increase of happiness. *Knowledge is Power*, says Lord Bacon. *Knowledge is Pleasure*, we may add with equal truth… Indeed, the pursuit of knowledge is so pleasurable, that I have often paused, and sat in amazement at the blindness and folly of those, who, with

---

[60] Alexander, *The American Mechanic*, 7-11, 16–28.

[61] Alexander, *The American Mechanic*, 34. Alexander believed that part of the reason for the discontentment among the working classes in urban areas was due to the unnatural working and living conditions in the crowded factory towns and industrial centers. While disagreeing with George Henry Evans' agrarianism, Alexander supported government policies that encouraged westward emigration. Writing to Hall in 1838, Alexander stated: "I am persuaded that it is our duty as Christian patriots, to encourage husbandry, and discourage overgrown manufactures. God has spread a wide country before us, yet thousands are herding in our factory towns, under influences ruinous to body and soul. These bloated establishments invite and receive some of the grandest villains of the old country. The policy engendered in these communities is necessarily agrarian; and the human race deteriorates, physically. I feel it to be incumbent on myself to say all I can for emigration to the West; and for the same reason I have come to look on a high protective Tariff as a great sin" (Alexander, *Forty Years' Letters*, 1:266).

[62] Alexander, *The American Mechanic*, 16–19.

[63] Alexander, *The American Mechanic*, 20.

every opportunity and free invitation, never enter this gar-
den.[64]

Almost half of *The American Mechanic* is made up of articles regarding
the acquisition of knowledge and self-education, giving suggestions to
the uneducated laborer so that he might acquire a useful and competent
knowledge across a wide range of fields. Starting with reading and writing, Alexander goes on to grammar, arithmetic, accounting, history, geography, natural philosophy, chemistry, and the Bible.[65] To encourage
working men in this pursuit, Alexander told the stories of numerous
self-taught men whose diligence and persistence helped them rise
above their circumstances, including Benjamin Franklin, Linnaeus,
Erasmus, and many others.[66] Hoping to encourage the working man to
better his own condition through self-education, Alexander stated:
"My great end will have been accomplished, if I can lodge deeply in the
reader's mind two convictions: first, that knowledge is *desirable*; secondly, that it is *attainable*. He who has received the due impression of
these two truths, may be safely left to himself."[67] Through self-education, the working classes might truly improve the quality of their lives,
perhaps even climbing up the socio-economic ladder through hard
work and self-discipline. Alongside these encouragements, Alexander
also took pains to warn laborers against various temptations that are
particularly destructive: alcohol, the love of money and material things,
misanthropy, despair, fraud, intemperance, and foolish associations.[68]
For all of these areas, Alexander used stories and anecdotes as a means
of counsel and practical encouragements to stay away from these common vices.

The Working-Man follows similar themes as *The American Mechanic*, though written for a slightly more advanced audience. It too

---

[64] Alexander, *The American Mechanic*, 168.
[65] Alexander, *The American Mechanic*, 224–280.
[66] Alexander, *The American Mechanic*, 185–210.
[67] Alexander, *The American Mechanic*, 216.
[68] Alexander, *The American Mechanic*, 24–28, 39–43, 55–62, 134–141.

commends such things as the enjoyment of home and family, self-education, and self-discipline.[69] It also contains a clear proclamation of the Christian gospel. Coming to the heart of his message to the working class, Alexander stated:

> The great truths of the Christian religion lie within a small compass. There is an agreement among all the conflicting sects of evangelical Christians as to a few cardinal points. They are such as these: that by nature men are children of wrath; that God will punish the impenitent; that we must be born again; that without faith it is impossible to please God; that he who believeth shall be saved, and he who believes will not be condemned. Further, the faith which saves us, regards chiefly the Lord Jesus Christ; that he is the Son of God; that he became man for our salvation; that he bore our sins in his own body on the tree; that he rose again from the dead, and ascended into heaven; and that we are justified by faith in him. He who believes thus, and manifests this belief by corresponding works, is a true Christian.[70]

Instead of setting "undue value...upon wealth and temporal prosperity," workers should seek that which will "secure them for eternity."[71] While such statements of the gospel are not abundant in his "Charles Quill" letters, neither are they absent. In making the bulk of this material not overtly religious, Alexander attracted a substantial readership with those outside the church.[72] In combining statements of the gospel

---

[69] Alexander, *The Working-Man*, 9–13, 27–38, 55–107, 144–182, 224–237.

[70] Alexander, *The Working-Man*, 286.

[71] Alexander, *The Working-Man*, 285–286.

[72] *The American Mechanic* went through three printings by 1847 and "went through a ready sale" (Alexander, *The American Mechanic and Working-Man*, 1:1). For an anecdote on their popularity, see Alexander, *Forty Years' Letters*, 1:279. A *Trenton State Gazette* article in 1847, revealing that Alexander was the man behind Charles Quill, stated: "In administering useful instruction to mechanics and working men, in counteracting utilitarianism so far as it is debasing and penurious, in teaching those to whom they are addressed, to live

with practical words of advice and instruction to the working classes, Alexander showed his ability to contextualize the gospel to a particular audience, even using a penname to further the reach of his message.[73]

Conservative Response to Utopian Socialism and Trade Unionism

Rather than viewing these movements as beneficial, Alexander viewed utopian socialism and trade unionism as destructive to society. Instead of incorporating whatever insights into the human condition they might offer, he opposed them with great vehemence. Their humanistic ideology and anti-Christian sentiments led people away from Christ and stirred up general discontentment and disorder. Alexander noted the effect that these movements were having, stating: "Inoculate any large class with antichristian opinions, and the contagious influence becomes horridly rife. An angry, relentless spirit of discontent, mutual distrust, lust of change, revolutionary fire, and general disquiet, plays on the features and inflames the language."[74] As a socially conservative Christian, Alexander's message to the working classes was, by contrast, a message which pointed people to Christ, godliness, virtue,

---

well and happily, these essays have no superiors" ("Charles Quill," *Trenton State Gazette*, January 16, 1847, in the Alexander Family Collection, 1:3, Department of Rare Books and Special Collections, Princeton University Library, Princeton, NJ).

[73] Alexander, *The American Mechanic and Working-Man*, 1:1. Alexander also wrote numerous articles for the working-classes in *The Princeton Magazine*, edited by his brother William. In one of these articles, Alexander stated: "My heart I own often glows, when I consider how happy the dwellings of our mechanical classes might be, in this blessed land of knowledge, freedom, and peace, if they could only be persuaded early to fix right principles, and shun those seductions which are as fatal to worldly wealth as to virtue; if they could only beautify and guard their homes by temperance, knowledge and true religion" (Charles Quill [James W. Alexander], "The Prospects of the Mechanic," *Princeton Magazine* 1 [1850]: 81). For more on *The Princeton Magazine* and Alexander's articles in it, see Alexander, *Forty Years' Letters*, 2:112.

[74] Alexander, *Discourses on Common Topics*, 29. For an additional comment on trade unionism and societal decline, see Alexander, *Forty Years' Letters*, 1:237.

contentment, and the common graces that God has bestowed upon all mankind.

As has already been mentioned, Alexander's response to the radicalism of utopian socialism and trade unionism was similar to the response of other social conservatives like Robert Walsh and Hannah More. Responding to "utopian notions and schemes," Robert Walsh stated:

> To the working classes, to all classes in our Union, four remedies may be urged as all-sufficient—Industry, Frugality, Temperance, and Domesticity. Whoever practices these cardinal points, will be prosperous and happy as far as the inherent and inevitable precariousness of human affairs will admit. We have noted domesticity in particular for these operatives, because those are likely to thrive most in their trades, and enjoy most happiness at home, who are the least intimately and zealously connected with clubs, and committees and caucuses. Doubtless, they are entitled, and even bound to give a certain degree of attention to politics and political economy; but a special and over-anxious devotion to those subjects, and the pursuit of projects for the removal of financial oppressions and disadvantages, must consume time and thoughts indispensable for success in business, and by rendering them fretful and uneasy, aggravate the common ills of life, and blight much of the enjoyment within their reach.[75]

Hannah More also commended hard work, faith in God, and contentment in the face of poverty in such writings as *The Shepherd of Salisbury Plain.*[76] In harmony with other social conservatives, Alexander called the working classes to contentment and virtue and away from discontentment, vice, and social upheaval. While utopian socialism and trade

---

[75] Walsh, *Didactics*, 2:39.

[76] Hannah More, *The Shepherd of Salisbury Plain, and Other Tales* (New York: Derby & Jackson, 1857), 7–40. For a critique of More's advice to the poor, see Mona Scheuermann, *In Praise of Poverty* (Lexington, KY: University Press of Kentucky, 2002).

unionism called for an economic and social revolution, Alexander sought to encourage a *moral revolution*, whereby the character of individuals and especially of families would be infused with virtue:

> The indispensable material of a happy State, is a body of good citizens. It is not territory, fertile soil, mines, cities, arts, navies, armies, monuments, laws, constitutions, or even liberty, which sustain and ennoble a people: but good citizens. That which makes good citizens, tends directly to the felicity and glory of a State. This will not be denied, in an age and country of which it is the genius to flatter, and almost deify the people. National virtue is the virtue of collected individuals. The power to be applied, for this result, will therefore operate to most advantage when brought to bear on the primary and constituent portions, *especially on each family and each individual.*[77]

Social reformers ought to focus on strengthening the moral fiber of individuals and families with the gospel and Christian instruction, not on social engineering. Since utopian socialism and trade unionism failed to address the fundamental root of social ills and spread a destructive humanism as the answer, Alexander strongly rejected them. By promoting humanistic solutions to social ills and by inflaming the sinful tendencies of men in the process, they were doing more harm than good.

Conclusion

Economic collectivism and egalitarianism were powerful forces in antebellum America. Closely connected with the Jacksonian spirit of the age, these movements attracted many who were discontented with their social standing and in poverty. In spite of the appeal of these movements to many, Alexander rejected them both. He rejected utopian socialism for its incompatibility with Christianity, its humanistic radicalism, and its ideological antagonism toward private property, traditional religion, marriage, and the family. He rejected trade unionism

---

[77] Alexander, *Thoughts on Family Worship*, 163 (emphasis mine).

for its promotion of discontentment, violence, and personal antagonism in American society.[78]

Alexander joined with other social conservatives who provided an alternative message to the working class, namely, a message of Christian virtue and the Christian gospel. His promotion of contentment and individual self-betterment set him apart from those who agitated for societal revolution. His emphasis on the spiritual needs of man, Christian virtue, and moral reform also set him apart from those who traced societal ills to economic inequalities. Alexander understood that man's problems go much deeper, and his Christian perspective set him apart from the essentially materialistic perspective of economic collectivism.

---

[78] For another rejection of socialism and trade unionism written shortly after Alexander's death, see Joseph P. Thompson, *The Workman: His False Friends and His True Friends* (New York: American Tract Society, 1879). Like Alexander, Thompson viewed socialism and trade unionism as incompatible with Christianity. See Thompson, *The Workman*, 229–231.

Chapter 4
The Rejection of Abolitionism

Alexander devoted himself to helping slaves and free blacks in antebellum America, but not in connection with the abolitionist movement. He rejected the abolitionists, and yet longed for the gradual emancipation of slaves. Following the British who had done so a year earlier, the United States outlawed the importation of slaves in 1808. Slavery itself, however, remained protected by law in the Southern states until shortly after Alexander's death. Anti-slavery activists prior to the 1830s did not have a unified answer to the legal, economic, and sectional problems surrounding the lingering existence of slavery, but the abolitionist movement from the 1830s onward had a clear solution: the immediate abolition of slavery and the immediate emancipation of all slaves.[1] Led by social reformers such as William Lloyd Garrison, abolitionism emerged as a powerful voice within antebellum American culture.[2] For multiple reasons, however, Alexander rejected the abolitionist movement as a beneficial expression of social reform.

Disapproval of Slavery and Sympathy for Slaveholders
Alexander saw the degrading effects of slavery on American society firsthand. As a student at Princeton Seminary, Alexander wrote John Hall regarding his plans for relocation after seminary: "my feelings and

---

[1] On slavery in the early national period of America, see Gordon S. Wood, *Empire of Liberty: A History of the Early Republic, 1789-1815* (New York: Oxford University Press, 2009), 508–542.

[2] For more on Garrison, see Henry Mayer, *All on Fire: William Lloyd Garrison and the Abolition of Slavery* (New York: W. W. Norton, 1998). For Garrison's central place in the abolitionist movement, see Howe, *What Hath God Wrought*, 425–428.

prepossessions would lead me southward, but *slavery appalls me*."[3] Despite his feelings about slavery, Alexander was in fact settled in the
South for his first pastoral charge, and there he was introduced to slave
society firsthand. As he transitioned to life in slave-holding Virginia,
Alexander wrote to Hall in 1826, stating:

> The whole face of society exhibits an appearance very differ-
> ent from what one perceives in the North. Slavery of itself is
> enough to stamp a marked character upon the Southern pop-
> ulation. The number of blacks which I met in the streets at
> first, struck me with surprise, but now every thing has become
> familiar. When I consider how much of the comfort, luxury,
> and style of Southern gentlemen would be retrenched by the
> removal of slave population, I can no longer wonder at the te-
> nacity with which they adhere to their pretended rights.[4]

Going on in this letter, Alexander describes to Hall how he found slavery to impoverish the lives of slaves, even though many were treated
kindly:

> The servants who wait upon genteel families, in consequence
> of having been bred among refined people all their lives, have
> often as great an air of gentility as their masters. The comfort
> of slaves in this country is greater, I am persuaded, than that
> of the free blacks, as a body, in any part of the United States.
> They are no doubt maltreated in many instances; so are chil-
> dren: but in general they are well clad, well fed, and kindly
> treated. Ignorance is their greatest curse, and this must ever
> follow in the train of slavery. The bad policy and destructive
> tendency of the system is increasingly felt.[5]

While living in Virginia, Alexander came to see more of this "destructive tendency" firsthand. Writing to Charles Hodge just a year later,

---

[3] Alexander, *Forty Years' Letters*, 1:37 (emphasis mine).
[4] Alexander, *Forty Years' Letters*, 1:93.
[5] Alexander, *Forty Years' Letters*, 1:93.

Alexander reported more of the evils incurred by "the curse of slavery," especially against female slaves:

> You can have no idea of the extent to which negro and mulatto women are prostituted to the lusts of the whites in this country. I could name married men of some repute, whose progeny fills their quarters. Young men and boys of age 15 are plunged into this slough of vice from day to day. The indulgence costs no trouble or expenses, and is seldom followed by the vindictive scourge which accompanies licentiousness in other places. This is an evil which the law does not reach, and which the preacher cannot mention.[6]

Seeing firsthand how slavery left moral and intellectual degradation in its wake, Alexander longed for the removal of slavery from American life. Writing to Hall in 1835, Alexander stated this as part of his considered position: "I abhor slavery, and think the public mind should be enlightened, and every lawful means immediately taken for an eventual and speedy abolition."[7]

While desiring the abolition of slavery, Alexander never condemned slaveholders *per se*. From his initial introduction to slave society, Alexander instead developed a sense of sympathy for certain slaveholders, recognizing the practical difficulties that hindered many of them from freeing their slaves. Writing to Hall in 1826, Alexander stated:

> You hear daily complaints on the subject [of slavery] from those who have most servants. But what can they do? Slavery was not their choice. They cannot and ought not to turn them loose. They cannot afford to transport them; and generally the negroes would not consent to it. The probable result of this

---

[6] Alexander to Hodge, May 14, 1827, James Waddel Alexander Manuscript Collection.

[7] Alexander, *Forty Years' Letters*, 1:228.

state of things is one which philanthropists scarcely dare con-
template.[8]

This sense of sympathy for slaveholders was deepened by certain close
friendships Alexander developed while living in Virginia.[9] After leaving
the South in 1828, Alexander continued to maintain his friendships
with Southern slaveholders through occasional visits to Virginia. As he
and his family were waited on by slaves at a Virginia plantation during
one stay in 1842, Alexander felt his sympathies only deepen for his
slave-holding friends. He reflected on this experience in a letter written
to Hall, stating:

> I am more and more convinced of the injustice we do the
> slaveholders. Of their feelings towards their negroes I can
> form a better notion than formerly, by examining my own to-
> wards the slaves who wait on my wife and mind my children.
> It is a feeling most like that we have to near relations.[10]

Personal experiences like this in slaveholding society only deepened Alexander's sympathy for kind and benevolent slaveholders.[11]

As abolitionist rhetoric against slaveholders intensified, Alexander's defended the Christian slaveholders he had come to know in a
more public way. In 1847, he published the following in his *Thoughts on
Family Worship*:

> For however the ignorant and unjust clamours of some may
> reiterate the contrary, we speak what we do know, and testify
> what we have seen, in asserting that pious householders at the
> south are accustomed to exert a direct religious influence on
> their servants. ...that the effort is conscientiously made in a

---

[8] Alexander, *Forty Years' Letters*, 1:93.

[9] Alexander, *Forty Years' Letters*, 2:19.

[10] Alexander, *Forty Years' Letters*, 1:352.

[11] Alexander, *Forty Years' Letters*, 1:309. See also Alexander, *Thoughts on Family Worship*, 70–71.

large number of blessed instances, we not only believe, but do testify.[12]

When Alexander journeyed across the Atlantic in 1851, he expressed a similar frustration with what he considered to be English ignorance of slaveholding in America. He wrote to Hall: "They [English Christians] all have the grossest views of our slavery, and lose temper when spoken to."[13] Out of this frustration, he refused to attend the meetings of evangelical organizations in England which excluded slaveholders. Writing again from England in 1851, Alexander stated to Hall:

> The Christian Evangelical Alliance meets on the 20th, and lasts twelve days. I do not expect to go, after their acts concerning American slave-holders. I declared to Dr. Hamilton that whatever my private opinions were on slavery, I would sit in no body where my Southern brethren were excluded.[14]

So while disapproving of the system of slavery overall, Alexander recognized that many slaveholders conscientiously and affectionately took care of their slaves. Sympathetic for the "Southern brethren" who were caught up in slaveholding, Alexander was thankful that he and Hall were not so entangled, stating: "I rejoice that you and I are not laden with negro souls and bodies."[15]

Reasons for Rejecting Abolitionism

Alexander had many reasons for rejecting the abolitionist movement of his day, the first being the vehement way it made a blanket condemnation of all slaveholders. Alexander saw a sharp contrast between the

---

[12] Alexander, *Thoughts on Family Worship*, 75. Alexander also defended Southern slaveholders in the *Repertory*. See James W. Alexander, "Religious Instruction of Negroes," *Biblical Repertory and Princeton Review* 17 (1845): 590–606.

[13] Alexander, *Forty Years' Letters*, 2:154.

[14] Alexander, *Forty Years' Letters*, 2:339.

[15] Alexander, *Forty Years' Letters*, 1:234.

militant abolitionism of Garrison and the patient, temperate efforts of earlier abolitionists like William Wilberforce, whom he deeply appreciated. Writing in the *Repertory* in 1838, Alexander stated:

> In truth, there is...the greatest possible contrast, between the hearts and lives of Wilberforce and the earlier abolitionists and the hearts and lives of those who have since usurped their names; the difference is that which exists between the refinement of the scholar and Christian gentleman, and the gross unmannered insolence of the upstart agitator of *canaille*. The one was warm and productive, but gentle and benevolent, ready to admit facts, weigh defense, and retract errors: the other is hot, heady, meddlesome, too often careless of truth, and seldom anxious to repair the injuries inflicted by a calumny set on fire of hell. The one abolished to a certain extent a nefarious trade, by most legitimate proceedings; the other threatens to carry fire and sword through half a nation, or if this be averted, to rend, without the least prospect of aught to indemnify for the loss, those bonds on which depend the triumphs of religion, truth and peace throughout the hemisphere. The early friends of the black man strenuously and even violently strove to remove a dreadful disease; the abolitionists, knife in hand, are ready to extirpate a cancer, though the patient die on the table.[16]

In Alexander's eyes, the abolitionists were guilty of bringing needless division and strife to the nation with their promotion of radicalism and anarchy.[17] He also noted how churches across the nation were being

---

[16] James W. Alexander, "The Life of William Wilberforce," *Biblical Repertory and Princeton Review* 10 (1838): 571.

[17] Alexander, "Life of William Wilberforce," 572. Garrison's political anarchism is widely recognized by historians. Garrison once called the United States Constitution, "a covenant with death and an agreement with hell" (Howe, *What Hath God Wrought*, 651). He also publicly burned a copy of the Constitution on July 4, 1854, stating, "So perish all compromises with tyranny" (Paul Johnson, *A History of the American People* [New York: Harper Collins, 1997], 447). For more on Garrison's political anarchism, see David

harmed by abolitionists, as racial tensions between whites and blacks were being inflamed by their acrimonious rhetoric.[18] As tensions rose between black and white believers in Princeton, Alexander wrote to Hall in 1837: "In consequence of the abolition movements the prejudice of the lower classes of whites against the [free] blacks has become exorbitant and inhuman."[19] Alexander was aware of disruptions being caused by abolitionists in other churches as well.[20] Since their strong rhetoric was producing such tensions and divisions, even among believers, Alexander did not associate in any way with the antebellum abolitionist movement.

Another reason why Alexander rejected abolitionism was because of its connection, in his mind, with the same anti-scriptural egalitarianism he saw in trade unionism, utopian socialism, and the "ultra-democracy" of his day. Certainly, some abolitionists were social utopians, like Robert Dale Owen and Frances Wright, who were both advocates of women's rights as well. Abolitionism was yet another expression of social radicalism in Alexander's eyes, built on the same foundation of secular ideology. With abolitionists, he lumped together all such social radicals, namely "those who abjure conjugal obedience, and feminine modesty, and deny all coercion of law."[21] Alexander believed the social

---

Torbett, *Theology and Slavery: Charles Hodge and Horace Bushnell* (Macon, GA: Mercer University Press, 2006), 143. Upon hearing Frederick Douglas in 1847, Alexander described his speech as follows: "It was Catilinarian and treasonable. He said, up and down, that he despised and hated the country and the Constitution, and invoked the aid of England" (Alexander, *Forty Years' Letters*, 2:69).

[18] As Gordon Wood has observed: "The anti-slavery movement that arose out of the Revolution inadvertently produced racism in America" (Wood, *Empire of Liberty*, 508).

[19] Alexander, *Forty Years' Letters*, 1:260.

[20] Alexander, *Forty Years' Letters*, 1:251.

[21] Alexander, "Life of William Wilberforce," 572. Critical of the "Female Anti-Slavery Associations" that were promoting feminist ideology through their abolitionism, Alexander quotes Wilberforce as saying: "All private exertions for such an object become their character, but for ladies to meet, to publish, to go from house to house stirring up petitions—these appear to

anarchism of the abolitionists was also connected with the revolutionary radicalism that lie behind the French Revolution.[22] Just as the
French Revolution hindered Wilberforce's work to end the slave trade,
so too were American abolitionists making life more difficult for those
they were seeking to help:

> The breaking out of the French Revolution impeded the work,
> precisely as the disorganizing jacobinism of certain abolition-
> ists among ourselves has hindered the evangelizing of our own
> negroes. It is no more to be questioned that the suspicion cast
> on the sacred labours of Wilberforce by the French excesses
> of the "Amis des Noirs," retarded the great event, than that
> the odious misrepresentation and violence of northern aboli-
> tionists have riveted the yoke on thousands of southern
> slaves.[23]

Just as had happened in England, Alexander found that the social radicals were doing more harm than good.

In its war against traditional authority structures, Alexander also
found the "disorganizing Jacobinism" of contemporary abolitionism,
as he called it, to be more humanistic than biblical.[24] In his *Thoughts on
Family Worship*, he described how the abolitionists' social

---

me proceedings unsuited to the female character as delineated in Scripture"
(Alexander, "Life of William Wilberforce," 572). For more on the abolition-
ists' connection with social anarchism and feminism, see Howe, *What Hath
God Wrought*, 648-653, and McDougall, *Throes of Democracy*, 203-209.

[22] Alexander, "Life of William Wilberforce," 571. David Calhoun con-
cludes that the Princetonians' commitment to "a stable and hierarchical society" and their sense of alarm at the "terrors of the French Revolution and the
disorders of Jacksonian democracy" kept them from supporting the abolitionist cause (David B. Calhoun, *Faith and Learning, 1812-1868*, vol. 1 of *Princeton
Seminary* [Edinburgh: Banner of Truth, 1994], 327).

[23] Alexander, "Life of William Wilberforce," 573-574. For more on how
the French Revolution hindered British abolitionism in the 1790s, see William
Hague, *William Wilberforce: The Life of the Great Anti-Slave Trade Campaigner*
(London: Harper Collins, 2007), 229-257.

[24] Alexander, *Forty Years' Letters*, 2:233.

egalitarianism was drawing individuals away from a biblical under-standing of authority:

> Few topics have been more largely or more angrily discussed in our day, than the relation of master and servant. We have had abundance of abstractions, and of unscriptural lamenta-tions, but so far as we can observe, no real profit has accrued to the inferior persons. If the present current of opinion goes on, we shall soon arrive at the point at which there will be no such thing as a *servant*. Out of a false delicacy, an irreligious spirit of levelling, a yielding to pride, and a mistaken view of the character of labour, even good people have been willing to banish the very word from their diction, corrupting at once their language and their morals. The generation which is now growing up among us, is exceedingly slow to recognise any proper authority in the master, or any obligation to obedience in the servant.[25]

Believing that the Bible condoned relationships of authority and sub-servience, Alexander stated to Hall in 1846:

> I can go a peg higher than you about slavery, and fail to see the scripturalness of much that is postulated now-a-days, respect-ing the popular idol, liberty. As existing, slavery is fraught with moral evil; the want of marriage, and of the Bible, and the separation of families, &c., &c., are crying sins; but I am to-tally unable to see the relation to be necessarily unjust. The moral questions are so various from the circumstances, that each must be decided apart.[26]

Writing to Hall in 1847, Alexander stated this fundamental disagree-ment with the abolitionists clearly: "I see no trace of the modern dog-mas about absolute freedom in the Bible."[27] For these significant

---

[25] Alexander, *Thoughts on Family Worship*, 71.

[26] Alexander, *Forty Years' Letters*, 2:52.

[27] Alexander, *Forty Years' Letters*, 2:65.

reasons, then, Alexander could not join with the abolitionists. Their ideology of equality, their over-estimation of individual liberty, and their blanket condemnation of slavery simply did not fit with Alexander's understanding of Scripture.[28]

A fourth reason why Alexander opposed abolitionism was because of a strong practical consideration in his mind: he did not believe that immediate emancipation would be the best thing for many of the slaves. He did not believe all slaves were adequately prepared to live as free individuals in antebellum America. Without education, without property, and faced with pervasive societal racism, Alexander observed that freed blacks at times ended up in a worse condition than slaves. These personal observations formed a powerful argument in Alexander's mind against total and immediate emancipation. Alexander made the following comment to Hall regarding the slaves of Virginia politician John Randolph and the fate of them after Randolph's death:

> They adored him [Randolph] as almost above the human standard, and preferred being his slaves to being free. It is perhaps (after all our abstractions) better for these negroes, as a set, that they are not freed. I say this seriously, founding my judgment on the following striking fact: Richard and John Randolph were brothers, and divided between them the estate of their father. Each took a moiety of the slaves. Richard set his free: John retained his on the estates. Col. Madison published the history of the former moiety and their offspring. They have almost become extinct; those who remain are wandering and drunken thieves, degraded below the level of

---

[28] Many abolitionists rejected Scripture, as it did not contain a blanket condemnation of slaveholding. William Lloyd Garrison rejected the authority of Scripture, crediting Thomas Paine's influence for his views on the Bible. Mark Noll quotes Garrison as stating: "To say that everything contained within the lids of the Bible is divinely inspired, and to insist upon the dogma as fundamentally important, is to give utterance to a bold fiction, and to require the suspension of the reasoning faculties. To say that everything in the Bible is to be believed, simply because it is found in that volume, is equally absurd and pernicious" (Noll, *The Civil War as a Theological Crisis*, 31).

humanity, and beyond the reach of Gospel means. The slaves of Roanoke are the descendants of the other moiety. They are nearly four hundred, and though not free, are sleek, fat, healthy, happy, and many of them to all appearance ripe for heaven. These I know to be facts, and they are worth more to me than a volume of dissertations on the right to freedom.[29]

As Alexander later observed the difficulties of the Irish and the freed blacks in New York City, he stated: "I can't help thinking how much better off the Southern slaves are, physically and morally, than the Irish. Who ever heard of slaves starving until the master starved? ...The wretchedest portion, by far, of the black race, is the free portion. Our New York negroes are lower than savages in many respects."[30] His observations led him to the conclusion that:

The most miserable portion, physically and morally, of the black race in the United States, is the portion which is free, I am as well assured as I can be of any similar proposition. That immediate emancipation would be a crime, I have no doubt; and therefore believe there are cases in which there is neither injustice nor inhumanity in holding [slaves].[31]

Because of what he observed of the plight of many freed blacks in America, Alexander rejected the abolitionists' call for immediate emancipation as impractical and potentially harmful to those they were seeking to help.

Alexander believed that simply freeing black slaves would not necessarily give them a better life, as long as racist attitudes prevailed in the minds of the white majority. Alexander stated that "the prejudice of colour and caste" was the "real hindrance" to the well-being of blacks in antebellum America, and he viewed white prejudice against

[29] Alexander, *Forty Years' Letters*, 1:270, cf. 271.
[30] Alexander, *Forty Years' Letters*, 2:65.
[31] Alexander, *Forty Years' Letters*, 2:52.

blacks as a significant societal evil to be addressed.[32] Without removing racial prejudice and the widespread disapproval of cross-racial marriages, among other things, simply freeing the slaves was an insufficient solution to alleviating their plight. Writing to Hall in 1845, Alexander stated:

> Amalgamation, say what they please, can go on, does go on, and will go on. ...leave [the emancipation question] out of view, and what becomes of our negroes, slave or free? Those called by mockery free people, are a race of Helots or Yahoos, in our estimation. We do not give them our dinners, or our daughters; we debar them from pulpits, pews, and omnibuses; we deny them actual citizenship. We smell their rancid odours, and hustle them off our streets more vehemently now that they are free, than when they were slaves. Educate them, and this prejudice makes them miserable.[33]

Alexander was more open to the idea of interracial marriage between blacks and whites than other Princetonians.[34] At the very least, he

---

[32] Alexander, *Forty Years' Letters*, 2:18.

[33] Alexander, *Forty Years' Letters*, 2:18-19.

[34] Charles Hodge argued strongly against the "amalgamation of distinct races" in the *Repertory*, stating: "There are natural laws which forbid the union of distinct races... The effects of amalgamation of distinct races is seen in the physically, intellectually and socially degraded mongrel inhabitants of Mexico and South America. In these cases the chief elements were the Spanish and Indians, elements less widely separated than the Anglo Saxon and the Negro. The amalgamation of these races must inevitably lead to the deterioration of both. It would fill the country with a feeble and degraded population, which must ultimately perish. For it is a well ascertained fact that the mulatto is far more frail than either the white man or the negro. We read in the disastrous physical effects of the amalgamation of the blacks and whites, a clear intimation that such amalgamation is contrary to the will of God, and therefore is not an end which statesmen ought in any way to facilitate" (Charles Hodge, "Emancipation," *Biblical Repertory and Princeton Review* 21 [1849]: 594). Nowhere, does Alexander give any indication that he holds to Hodge's views on this matter; in fact, he seems to indicate an openness to interracial marriage

understood that racial prejudice and animosity was the main hindrance to the elevation of blacks in antebellum America. Since abolitionism did not address the more fundamental issue of racism, Alexander was not convinced that its goal of immediate emancipation would truly better the condition of blacks in American society. Racial prejudice was the deeper issue and social evil that needed to be addressed.

Hodge and Alexander on Slavery

In his views on slavery, Alexander was in overall agreement with Princeton's leading theologian and chief spokesman on the issue, Charles Hodge.[35] Along with Hodge, Alexander disagreed with abolitionists like Garrison, who viewed slavery as an absolute sin, and also with Southerners like James Henley Thornwell, who came to assert the position that slavery was a positive social good.[36] Hodge published his views on slavery in numerous books and articles, and Alexander found himself in agreement with Hodge's position.[37] Writing to Hall in 1856,

and expressed appreciation for individuals of mixed ethnicity (see Alexander, *Forty Years' Letters*, 2:18–19).

[35] While many New School Presbyterians embraced abolitionism, many of the Old School Presbyterians in the North held views similar to those expressed by Hodge. We could almost speak of a "Princeton position" on slavery (Calhoun, *Faith and Learning*, 325). For others of this "school," see Cortlandt Van Rensselaer, *Miscellaneous Sermons, Essays, and Addresses* (Philadelphia: J. B. Lippincott, 1861), 243–410; Robert J. Breckinridge, "Hints on Colonization and Abolition" *Biblical Repertory and Theological Review* 5 (1833): 281–305; Miller, *Life of Samuel Miller*, 292–300.

[36] Noll, *The Civil War as a Theological Crisis*, 2. For more on Thornwell's view on slavery, see James Henley Thornwell, "The Christian Doctrine of Slavery" in *The Collected Writings of James Henley Thornwell*, ed. John B. Adger and John L. Girardeau (Richmond: Presbyterian Committee of Publication, 1873), 4:398–436.

[37] For Hodge's position on slavery see the following articles and books by Hodge: "Slavery," *Biblical Repertory and Princeton Review* 8 (1836): 268–305; "West India Emancipation," *Biblical Repertory and Princeton Review* 10 (1838): 602–644; "Abolitionism," *Biblical Repertory and Princeton Review* 16 (1844): 545–581; "Emancipation," *Biblical Repertory and Princeton Review* 21 (1849): 582–607; "Civil Government," *Biblical Repertory and Princeton Review* 23

Alexander stated: "Dr. Hodge has most admirably stated the slavery doctrine, in his [commentary on] Ephesians. ...How nobly this clear enunciation of Scriptural principle towers above all the extravagancies of both sides!"[38]

Regarding his position on slavery, Hodge could be labeled a "gradual emancipationist."[39] He believed that a host of efforts should be exerted to bring about the gradual removal of slavery. With post-millennial optimism, he also believed that God would eventually bring an end to slavery and to imprudently run ahead of God's providential working would only bring harm to the slaves.[40] Like Hodge, Alexander also believed in a gradual approach toward the removal of slavery, writing to Hall in 1847: "I am more and more convinced that our endeavours to

---

(1851): 125-158; *A Commentary on the Epistle to the Ephesians* (New York: Carter & Brothers, 1856; repr., Edinburgh: Banner of Truth, 1991); "The Unity of Mankind," *Biblical Repertory and Princeton Review* 31 (1859): 103-149; "The State of the Country," *Biblical Repertory and Princeton Review* 33 (1861): 1-36; "The Church and the Country," *Biblical Repertory and Princeton Review* 33 (1861): 322-376; "Diversity of Species in the Human Race," *Biblical Repertory and Princeton Review* 34 (1862): 435-464; "The War," *Biblical Repertory and Princeton Review* 35 (1863): 140-169; and "The Princeton Review on the State of the Country and of the Church," *Biblical Repertory and Princeton Review* 37 (1865): 627-657. For analysis of Hodge's position on slavery see: Torbett, *Theology and Slavery*, 55-114; Stewart, *Mediating the Center*, 67-110; Allen C. Guelzo, "Charles Hodge's Antislavery Moment," in Stewart and Morehead, *Charles Hodge Revisited*, 299-325; and Barker, "Social Views of Charles Hodge," 6-14.

[38] Alexander, *Forty Years' Letters*, 2:225. The moderate position of Hodge and Alexander was the position adopted by the Old School Presbyterian Church at its 1845 General Assembly. See Charles Hodge, "The General Assembly," *Biblical Repertory and Princeton Review* 17 (1845): 437-441. For Alexander's hearty endorsement of the 1845 General Assembly's position, see Alexander, "Religious Instructions of Negroes," 605-606.

[39] See Hodge, "Slavery," 275. Mark Noll labels Hodge a "moderate emancipationist" (Noll, *The Civil War as a Theological Crisis*, 128).

[40] Hodge, "Slavery," 268-269; Hodge, "West India Emancipation," 606. For more on Hodge's views on providence in connection with slavery, see Noll, *The Civil War as a Theological Crisis*, 81-84.

do at a blow, what Providence does by degrees, is disastrous to those whom it would benefit."[41]

Hodge believed that slavery would gradually pass away under God's providence as biblical norms and principles were spread throughout society by the church.[42] He referred to this as "the gospel method of extinguishing slavery."[43] One set of biblical principles the church should be bold in declaring was the clear and specific scriptural directives given to masters regarding the treatment of their slaves.[44] Hodge believed that Scripture required slaveholders to provide for all the educational, social, and religious needs of their slaves and that it was unjust for a slaveholder to "withhold a reasonable compensation for the labour of his slaves."[45] By reforming slave laws according to scriptural norms, so as to allow slaves to become educated and to accrue personal property, Hodge believed that slaves could be elevated and bettered *as slaves* and thus prepared for freedom.[46] Alexander also believed that reforming slave laws would help slaves transition to freedom, stating: "Our church, I am clear, ought to protest against the laws about reading, &c. As clear am I, that our States should regard slavery as a transition-state, to be terminated as soon as possible, and that they should enact laws about the *post-nati* [slaves who came to reside in the

---

[41] Alexander, *Forty Years' Letters*, 2:65.

[42] Hodge, *Ephesians*, 267, 273; Hodge, "Slavery," 286.

[43] Hodge, "Slavery," 300.

[44] Hodge, "Slavery," 280.

[45] Hodge, "Abolitionism," 576. Alexander commended Hodge's attack on southern slave laws by quoting this section of Hodge's Ephesians commentary in a letter to Hall: "It is just as great a sin to deprive a slave of the just recompense for his labour, or to keep him in ignorance, or to take from him his wife or child, as it is to act thus towards a free man" (Alexander, *Forty Years' Letters*, 2:225). See also Hodge, "Slavery," 483.

[46] Hodge believed that such preparation for emancipation might be necessary to help slaves live as free and responsible individuals (Hodge, "West India Emancipation," 625). Along these same lines, Alexander called the evangelism of slaves "the best preparative for freedom" (Alexander, *Forty Years' Letters*, 1:272).

United States after the Declaration of Independence]."[47] By patiently appealing to slaveholders to deal with their slaves according to scriptural principles and to reform the slave laws of their separate states, Hodge and Alexander both believed that slaves would be healthily transitioned out of slavery and truly bettered in the long run.[48]

Many gradual emancipationists like Hodge and Alexander believed that sending freed slaves back to West Africa as colonists was in the best interests of both blacks and whites.[49] Hodge argued for African colonization along sociological lines:

> There are natural laws which forbid the union of distinct races in the same commonwealth... It is a law that the stronger and more numerous race should displace the weaker. The weaker may be absorbed and assimilated, where the difference is slight, but if the difference is so great as to keep the races apart, one of two results seems invariably to follow, either the weaker race dies out, or it is reduced to a state of bondage.[50]

Since Hodge believed that blacks and whites could not be happily assimilated into one "commonwealth," he supported the plans for African colonization. Alexander also supported African colonization, but he argued for it more as a means of effectively spreading Christianity,

---

[47]Alexander, *Forty Years' Letters*, 2:52.

[48] For a statement of Alexander's optimism, see Alexander, *Forty Years' Letters*, 2:65. For a further statement on reforming the slave laws, see Alexander, *Forty Years' Letters*, 2:217–218.

[49] Alexander's father, Archibald Alexander, was an enthusiastic proponent of "African colonization." Alexander told Hall in 1840 that his father "has this more at heart than any thing in the world" (Alexander, *Forty Years' Letters*, 1:297). Archibald Alexander wrote a large book in support of the Colonization movement, entitled *A History of Colonization on the Western Coast of Africa* (Philadelphia: William S. Martien, 1846). Many American supported African colonization, including Abraham Lincoln, who supported colonization both before and after the Emancipation Proclamation. See Phillip W. Magness and Sebastian N. Page, *Colonization after Emancipation: Lincoln and the Movement for Black Resettlement* (Columbia, MO: University of Missouri, 2018).

[50] Hodge, "Emancipation," 594–595.

believing that the Christian faith is most effectively spread by transplanting a communal expression of Christian culture into a foreign land.[51] By sending Christians to form a Christian society in the midst of paganism, Alexander believed, the gospel might be powerfully spread in unevangelized lands. Writing to Hall in 1840, Alexander stated:

> My mind expands when I look at the mighty conquests of our language. If we could only pour in the gospel with this tide of conquest and colonization! Since, in our day, God so signally blesses colonies for the spread of civilization, ought we not to follow the lead of Providence, and strike in as much as possible with the divine plan? The hope of great effects is more reasonable from such efforts than from insulated assaults on the mass of heathenism. It is the difference between firing a ball against a walled town, and entering a breach with a victorious army.[52]

Alexander rejoiced to hear in 1849 that large numbers of Christians were relocating to California to set up Christian communities. Writing to Hall about this, he stated: "Having long believed colonies to be the best missions, I see in this a most hopeful means for spreading the gospel. California churches can send missions with ease to China, Japan, and Polynesia."[53] Viewing Christian colonization in general as "God's means of civilizing and Christianizing the world," Alexander enthusiastically supported African colonization and colonization to all parts of the world.[54] His stated reasons for doing so were evangelistic.

Alexander's Efforts on behalf of Blacks

In contrast with the abolitionists, Alexander was more concerned with the spiritual condition of blacks in America than with freeing blacks who were still in a state of slavery. While many were consumed with

---

[51] Alexander, *Forty Years' Letters*, 1:228.
[52] Alexander, *Forty Years' Letters*, 1:301.
[53] Alexander, *Forty Years' Letters*, 2:92.
[54] Alexander, *Forty Years' Letters*, 1:308.

the slavery question, Alexander believed that Christians should be more concerned with the souls and eternal well-being of slaves than with their temporal circumstances. Writing to Hall in 1847, Alexander stated: "To give the gospel to the slaves, is a duty pressing above all others."[55] By their misplaced efforts at social reform, Alexander believed that abolitionists were bringing real harm to slaves, when so much good might be brought to them simply through the gospel evangelism, teaching, and discipleship. Writing from Virginia in 1838, Alexander stated:

> The law (thanks to the meddling of anti-slavery societies) forbids schools, and public teaching to read; it was not so when I lived here: but I hold it to be our business to *save their souls;* and however criminal slavery might be, I see with my eyes that God has so overruled it, as that the slaves are more open to Gospel truth than any human beings on the globe.[56]

Instead of calling for immediate emancipation, then, Alexander pressed slaveholders to labor at evangelizing their slaves. Alexander stated in his *Thoughts on Family Worship*, "Providence has placed the master of African servants in a position where he can reach a great number of immortal souls; more accessible, we think, to religious impression than any persons in the world. The first great duty is to give them the gospel, and to seek their salvation." [57]

Alexander commended slaveholders he knew who were faithful in evangelizing and giving Biblical instruction to their slaves. One such slaveholder was Paulina Le Grand. When Alexander was a pastor in Virginia, he resided on the estate of Le Grand, and she became a close friend.[58] Writing of her in 1827, Alexander described her spiritual concern for her slaves to Hall:

---

[55] Alexander, *Forty Years' Letters*, 2:65.
[56] Alexander, *Forty Years' Letters*, 1:272.
[57] Alexander, *Thoughts on Family Worship*, 78.
[58] Alexander, *Forty Years' Letters*, 1:102, 2:19.

Mrs. Le Grand lodges and boards a good Episcopalian...for this business [of evangelism] among her slaves. ...Now it is my deliberate belief, that more of these slaves are likely to go to heaven, than of an equal number of servants of pious people in our Middle States; and such being the hopefulness of the work, how earnestly ought Christians to engage in it! Thousands might be got to attend public preaching, as hundreds now do.[59]

Upon Le Grand's death in 1845, Alexander recounted her relationship with her slaves with great admiration:

She was distressingly exercised about slavery. But what could she do? She often asked me, but I was dumb. She had as many as possible taught to read, and this up to the present time. A large number of her slaves are real Christians, not to speak of perhaps a hundred who have gone to heaven. I fully believe that more of them have secured eternal life, than would have been the case in any freedom conceivable. And surely, if eternity is more than time, this is a consideration to be pondered. But she saw no escape; individual opinion was inert.[60]

Another individual who Alexander commended in his letters was Charles Colcock Jones. Jones was a graduate of Princeton Seminary, and Alexander was very enthusiastic about his work among slaves.[61] Writing to Hall in 1841, Alexander stated: "C. C. Jones, of S.C., preaches to the slaves three times on Sunday, and every evening in the week. Yet this is the man whom the young Andoverians would not let

---

[59] Alexander, *Forty Years' Letters*, 1:272.

[60] Alexander, *Forty Years' Letters*, 2:19.

[61] The correspondence of Jones and his family has been published in the following volumes: Robert Manson Myers, ed., *The Children of Pride: A True Story of Georgia and the Civil War* (New Haven: Yale University Press, 1972); and Robert Manson Myers, ed., *A Georgian and Princeton* (New York: Harcourt Brace Jovanovich, 1976). For a recent sketch of Jones's life see: Iain H. Murray, *Heroes* (Edinburgh: Banner of Truth, 2009), 175–256.

preach in their chapel. *Sit anima mea cum Jonesio!* [My spirit is with Jones!]"[62] In 1847, Alexander put his appreciation for Jones in print:

> In the great day of reckoning, we doubt not that the silent, un-obtrusive self-denying labours of Dr. C. C. Jones, and his faithful coadjutors, will shine forth in colours of a brighter philanthropy, and will be acknowledged as more full of love for the slave, than all the inflammatory harangues of a hundred misguided and disorganizing zealots.[63]

Alexander knew of others like Jones, and he similarly commended their work in slave evangelism, stating: "I know of five or six men who are silently wearing out life in most devoted labour among the slaves. Slavery must and will end; I hope peaceably; but, anyhow, we ought to save the souls of this generation."[64] Alexander personally labored in slave evangelism and was so enthusiastic about it that he worked to recruit others to join him.[65] He frequently commended such work to Hall and in 1843 posed this question to him:

> Quere: whether all missionary enterprises among us ought not to yield precedence to the work of evangelizing the Southern slaves? Ministers ought to be among them, in sufficient numbers, even if they were to be emancipated to-morrow; so that the question has no limitation from that of Abolition. Next in order, I think, come the Indians, whose condition is now more favourable than that of any heathen tribes on earth, for receiving the gospel. The prestige, however, of this mission = 0.[66]

---

[62] Alexander, *Forty Years' Letters*, 1:337.
[63] Alexander, *Thoughts on Family Worship*, 80.
[64] Alexander, *Forty Years' Letters*, 1:319, cf. 351.
[65] Alexander, *Forty Years' Letters*, 1:272, cf. 353.
[66] Alexander, *Forty Years' Letters*, 1:377.

After Alexander moved from Virginia, he continued to personally engage in slave evangelism whenever his travels took him back to the Southern states.[67]

Alexander's labor among slaves in Virginia was exceeded by his work with freed blacks in the North. As a pastor in Trenton, Alexander preached regularly to groups of freed blacks and tried to set up a Bible class for them, though he found the blacks in Trenton to be "strangely averse to white interference."[68] While in New York, he attempted to start a black congregation as well.[69] While serving in Princeton as the Professor of Rhetoric and *Belles Lettres* at the College of New Jersey, he preached weekly to a black congregation and was the founding pastor of a black church, Witherspoon Street Presbyterian Church.[70] Alexander recounted how he was scorned by "some of the lowest of the white canaille" in Princeton as "the preacher to the blacks," but in this ministry he found great satisfaction nonetheless.[71] Alexander wrote to Hall in 1835: "I believe my happiest hours are spent on Sunday afternoons in labouring among my little charge [the congregation of blacks]."[72] Although he delighted to serve this black congregation in New Jersey, Alexander found the black slaves of Virginia to be even more receptive to the gospel.[73]

Alexander's approach to blacks and black slavery in antebellum America reflects his socially-conservative and evangelical convictions. Summarizing his overall views on the plight of blacks in one lengthy

---

[67] Alexander, *Forty Years' Letters*, 1:271.

[68] Alexander, *Forty Years' Letters*, 2:65; 1:162–163.

[69] Alexander, *Forty Years' Letters*, 2:65.

[70] Alexander, *Forty Years' Letters*, 1:301, 334. This church grew out of the heightened racial tensions between blacks and whites in Princeton in the 1840s (Calhoun, *Faith and Learning*, 330). For more information on the state of blacks in Princeton, see Torbett, *Theology and Slavery*, 69-73.

[71] Alexander, *Forty Years' Letters*, 1:263.

[72] Alexander, *Forty Years' Letters*, 1:227. The bracketed insertion was provided by Hall.

[73] Alexander, *Forty Years' Letters*, 1:351; 2:65.

passage, Alexander wrote the following to Hall while visiting the estate of Mrs. Le Grand in 1842:

> My mind has been, and is, filled with the negroes. What I say on this point I say with, I do believe, as much love for the race as any man feels; and with an extent of observation perhaps as large as I can pretend to on any subject, having seen the worst as well as the best of their condition. And the result of all, increasingly, is, what you I am sure would agree to if you were on the spot, that the *average physical evils* of their case are not greater than of sailors, soldiers, shoeblacks, or low operatives; while their *moral evils* are unspeakably great. My point is this, then: The soul of the negro is precious and must be saved. Aim at this, at this first, at this directly, at this independently of their bondage, and the other desirable ends will be promoted even more surely than if the latter were made the great object. A gradual emancipation is that to which the interior economy of the North-Southern States was tending, is tending, and will reach; it is desirable; in my view it is inevitable; it is craved by thousands here; but an emancipation even gradual may arrive in such sort as to leave a host of blacks to be damned, who, by the other means, may be Christianized, while their eventual freedom is not less certain. It is the salvation of the slave, which is infinitely the most important, which moreover Southern Christians *can* be led to seek, and of which the very seeking directly tends to emancipation. I say this, on the obvious principle, that when the owner by seeking the salvation of his slave, gets (as he must) to love him, he will not rest (I speak of the mass) without trying to make him a free-man. I cannot describe the pleasure I have had in preaching and talking to the slaves: if I have ever done any good, this is the way.[74]

Through the spread of Christian truth to slaves and slave-holders, "the other desirable ends" of society reform would be promoted and gradually attained. By thus making social reform secondary to the eternal

---

[74] Alexander, *Forty Years' Letters*, 1:354.

needs of man, Alexander approached slavery and racial oppression from a fundamentally different perspective than the abolitionists of his day. Their approach was this-wordly and materialistic, but Alexander's evangelical perspective caused him to see the problems of this world from an eternal perspective.

Conclusion

Alexander rejected abolitionism as a social reform movement for many reasons. The social radicalism of the abolitionists clashed with his social conservatism, and he viewed their zealous activism as divisive and antagonistic to the peace of both church and state. Alexander believe that their egalitarianism and exaltation of individual liberty was yet another expression of the "Jacobin" and Jacksonian spirit of the age, driven more by humanistic ideology than by the teaching of Scripture. He also rejected the abolitionists' blanket condemnation of slaveholders, and he did not believe that immediate emancipation was necessarily the best in every particular case.

Alexander desired the abolition of slavery, but he believed it should be sought gradually and by scriptural means. As he considered the overall condition of the slaves, he prioritized doing good to their souls, and he believed that this is where the focus of Christian philanthropy toward slaves should be. His moderate position caused him and others like him at Princeton to differ both from the abolitionists and from Southern Presbyterians within their own denomination.[75] They stood apart from both these groups largely because of their commitment to scripture and their critical interaction with popular social philosophies in antebellum American culture.

---

[75] For the unpopularity of the Princetonians' mediating position on slavery and the negative reaction it received in their own day, see Hodge, "*Princeton Review* on the State of the Country and Church," 637–641, 657.

Chapter 5
The Rejection of Secularized Education

Alexander knew how important a general education was for bettering the condition of the poor. He spelled this out in his Charles Quill letters in *The American Mechanic* and *The Working-Man*.[1] In one of these letters, Alexander rejoiced that "within a few years past, the cause of popular education, in all free [Northern] States, has begun to assume its just rank."[2] While the spread of "popular education" was celebrated by Alexander, he did not approve of the growing trend to remove religious teaching from public education. While education in general was viewed by Alexander as beneficial to society, he never considered the promotion of a general education to be a sufficient means of social reform. In fact, Alexander viewed the spread of a purely secularized system of education to be dangerous and harmful to society. Given his position on secular education, Alexander stood apart from yet another significant social reform movement in antebellum America.

The Rise of Secular Education in Antebellum America

Education in colonial America was closely connected with its religious institutions.[3] This connection continued long after American independence, with Christian organizations involved with many of America's educational institutions well into the nineteenth century.[4] With the advance of secular thought in antebellum America, the role of

---

[1] See especially Alexander, *The Working Man*, 161–178.

[2] Alexander, *The Working Man*, 179.

[3] John Pulliam, *History of Education in America*, 2nd ed. (Columbus, OH: Charles Merrill Publishing, 1976), 54.

[4] Howe, *What Hath God Wrought*, 449–451.

religion in government-sanctioned education was altered dramatically. As religious institutions lost their place of influence in the culture at large, they also lost their position of influence in the educational system.

An early advocate of severing education from religion in America was Thomas Jefferson. Jefferson believed that education was essentially a state affair, given the needs of a free republic for an educated citizenry. He also believed that religion should be kept separate from all affairs of state, including state-run education.[5] While a member of the Virginia legislature, Jefferson tried unsuccessfully in 1779 to implement a state-run school system that would make three years of education in reading, writing, mathematics, and history available for free, without any religious elements attached to them.[6] Although Jefferson's educational plan was never enacted, he successfully established the University of Virginia in 1819, a university committed to "free inquiry" unrestrained by any religious institution or creed.[7] The establishment of this university was opposed by many clergymen, including Presbyterians like John Holt Rice.[8]

---

[5] For an overview of Jefferson's views on education see, Cameron Addis, *Jefferson's Vision for Education, 1760–1845* (New York: Peter Lang Publishing, 2003); and Gerald L. Gutek, *Historical and Philosophical Foundations of Education: A Biographical Introduction*, 3rd ed. (Upper Saddle River, NJ: Prentice Hall, 2001), 149–167.

[6] Gutek, *Historical and Philosophical Foundations of Education*, 163–164.

[7] Gutek, *Historical and Philosophical Foundations of Education*, 165–167.

[8] Addis, *Jefferson's Vision for Education*, 68-87. Alexander also disliked Jefferson's "antichristian plans" for the University of Virginia (Alexander, *Forty Years' Letters*, 2:71). Alexander also shuddered at the prospects of Girard College, a secular school established in Pennsylvania for orphans. This college was established by the will of Stephen Girard, which stipulated that no minister of any denomination was to be allowed ever to enter, even as a visitor (Alexander, *Forty Years' Letters*, 1:241). Daniel Webster argued against the legality of such a stipulation before the United States Supreme Court in 1844. See Daniel Webster, *Defence* [sic] *of the Christian Religion and the Religious Instruction of the Young* (New York: Mark H. Newman, 1844). Alexander expressed his appreciation for Webster's speech, calling it "a noble defence of

Jefferson's ideas for secular education were not widely embraced during his lifetime, but they were indicative of a growing trend. Jefferson's vision for a secularized public education anticipated in some respects the "common school" movement championed by Horace Mann.[9] In the 1830s, Mann emerged as an educational leader who pushed for the exclusion of religious materials and instruction that could in any way be considered "sectarian." A Unitarian himself, Mann was made the secretary to the Massachusetts State Board of Education in 1837, and from this role he championed a state-wide school system which would become the model for education far beyond Massachusetts.[10] According to Mann's interpretation of Massachusetts law, the Bible was to be used in Massachusetts schools only as a "reading text," and the schools in Massachusetts were also to teach a common ethic of piety, patriotism, and morality. In removing specific religious viewpoints from the classroom, Mann promoted a form of moral education, "creating in effect a common religion for a common school."[11] Mann's vision for "common schools" was largely driven by his vision for social reform. He believed that a common education containing the "moral aspects" of religion would be "an effective attack on poverty, crime, and social conflict," and it was largely for these social ends that Mann argued his case for a "nonsectarian" common school.[12]

---

the Bible, the ministry, and religious training" (Alexander, *Forty Years' Letters*, 1:391). The court did not rule in favor of Girard's wishes.

[9] Gutek, *Historical and Philosophical Foundations of Education*, 162, 164.

[10] For a selection of Mann's writings on education, see Horace Mann, *The Republic and the School*, ed. Lawrence A. Cremin (New York: Teachers College Press, 1957). For an overview of Mann's life and educational views, see William Hayes, *Horace Mann's Vision of the Public Schools: Is It Still Relevant?* (Lanham, MD: Rowman and Littlefield, 2006); and Gutek, *Historical and Philosophical Foundations of Education*, 188–208.

[11] Herbert M. Kliebard, ed., *Religion and Education in America: A Documentary History* (Scranton, PA: International Textbook Company, 1969), 6.

[12] Kliebard, *Religion and Education in America*, 5.

Using the Bible in publicly-funded schools, even as a reading text, met with opposition in some parts of antebellum America, partly due to the explosive population growth of Roman Catholic immigrants.[13] The growing presence of Catholics, who did not approve of the indiscriminate reading of the Bible by laity, put pressure on many states to remove religious teaching from their schools altogether. In 1854, Charles Hodge lamented "the irreligious character of education provided by the State," stating that it was "under the instigation of Papists" that "the State authorities began to exclude the Bible."[14] As America's Protestant hegemony gave way to a greater religious diversity, schooling which tried to teach only what was common to all religious perspectives had increasingly little religious material to teach.[15]

Alexander and Packard on Christian Education

It is clear from Alexander's letters to John Hall that he was not satisfied with the growing trend toward secularization in American education. Alexander believed that a truly beneficial education had to have the teaching of the Bible at its heart. Writing to Hall in 1834, Alexander stated: "I am filled with enthusiasm about having the Bible more taught. Instead of a mere *reading-book* in schools, it must be taught, after the Sunday School fashion; geography, archaeology and all. ...The Bible—the Bible—it is this which must save America."[16] Writing a few weeks later, Alexander again stated: "I am a little wild on the subject of

---

[13] Kliebard, *Religion and Education in America*, 7.

[14] Charles Hodge, "The Education Question," *Biblical Repertory and Princeton Review* 26 (1854): 535-536.

[15] The presence of Protestants who held to universalism and who denied the Trinity also made a common religious teaching in early America difficult to arrive at. For Mann's rejection of certain religious truths "offensive to Universalists," see Kliebard, *Religion and Education in America*, 71.

[16] Alexander, *Forty Years' Letters*, 1:219. Contrary to Horace Mann and other educational reformers, Alexander believed that the Bible must be kept in view when trying to teach basic virtues and ethics. See James W. Alexander, "Necessity of Popular Education," *Biblical Repertory and Princeton Review* 7 (1835): 51.

making the Bible the grand organ of mental and spiritual development. Suppose one knows the Bible, and from it as a centre radiates into the thousand subsidiary knowledges, will he not know all he needs?"[17] Since he considered knowledge of the Bible to be at the heart of a beneficial education, Alexander strongly disagreed with educational reformers who sought to remove it or limit its use.

Alexander's friend John Hall became the editor of the weekly journal published by the American Sunday School Union in 1832, and Alexander hoped that Hall would use this journal to promote his vision of a Bible-centered education.[18] Writing to Hall shortly after he had assumed this position, Alexander stated: "You ought...to have always before you the great idea, that the Bible is the central instrument in universal Education; that beginning with this, the whole Encyclopedia may be traversed."[19] Writing to Hall two years later, Alexander again encouraged Hall along these lines:

> Let me beg of you to take it as a prominent perpetual object of selections, &c. for your Journal, to hold up the great truth, that *the Bible is the book to educate the age*. Why not have it the *chief* thing in the family, in the school, in the academy, in the university? The day is coming; and if you and I can introduce the minutest corner of this wedge, we shall be benefactors of the race.[20]

It is likely that Hall shared Alexander's overall views on the importance of keeping the Bible at the center of education in America. Only by doing so would American society truly benefit from increased accessibility to schools and education.

In his position at the Sunday School Union, Hall came to work very closely with Frederick Adolphus Packard, an outspoken advocate

---

[17] Alexander, *Forty Years' Letters*, 1:220.
[18] Alexander, *Forty Years' Letters*, 1:192.
[19] Alexander, *Forty Years' Letters*, 1:193.
[20] Alexander, *Forty Years' Letters*, 1:217.

of Christian education. Packard had been a successful lawyer in Massachusetts before becoming the general editor and secretary of the American Sunday School Union in 1829.[21] For a number of years, Packard strenuously opposed Horace Mann's vision of a "nonsectarian" education, arguing that it amounted to an essentially nonreligious education.[22] In 1838, Packard entered into a series of exchanges with Mann, centering around whether certain books published by the American Sunday School Union were to be regarded as "sectarian" and therefore not suitable for a general education. These exchanges quickly grew heated and became public.[23] Packard went on to write a series of anonymous newspaper articles berating Mann and the Massachusetts Board of Education for excluding evangelical instruction as "sectarian."[24] Packard even attempted to overturn the Board's position politically, an effort which proved unsuccessful.[25]

Packard's labor in championing Christian education in the public schools was appreciated by Alexander. He shared Packard's opposition to the secularization of public education, and he wrote to Hall in 1840 with this request:

> Tell [Packard] that I beseech him to write an off-hand article
> for the Repertory, on the subject he once touched in some

[21] Packard served in this role until 1867, editing over two thousand titles published by the Union (*The Biblical Repertory and Princeton Review Index Volume*, 73). For more on Packard, see: Edwin Wilbur Rice, *The Sunday-School Movement, 1780-1917, and the American Sunday School Union, 1818-1917* (Philadelphia: American Sunday School Union, 1917), 174–177.

[22] Frederick M. Binder, *The Age of the Common School, 1830-1865* (New York: John Wiley & Sons, 1974), 60–61.

[23] This conflict is described at length in Raymond B. Culver, *Horace Mann and Religion in the Massachusetts Public Schools* (New York: Arno Press, 1969), 55–110. For the extant text of the series of letters between Mann and Packard, see Culver, *Horace Mann and Religion*, 241–284.

[24] For information on these newspaper articles, see Culver, *Horace Mann and Religion*, 83–110.

[25] For a complete account of the legislative attempts to reverse the Massachusetts position, see Culver, *Horace Mann and Religion*, 127–180.

letters; viz., the danger and folly of an un-religious Education for the country. Let him fill it with his British recollections, &c. He is precisely the man to do it. The call is imperative, and this is the nick of time. I wish I could make him know how earnestly I desire this. ...If this is not our vocation just now, I know not what is. I am afraid the devil is getting hold of the common-school crank... Talk fully with [Packard] about the religious-education-literature, (as above,) for I think it *the* question of our age and land. If we could leave that matter on its right foot, we might die. If I were a raging, athletic, outdoor man, I would stake every thing upon it.[26]

Packard complied with this request, and in 1841 his first article appeared in the *Repertory*, entitled "Religious Instruction in Common Schools."[27] In this article, Packard argued that public education should be a matter of local funding and local control, with the inhabitants of each school district free to choose their own teachers and curriculum according to whatever religious perspective they preferred.[28] With the majority of school districts still likely to run their schools according to evangelical convictions, Packard believed that this approach would result in "the efficient, practical, intelligent, constant inculcation of Scriptural truth as received by the great body of Protestant Christians in the United States" in the public schools.[29] All schools which

---

[26] Alexander, *Forty Years' Letters*, 1:312–313.

[27] Frederick A. Packard, "Religious Instruction in Common Schools," *Biblical Repertory and Princeton Review* 13 (1841): 315–368. Packard wrote many other articles for the *Repertory* pertaining to education, including: "Irish School System," *Biblical Repertory and Princeton Review* 14 (1842): 87–119; "English School Systems," *Biblical Repertory and Princeton Review* 15 (1843): 1–22; and "Horace Mann," *Biblical Repertory and Princeton Review* 38 (1866): 74–94. In his critical biography of Robert Owen, the utopian socialist, Packard addresses Owen's secular philosophy of education throughout. See Packard, *Life of Robert Owen*, 112–117, 144–158, 168–174, 251–254. For more information on Owen's educational philosophy, see Gutek, *Historical and Philosophical Foundations of Education*, 211–226.

[28] Packard, "Religious Instruction in Common Schools," 340–342.

[29] Packard, "Religious Instruction in Common Schools," 355.

excluded religious instruction altogether should not be the recipient of public funds, Packard argued, as the maintenance of Protestant Christianity and the spread of biblical truth were in the best interest of the state.[30] Packard ended his article by stating: "We appeal to Christian men of all Protestant denominations and parties to renounce all connexion with any system of public instruction which does not fully and distinctly recognise the religion of Jesus Christ, revealed in the gospel, as the ground work of the whole scheme."[31] With this appeal, Packard closed the article he had written at Alexander's request, responding to what Alexander's considered to be "*the* question of our age and land."[32]

Presbyterian Parochial Schools

It is not clear how Alexander felt about all the aspects of Packard's plan for publicly-funded religious education advocated in his 1841 article. As the trend to remove religious instruction from public schools failed to be abated by the efforts of Packard and others, Alexander virtually gave up on the attempt to secure Christian education within the public school system. Out of increasing disappointment in the secular direction of public education, Alexander turned in the mid-1840s to lend his support to parochial schools being set up within the Presbyterian Church.[33]

Of Old School Presbyterians, Alexander was not alone in his concern with the secularization of public education. He was also not alone in advocating increased denominational involvement in providing a

[30] Packard, "Religious Instruction in Common Schools," 355–356.
[31] Packard, "Religious Instruction in Common Schools," 367. For an extended defense of public religious education expressing views similar to Packard, see George B. Cheever, *Right of the Bible in our Public Schools* (New York: Robert Carter & Brothers, 1859).
[32] See also James W. Alexander, "Teaching a Science," *Biblical Repertory and Princeton Review* 20 (1848): 56.
[33] The attempt by Old School Presbyterians to launch a system of parochial schools is told in Lewis Joseph Sherrill, *Presbyterian Parochial Schools, 1846–1870* (New Haven: Yale University Press, 1932).

general education.[34] Many of those connected with Princeton Seminary had considered parochial education for some time. In 1838, the Presbyterian General Assembly had formed a committee consisting of Samuel Miller, Charles Hodge, Archibald Alexander, Joseph Addison Alexander, and James Carnahan to explore the subject of Christian education and what role the church should play in it.[35] A report written by Samuel Miller came out of this committee in 1840, calling for a system of "Church Schools" to be established.[36] Although the report was accepted and adopted by the General Assembly, little was done to implement such a system over the next few years.[37] In 1844, another committee was formed "to consider the expediency of establishing Presbyterian Parochial Schools."[38] Alexander chaired this committee and wrote its report, which was presented to the General Assembly of 1846.[39]

In his report to the Assembly, Alexander called the church to embrace the ideal of having a parochial school established out of every local church.[40] This, he believed, was called for by the condition of public education. He opened his report stating the reasons why government schools were to be rejected as adequate dispensers of religious education, even where the Bible was used as a textbook:

---

[34] In 1828, Charles Hodge had advocated for "the time-honored teaching of religion in common schools" (Sherrill, *Presbyterian Parochial Schools*, 7). In the 1840s, however, he too came to be an advocate for the fledgling Presbyterian parochial school movement.

[35] Sherrill, *Presbyterian Parochial Schools*, 7.

[36] Sherrill, *Presbyterian Parochial Schools*, 7–8. For the text of Miller's report, see Samuel Miller, *The Christian Education of the Children and Youth in the Presbyterian Church* (Philadelphia: Presbyterian Board of Publication, 1840). For more on Miller's views on Christian education, see Miller, *Life of Samuel Miller*, 2:417–428.

[37] Sherrill, *Presbyterian Parochial Schools*, 8.

[38] Sherrill, *Presbyterian Parochial Schools*, 20.

[39] This report is contained in *Minutes of the General Assembly of the Presbyterian Church in the United States of America, Volume 11* (Philadelphia: William S. Martien, 1846), 227–232.

[40] *Minutes of the General Assembly, Vol. 11*, 229.

Our State schools, in their best estate, can teach no higher morals or religion, than what might be called the *average* of public morals and religion. So long as the majority do not receive the truths of grace, State schools, their creature, can never teach the gospel. In some States, it is already a matter of debate, whether the word of God shall be admitted, and even if this were settled to our wishes, it needs scarcely be said, our necessities demand something far higher than the bare reading of the Bible. In our State schools—Bible or no Bible—we have every assurance that Christ, and grace, and gospel liberty, cannot, by authority, be so much as named; and without these there can be no Christian education.[41]

Alexander went on to condemn "the system of such compromise" that existed in some states, whereby "the child's creed shall be so dilute [*sic*] as to be equally palatable to the Socinian, Jew, or Mussulman [Muslim]."[42] Recognizing education to be "incomplete" without instruction in Scripture and "the doctrines of grace," Alexander's report concluded with a series of resolutions commending parochial education for serious consideration and approving all such churches that had already begun a parochial school.[43] Alexander's report stirred up a spirited debate at the Assembly, with some individuals speaking against the formation of parochial schools, arguing that working within the government system was a better approach.[44] One individual who argued this was Robert J. Breckinridge of Kentucky. Breckinridge strongly resisted the notion of a parochial school, arguing that Christians ought to put all their efforts into making the state-run schools as suitable as possible.[45]

---

[41] *Minutes of the General Assembly, Vol. 11*, 228.

[42] *Minutes of the General Assembly, Vol. 11*, 228.

[43] *Minutes of the General Assembly, Vol. 11*, 232.

[44] For Hodge's description of the debate sparked by Alexander's report, see Charles Hodge, "The General Assembly," *Biblical Repertory and Princeton Review* 18 (1846): 433–441.

[45] For Breckinridge's arguments against parochial schools, see Robert. J. Breckinridge, "Denominational Education," *Southern Presbyterian Review* 4 (July 1849): 1–19.

While most of the Princetonians tended to support parochial education, many prominent Southern Presbyterians did not, holding on to the belief that the public schools might yet be able to provide an acceptably Christian education.[46]

The Assembly eventually adopted Alexander's report, and Alexander was surprised at the debate generated by what he viewed as a modest and cautiously-worded proposal. Writing to Hall on May 28, 1846, Alexander stated: "My little report on Parochial schools has made a breeze in our Assembly, which I was unprepared for. The resolutions appear to me milk-and-water enough for anybody. Yet I feel no zeal for them, beyond this, that I should like the skirt of the Assembly to be cast over those who are attempting church-schools."[47] While a proponent of parochial schools, Alexander had no desire to involve himself in controversy over it or in leading the denomination in the hard administrative work of implementing such a system. He was more committed to supporting the Sunday School movement with his efforts. Leadership of the Presbyterian parochial school movement fell to Charles Hodge and Cortlandt Van Rensselaer, a clergyman who was elected that same year to become the secretary of the Presbyterian Board of Education.[48] At the following General Assembly, Van Rensselaer prepared a stronger resolution than the one put forward by Alexander in the previous year, committing the Presbyterians even further

---

[46] James Henley Thornwell was another Southern Presbyterian who opposed the plan of parochial schools, largely on the grounds that it wasn't the church's role as a "spiritual" organization to involve itself in providing a general education (Sherrill, *Presbyterian Parochial Schools*, 37). Sherrill notes that "the attack from within the church upon the parochial system came almost entirely from the South" and that both Thornwell and Breckinridge were "connected officially with state education" (Sherrill, *Presbyterian Parochial Schools*, 43).

[47] Alexander, *Forty Years' Letters*, 2:52.

[48] Sherrill, *Presbyterian Parochial Schools*, 176. For more on Van Rensselaer, see Charles Hodge, *Memorial of Cortlandt Van Rensselaer* (Philadelphia: C. Sherman & Son, 1860). For more on Hodge's views on parochial education and Van Rensselaer, see Archibald Hodge, *Life of Charles Hodge*, 408–410.

to the cause of parochial schools.[49] One of Van Rensselaer's resolutions called for "immediate and strenuous exertions...by every congregation to establish within its bounds one or more Primary Schools...in which together with the usual branches of secular learning, the truths and duties of our holy religion shall be assiduously inculcated."[50] With Hodge giving a compelling sermon to the Assembly on this subject, the Van Rensselaer's resolution passed without as much debate as the year before.[51]

The Spread of Secular Education and Societal Decline

Alexander's advocacy of parochial schools did not cause him to disparage altogether the advances of public education. In fact, Alexander was quite supportive of the spread of public school education in general:

> When I say that these [public schools] do not attain to the utmost of what we need, it is with no intention of disparaging these institutions. Free education for the people is a sublime conception and a really patriotic work. The structure in the State of which I am a citizen [New York] is more glorious than the pyramids... Whatever defects may exist, we bless God for the institution and would wish it perpetuity. Far be it from us or ours, under any pretext of religion, to lay on it the ruthless

---

[49] This report was printed in full in Cortlandt Van Rensselaer, ed., *Home, the School, and the Church; or The Presbyterian Education Repository, Volume 2* (Philadelphia: C. Sherman, 1852), 33–57. For Hodge's account of the Assembly's handling of this matter, see Charles Hodge, "The General Assembly," *Biblical Repertory and Princeton Review* 19 (1847): 425–426.

[50] Hodge, "The General Assembly," (1847), 425.

[51] Sherrill, *Presbyterian Parochial Schools*, 26-27. For Hodge's sermon, see Charles Hodge, "Public Religious Education Enforced in a Discussion of Different Plans," in *Home, the School, and the Church; or The Presbyterian Education Repository, Volume 1*, ed. Cortlandt Van Rensselaer (Philadelphia: William S. Martien, 1850), 95–107. For another important article by Hodge in support of parochial schools, see Hodge, "The Education Question," 504–544. Even with Hodge's support, the Presbyterian parochial school movement never gained broad support. It was formally abandoned in 1870 (Sherrill, *Presbyterian Parochial Schools*, 68).

hand of spoliation. Far be it from the Christians of America to withdraw from it that support and influence which, by God's blessing, may yet avail to modify what is erroneous and supply what is wanting.[52]

Even though the public schools weren't providing the Christian education that they should, they were still to be appreciated. Again, Alexander stated: "Our public schools are, in a worldly sense, the glory of our States. Those palaces where thousands are taught, let it be repeated, merit the visits and admiration of strangers more than any or all the luxurious mansions of the proud. But the Bible is not that which these are instituted to teach."[53] Viewing the concept of government-run schooling favorably, Alexander was critical of the public system *solely* because of its secularism and refusal to teach the Bible, not because he was against public education in general.

Holding that "the actual condition of American society" demands "a general religious education," Alexander stated that: "our State schools, with all their power and secular advantages, fail of the objection which we hold to be paramount, *because they lack the religious element.*"[54] Because Alexander viewed education as "the training of the whole nature for usefulness and happiness," he viewed secular education to be seriously "incomplete," in that it "ignores our ruined state, our means of recovery, and our evangelical duty."[55] Schools that "exclude or omit all that is spiritual and evangelical" were insufficiently providing a beneficial education, and such an exclusion would ultimately work "wide-spread disaster" in furthering the advance of secularism in society.[56] According to Alexander, "If Knowledge is Power, it is, when separate from religion, disastrous power."[57]

---

[52] Alexander, *Sunday School and Its Adjuncts*, 34.

[53] Alexander, *Sunday School and Its Adjuncts*, 115–116.

[54] Alexander, *Sunday School and Its Adjuncts*, 13, 37 (emphasis his).

[55] Alexander, *Sunday School and Its Adjuncts*, 37.

[56] Alexander, *Sunday School and Its Adjuncts*, 40.

[57] James W. Alexander, "The Evils of an Unsanctified Literature," *Biblical Repertory and Princeton Review* 15 (1843): 73.

It bears repeating that Alexander did not view the government's involvement in education to be problematic *per se*, but what was alarming to Alexander was that educational reformers were establishing and furthering the advance of secularism and godlessness in America. Alexander believed that the rejection of religion in public education was connected with a much broader rejection in society of the Christian faith. According to Alexander,

> Our State schools, it seems to be well determined, will not furnish any thing for the soul. With some the Bible is sectarian; and it certainly does contain very strong tenets of a 'sect which was everywhere spoken against' in old times, and which is still eminently distasteful to all the varieties of antichristian craft and infidel looseness.[58]

Alexander viewed the secularization of education as one further step of religious and spiritual decline in American society, a society that had seen "disastrous changes" since the days of "the early colonists."[59] Alexander described the overall decline of American society according to these terms:

> The zeal for material prosperity and worldly success has not been accompanied with an equal zeal for light and religion... Industry has begotten wealth; wealth has engendered luxury and pride; these have weakened the principle of holiness; and the children of the church have grown up in conformity to the world, and have been followed by another generation, still further off from the frugality, strictness and reflection of the fathers... In a state of things like this, unbounded liberty of opinion has led to latitudinary doctrines, or to the denial of all Christian doctrine. This would be true even if our nation comprised only the descendents of the original stock. But we have to add a new ingredient in the accession, by myriads of

---

[58] Alexander, *Sunday School and Its Adjuncts*, 97. See also Alexander, *Sunday School and Its Adjuncts*, 106.

[59] Alexander, *Sunday School and Its Adjuncts*, 17.

foreigners, sometimes infidel, sometimes Popish, and, in a majority of instances, less addicted to religious sentiment than even those to whom they come. It need cause no surprise, therefore, that sagacious observers augur gloomily for the future and believe that the moral tone of society at large is suffering a depression. ...bad must grow worse in a fearfully-augmenting proportion unless some vigorous instrumentality be applied to arrest the plague.[60]

With American society declining into "irreligious ignorance," the need for religious education, Alexander believed, could not have been more pressing.[61]

Even though American society was growing increasing secular, Alexander believed that state-run schools should be obligated to teach Christianity and that "a clear majority of American Christian parents have a right to demand that [the Bible] should not be shut off from the minds of their offspring."[62] He resisted the notion that America was a secular state, and he believed that evangelical Protestantism should enjoy the explicit sanction of the American government, being the religion of America's founding generation and of the majority of Americans still. He believed that the pernicious idea of America as a secular state lay behind the spread of a secularism in public education: "As the State, *according to doctrines lately avowed*, has no religion and can favour none, the schools which are its creatures refuse to teach that which is sectarian. And under this designation they are pleased to comprehend not

---

[60] Alexander, *Sunday School and Its Adjuncts*, 18-20. Alexander was quite critical of the materialism of antebellum America, and he referred to money as "the God of Americans" (Alexander, *Forty Years' Letters*, 1:232). See also Alexander, *Forty Years' Letters*, 1:288-289, 341. Like political conservatives Edmund Burke and Alexis De Tocqueville, Alexander believed society should be built upon virtue instead of on "egalitarian materialism" (Bruce Frohnen, *Virtue and the Promise of Conservatism: The Legacy of Burke and Tocqueville* [Lawrence, KS: University Press of Kansas, 1993], 13, 148, 151).

[61] Alexander, *Sunday School and Its Adjuncts*, 49.

[62] Alexander, *Sunday School and Its Adjuncts*, 40. See also Alexander, *Sunday School and Its Adjuncts*, 35.

only the creeds of the respective sects, but that holy document which is the avowed basis of all."[63] In contrast with political secularists, Alexander viewed America as "a Christian land," stating that "it is the right of the people to have Christian Schools."[64] These comments illustrate

---

[63] Alexander, *Sunday School and Its Adjuncts*, 37 (emphasis mine). The role religion was intended by America's founders to have in affairs of state is a much debated issue. For an early and official statement of America's secular self-identity, see "Treaty of Peace and Friendship between the United States and the Bey and Subjects of Tripoli, of Barbury," November 4, 1796, *United States Statutes at Large* 8, 155. For the argument that America was established as a "Christian nation," see Charles B. Galloway, *Christianity and the American Commonweath* (Nashville: Methodist Episcopal Church, 1898); and Colwell, *Position of Christianity in the United States*, 9–67. Colwell and Alexander both believed that America was a "Christian nation," and they agreed that the State was therefore obligated to provide a Christian education to its citizenry. See Colwell, *Position of Christianity in the United States*, 89–121. For a helpful treatment of this topic in general, see Mark David Hall, *Did America Have a Christian Founding?: Separating Modern Myth from Historical Truth* (Nashville: Thomas Nelson, 2019).

[64] Alexander, *Sunday School and Its Adjuncts*, 242. Alexander was not alone among Princetonians who believed that America should legitimately be considered "a Christian nation." Charles Hodge, for one, lent his support to the National Reform Association, a group which organized to petitioned the government to amend the United States Constitution to read as follows: "We, the people of the United States, *humbly acknowledging Almighty God as the source of all authority and power in civil government, the Lord Jesus Christ as the Ruler among the nations, His revealed will as the supreme law of the land, in order to constitute a Christian government, and* in order to form a more perfect union..." (Archibald Hodge, *Life of Charles Hodge*, 411 [emphasis mine]). For more on the National Reform Association, see National Reform Association, *Proceedings of the National Convention to Secure the Religious Amendment of the Constitution of the United States* (Philadelphia: James B. Rogers, 1872).

One of the leaders of the National Reform Association was Charles P. McIlvaine, who led a delegation to Washington to meet formally with President Lincoln about the matter. This delegation met with him on February 9, 1864, with the President subsequently voicing his general approval (National Reform Association, *Proceedings of the National Convention*, viii-x). Although an Episcopalian, McIlvaine was a graduate of Princeton College. He also attended Princeton Seminary, studying under Archibald Alexander and Samuel Miller. See William Carus, ed., *Memorials of the Right Reverend Charles Pettit*

how Alexander's resistance to secularism in education was undoubtedly tied in with his overall political and social conservatism, which resisted secularism in all areas of public thought and life.

As Alexander contemplated the long-term effects of secular education, he could only envision what American society would look like with the religious elements removed from the education of America's youth:

> Another generation must arise before we shall be able to discern the fruits of the present system of common education. What will be the character of hundreds of thousands, let loose on society, or rather constituting that society, whose childhood and youth shall have been passed in schools and libraries, from which every particle of evangelical doctrine has been filtrated, and who shall have grown up to a ferocious acquaintance with the surface of all sciences, yet without the inculcation of one purely saving doctrine of the New Testament; our children will know![65]

While the spread of a secularized education might benefit individuals and society in some ways, Alexander did not believe it would necessarily lead to a better society.[66] Overall, he agreed with Packard in this

---

McIlvaine, D. D., D.C.L. (New York: Thomas Whittaker, 1882), 9–11. Joshua Hall McIlvaine, who attended Princeton College and Seminary as well, also published an article in the *Repertory* expressing his understanding of America as "a Christian nation." See Joshua H. McIlvaine, "A Nation's Right to Worship God," *Biblical Repertory and Princeton Review* 31 (1859): 664–697. Joshua McIlvaine, like Alexander, traced the secularization of education to the broader secularization of American society and political thought. See Joshua H. McIlvaine, "Covenant Education," *Biblical Repertory and Princeton Review* 33 (1861): 238–261.

[65] Alexander, "Teaching a Science," 54.

[66] Alexander's views on the importance of religious education were shared by others in early America. Benjamin Rush, a signer of the Declaration of Independence, stated in a letter written in 1791: "We profess to be republicans, and yet we neglect the only means of establishing and perpetuating our republican form of government, that is, the universal education of our youth

regard, who stated that "education without religion is at least as likely to prove a curse as a blessing."[67] If godlessness and increased secularism were spread by social reforms intended to make education more broadly available, such reforms would only prove to be detrimental in the end.

Conclusion

Alexander was supportive of plans to expand public education to the general population, but he did not want that education to be purely secular. Alexander, like Frederick Adolphus Packard, believed that the state should provide a general education to its citizens, but he believed that it should teach the Bible from a Protestant perspective and have this at the center of its curriculum. When it became increasingly clear that an educational program of this kind would not be implemented in America's increasingly secular climate, Alexander lent his support to the Presbyterian parochial school movement, which was supported by many other Princetonians as well. Notwithstanding its popular appeal, Alexander ultimately rejected the "common school" movement not so much for its democratic or egalitarian impulse, but for its secularism and antagonism to Biblical instruction. He supported it in its attempts to make education more generally available, but he opposed it as a purveyor of secularism and infidelity to the Christian faith.

---

in the principles of Christianity, by means of the Bible; for this divine book, above all others favours that equality among mankind, that respect for just laws, and all those sober and frugal virtues, which constitute the soul of republicanism" (Benjamin Rush, "A Defence of the Use of the Bible as a School Book," in *Essays: Literary, Moral, and Philosophical*, 2nd ed. [Philadelphia: Thomas and William Bradford, 1806], 112–113). Rush was a graduate of Princeton College.

[67] Packard, "Religious Instruction in Common Schools," 351.

Chapter 6
Alexander's Vision of Social Reform

Alexander was out-of-step with his times. As we have seen, he rejected a whole variety of social reform movements that emerged from a secular understanding of society and social ills. He believed that certain social and political movements like Jacksonian "ultra-democracy," utopian socialism, trade unionism, and abolitionism were built more on secular notions of man and social egalitarianism than on scriptural norms and principles. The common school movement he viewed in a more favorable light, applauding its intention to bring a general education to the masses. He could not support it, however, when it began to exclude religious instruction and became a purveyor of state-sanctioned secularism.

In his disagreement with these movements, Alexander was influenced by a deeply conservative and evangelical perspective.[1] His critique of popular social reform movements was not based on their overall intention to help the oppressed, but in their secular foundations and egalitarian vision of American society. The proposals that many were

---

[1] Alexander's overall perspective on social reform was shared with his brother, Addison. Addison published a sermon on Proverbs 22:2 in which he too rejected the same social reform movements his brother rejected. Specifically, Addison rejected the remedy of "obliterating social inequalities by a coercive distribution of all property," the remedy of "securing an equality of civil rights," and the remedy of "intellectual increase of knowledge and refinement of taste" (Joseph Addison Alexander, *Sermons*, 2 vols. [New York: Charles Scribner, 1862], 1:233-236). Addison Alexander's entire sermon on the subject of social reform illustrates how similar the two brothers were in their views on this subject. Prior to the Civil War, it seems that most of those at Old Princeton, apart from Colwell, held similarly to these views.

promoting to solve social ills were actually indicative of deeper ideological problems in antebellum America. In fact, in as much as these so-called "solutions" promoted anti-biblical ways of thinking, the solutions themselves were a part of the deeper problem—the problem of a culture becoming less biblical in its outlook.

Alexander was not content to be a critic of social reform efforts with which he disagreed. His writings reveal that he thought a great deal about what positive steps should be taken to address the social ills of antebellum America. He also engaged in many activities himself and promoted various causes which he believed would benefit American society. In all his writings and activities for social reform, Alexander advanced his own evangelical agenda, one that proceeded from Christian principles and had the spread of Christian truth at its heart.

Christianity, the Bible, and Social Reform

As an evangelical Christian, Alexander believed that the root of all social ills was found in the sinfulness of man. No proposed remedy of social reform which failed to reach to this fundamental root could truly bring about beneficial results in the long run. Lasting societal reform would come to a society only as the mass of its individuals were genuinely made into sincere Christians. It would not come about through the mere renovation of political, economic, or social structures.[2] Only the spiritual renovation that comes to individuals through the Christian faith could transform society in any deeply meaningful way. Alexander expressed this point as follows:

> To do good to men, is the great work of life; to make them true Christians is the greatest good we can do them. Every investigation brings us round to this point. Begin here, and you are like one who strikes water from a rock on the summits of the mountains; it flows down over all the intervening tracts to the

[2] Alexander, *Sunday School and Its Adjuncts*, 268-269.

very base. If we could make each man love his neighbour, we should make a happy world.[3]

Making followers of Christ is the way to reform and transform society. It is the way of true social reform. In his fullest statement of this central principle, Alexander wrote:

We must bring Christian principles to bear more on the masses of men. We must show them that what they seek by vain philanthropy, is realized wherever true Christianity takes effect. *If all men were good Christians, the evils of society would be in a good degree abated.* Prescriptive wrongs would cease. Property would be equalized. The rich would communicate of their wealth, and the poor would rise by industry, temperance, frugality, and wisdom. The Bible is made for all ages, and with every new discovery in science, it meets us and shows a coincidence. The worldly philosopher and philanthropist dreams of a perfect state of society—good-will among men and universal peace. Now, the Bible not only predicts this, but shows how it is to be attained. The principles of Christianity tend to produce that very state. All the high civilization and humanity of the best nations is in fact the product of Christianity. In countries where science, literature, and the arts are in a high state without true religion, we see luxury, excessive pleasure, hardness of heart, false honour, dueling, and suicide. Of this France is a great instance. *The true way then to benefit, and even remodel society, is to make it Christian.* This method is as simple as it is powerful. It proceeds upon no false or doubtful hypothesis, either of politics or economy. While men endlessly differ and dispute about these, and change one experiment for another in an endless round, loosing their beginnings by the change, and destroying human peace in the fruitless and soon abandoned trials, the humble Christian endeavours are going forward, with a noiseless but mighty efficacy. Place a thousand men in a Utopian community, such as Owen's, and try to mould them by the visionary principles of the 'New Social

[3] Alexander, *Thoughts on Preaching*, 41.

World,' and the result is discord, failure, and misery. But place a thousand men anywhere in the world, and make them true Christians, and you attain really all the good ends sought in the former experiment, and render them as happy as men can be in our world. Hence the man who does most to bring over those around him to the principles and practice of true religion, is the truest philanthropist.[4]

Alexander expressed the same central idea to John Hall in 1839, stating: "The great work is to save souls. All our economical, political, and literary reformations are mere adjusting of the outer twig; religion changes the sap of root and trunk. This I never felt more than now. I see that when a people become godly, all the rest follows."[5] Instead of focusing on man's outward condition, social reformers should focus first and foremost on man's deep spiritual needs, for "doing good to men's souls brings other relief in its train."[6]

While a professor at Princeton College, Alexander published a small book in 1844 to promote this perspective of Christian social reform entitled, *Good, Better, Best; or, Three Ways of Making a Happy World.*[7] Alexander wrote this book in the form of an entertaining story intended for an adult audience.[8] In the narrative of this story, Alexander speaks through the learned character of Dr. Lee, who explains that while doing good to men's bodies (i.e. feeding the poor) is *good* and doing good to men's minds is *better*, doing good to men's souls is the *best*

---

[4] Alexander, *Thoughts on Preaching*, 71-72 (emphasis mine).

[5] Alexander, *Forty Years' Letters*, 1:289.

[6] Alexander, *Forty Years' Letters*, 1:388.

[7] James W. Alexander, *Good, Better, Best; or, The Three Ways of Making a Happy World* (Philadelphia: American Sunday School Union, 1844; repr., Birmingham, AL: Solid Ground Christian Books, 2009). This book was republished in London in 1856, with a foreword by Robert S. Candlish.

[8] Alexander, *Forty Years' Letters*, 1:388. While this book was published in 1844, Alexander had been working on it since at least 1840. See Alexander, *Forty Years' Letters*, 1:294-295.

way of reforming society and of "making a happy world."[9] By promoting true religion and piety in the soul of a man, good might be brought effectively to his mind and body also, since a spiritual transformation generally brings about an intellectual and practical transformation as well.[10] Because "the want of religion" is "the principle want of our depraved race," the spread of the Christian religion and Christian truth would reach to the heart of social ills.[11] As the souls and minds of men are transformed through the power of Christianity *en masse*, real societal reform will come about as a result.[12]

Alexander's *Good, Better, Best* contains some of the same critiques of other social reform movements found in his other writings. The social radicalism and secularism of the French Enlightenment philosophers is disparaged in *Good, Better, Best* at length.[13] The utopian socialism of St. Simon, Robert Owen, and Frances Wright is also condemned in passing.[14] A large portion of the book also focuses on addressing those who see "popular ignorance as the grand source of [social] evil."[15] The overall thrust of the book, however, is not to criticize the "well-meant efforts of others."[16] Instead, the main theme is to

---

[9] Alexander, *Good, Better, Best*, 215. Alexander believed the central point of his *Good, Better, Best* was well illustrated and expanded upon in "Backhouse's *Visit to the Mauritius and South Africa*," *North British Review* 2 (November 1844): 105-135. See Alexander, *Forty Years' Letters*, 2:12. The book under review in this article is James Backhouse, *A Narrative of a Visit to the Mauritius and South Africa* (London: Hamilton, Adams, 1844).

[10] Alexander, *Forty Years' Letters*, 1:295.

[11] Alexander, *Good, Better, Best*, 145.

[12] Alexander pointed to the social reforms brought about by "early Methodism" as an example of how the spread of Christianity "works wonders in nations beyond the circle of those who are truly converted" (Alexander, *Sunday School and Its Adjuncts*, 263). Alexander credits William Wilberforce with making this observation.

[13] Alexander, *Good, Better, Best*, 127-133.

[14] Alexander, *Good, Better, Best*, 62, 134.

[15] Alexander, *Forty Years' Letters*, 295. See Alexander, *Good, Better, Best*, 75-146.

[16] Alexander, *Good, Better, Best*, 4.

illustrate the effects of the Christian religion for transforming society. Through the words of Dr. Lee, Alexander states:

> You cannot give men religion *alone*. You cannot give men religion, without giving them a multitude of lesser benefits. These benefits are those on which mere worldly philanthropists expend all their strength; benefits, moreover, which, after all their labours, they utterly fail to give, without religion. Knowledge and personal comfort—the great boon which deluded, suffering man craves—do not include religion: but religion includes and infers them. ...whether we speak of the individual or of society, "*seek ye first the kingdom of God and his righteousness*, AND ALL THESE THINGS SHALL BE ADDED UNTO YOU."[17]

Since the spread of Christianity gives new motives and desires to man, this alone can bring about the societal transformation sought by philanthropists and social reformers.[18]

Since the prospect of genuine social reform lies in the spread of Christianity, Alexander believed that the focus of social reform should be on bringing the transformative message of the Bible to the masses.[19] In the words of Dr. Lee, Alexander stated in *Good, Better, Best*: "The Bible is the great elevator of our race. The Bible is the great corrector of moral evils. The Bible is the great preventer of false opinion. The Bible is the great preserver of society, and renovator of the social state.

---

[17] Alexander, *Good, Better, Best*, 165–167 (emphasis his).

[18] Alexander, *Good, Better, Best*, 161. Alexander's brother Addison agreed with him, stating that "the true corrective of all social inequalities, so far as they are evil, must be furnished, not by human institutions and arrangements, but derived from a higher and an independent source. In other words, the only practicable efficacious remedy for social evils of the kind in question, is and must be, a religious one. *i.e.*, one founded not in mere prudential changes of man's mutual relations, but in their common relation to their common God" (Joseph Addison Alexander, *Sermons*, 1:232).

[19] Alexander, *Good, Better, Best*, 144.

What then can we teach, if we do not teach the Bible?"[20] Alexander believed that God works to transform the souls of individuals (and thereby society) through the Bible. Therefore, he was eager to teach the Bible and see it taught to others.[21] Writing to Hall in 1835, Alexander stated: "How pleasing it would be, if we could be all the time engaged in labours for the conversion of souls, and the exaltation of the Bible!"[22]

Alexander believed that all individuals should be led to master the content and literature of the Bible, and not just the bare system of theology it contained. Bible history, Bible geography, and Bible archeology should all be taught to the general population if an adequate knowledge of the Bible was to be spread.[23] Along with his brother Addison, Alexander produced in 1830 an introductory level book on biblical geography.[24] In order to help make the Bible more accessible to the young and those lacking a background in Bible knowledge, Alexander published a

---

[20] Alexander, *Good, Better, Best*, 114. In his advocacy for religious education, Packard likewise stated: "The Bible is the preserver of society. It is the grand repository and illustration of those principles of justice, purity, temperance, industry, frugality, and moderation, upon the observance of which the very existence of a commonwealth depends. Whence come the modern theories of agrarianism, socialism, and a train of still more destructive and delusive notions about new modifications of human society, and enlarged liberty for human reason and passion? Do they come from those who believe, or from those who despise the Bible? With an early, intelligent, and thorough acquaintance with this sacred volume, the youth of our country will not suddenly become the dupes of imposture or the victims of atheism and corruption" (Packard, "Religious Instruction in Common Schools," 366).

[21] For a similar emphasis by contemporaries, see Ransom Hebbard Tyler, *The Bible and Social Reform, or, The Scriptures as a Means of Civilization* (Philadelphia: James Challen & Son, 1860); John Matthews, *The Influence of the Bible in Improving the Understanding and Moral Character* (Philadelphia: Presbyterian Board of Education, 1864); and James McFarlane Mathews, *The Bible and Civil Government* (New York: Robert Carter & Brothers, 1851).

[22] Alexander, *Forty Years' Letters*, 1:232.

[23] Alexander, *Forty Years' Letters*, 1:219.

[24] James W. Alexander and Joseph A. Alexander, *A Geography of the Bible* (Philadelphia: American Sunday School Union, 1830). This book was based on Addison's notes, which Alexander worked into a book. See Alexander, *Forty Years' Letters*, 1:134.

book in 1838 entitled, *The Scripture Guide.*[25] He viewed this book as "very needful" and wrote it to help introduce the content of the Bible.[26]

Alexander's desire to spread a knowledge of biblical content versus a bare system of theology reflects the emphasis he himself placed on biblical and exegetical studies.[27] Writing to Hall in 1832, Alexander stated:

> I have never read through any system of theology [except Calvin's Institutes]; I read as much in Wesley and Watson as in Turretine. My days are almost entirely spent in studies purely exegetical, in which it has been my principle for a long time, not to approach a commentary until, if possible, I had arrived at some rationale exposition of the passage... The noblest help in New Testament study is the Greek Concordance, which is better than any dictionary.[28]

---

[25] James W. Alexander, *The Scripture Guide: A Familiar Introduction to the Study of the Bible* (Philadelphia: American Sunday School Union, 1838).

[26] Alexander, *Forty Years' Letters*, 1:190. See also Alexander, *Forty Years' Letters*, 1:347.

[27] Alexander, *Forty Years' Letters*, 1:295. See also Alexander, *Forty Years' Letters*, 1:181, 255.

[28] Alexander, *Forty Years' Letters*, 1:187 (bracketed information supplied in a footnote by Alexander). While it was common to educate upper-society girls with a basic knowledge of French, Alexander wished that these girls would instead be taught New Testament Greek (Alexander, *Forty Years' Letters*, 1:219). Alexander stated to Hall in 1834: "Why may not our female friends be made to read the Greek Testament? I will engage to teach any of the poor things that lose their time on French, to read the New Testament in less time" (Alexander, *Forty Years' Letters*, 1:220). Again he stated in 1843: "I don't see why everybody should not learn Greek enough to read the New Testament. It would be worth ten times as much as the nonsensical boarding school French, which never does any good to anybody" (Alexander, *Forty Years' Letters*, 1:367).

Alexander certainly valued systematic theology and saw himself within a clearly defined theological tradition.[29] But however valuable theological systems might be, Alexander believed that they were to be kept always subsidiary to the Bible and serve as an aid in the exegetical study of Scripture.[30] Rather than merely dispensing systems of theology, he believed that helping individuals comprehend the complete literature of the Bible was of the utmost importance.[31]

Along with the entire scope of biblical content, the main portion of the Bible that was to be spread to the masses was the gospel of Jesus Christ. Writing to Hall in 1839, Alexander stated: "Methinks no work of the age is more important than the getting the mob of our cities in contact with Gospel-truth."[32] In the words of Dr. Lee, Alexander also stated that "Our chief business in life, whether we are clergymen or laymen, men or women, old or young, is to convey the gospel, the blessed means of salvation, to the minds of our fellow creatures."[33] Since spiritual transformation is brought about in the souls of men through the biblical gospel, only by spreading the knowledge of this truth would society be transformed.

Preaching and Social Reform

Alexander viewed powerful and instructive preaching as the best means available for spreading the truth of the Bible to the souls of men.[34] He considered preaching to be God's special means for bringing the truth of his Word to mankind.[35] Alexander called preaching "God's great

---

[29] The great value Alexander placed on catechetical instruction in his ministry has already been noted.

[30] See James W. Alexander, "On the Use and Abuse of Systematic Theology," *Biblical Repertory and Theological Review* 4 (1832): 187.

[31] Alexander, *Sunday School and Its Adjuncts*, 119, 123–124.

[32] Alexander, *Forty Years' Letters*, 1:276.

[33] Alexander, *Good, Better, Best*, 168.

[34] Alexander, *Forty Years' Letters*, 1:289.

[35] Alexander greatly enjoyed preaching and was widely regarded as an excellent preacher (Alexander, *Forty Years' Letters*, 1:203; Anderson, "Religious Rhetoric of James W. Alexander," 5–6). He once wrote to Hall that

ordinance," and he believed he held to a higher view of preaching than either his friends Hodge or Packard.[36] As Alexander presents his positive vision for social reform in *Good, Better, Best*, a prominent role is given to the place of preaching.[37] Writing to Hall in 1847, Alexander stated how important powerful and zealous preaching was for the growth and expansion of the church:

> Presbyterianism has never and nowhere made striking advances, except when the body of preachers and people has been animated with a zeal for truth and saving souls, such as at the very time has been a little too strong, methodistical, pietistical, enthusiastical, in the eyes even of many sound, good sort of brethren... Our real aggression has always been by warm pushing of our evangelical tenets.[38]

Warm, zealous preaching was the primary way, in Alexander's mind, that the Christian faith would be advanced in society.

Alexander understood preaching to be a means not only of exhortation but of solid Biblical instruction. In 1838, Alexander expressed his conviction of this to Hall, in spite of the errors he felt he had made in the past:

> Hortation seems to me to be the pulpit-error of the age, which has emasculated the church... In this matter of preaching...I

"Preaching Christ is the best, hardest, sweetest work, on this side of beholding him" (Alexander, *Forty Years' Letters*, 1:291).

[36] Alexander, *Forty Years' Letters*, 1:400.

[37] Alexander, *Good, Better, Best*, 1:157–160. Regarding the social renovation of the fictional town of Woolfall, Alexander (speaking through the character of Dr. Lee), called preaching "the grand instrument" of reform (Alexander, *Good, Better, Best*, 160). The main preacher used in Alexander's story is a "Mr. Gay," a Methodist. While Dr. Lee states that "I am no Methodist, and you know I was brought up with some prejudices against that people," his apprehensions are soon put at ease as Mr. Gay's preaching wrought "an awakening" and brought about "a total change...in the whole structure of society" (Alexander, *Good, Better, Best*, 157–158).

[38] Alexander, *Forty Years' Letters*, 2:74.

feel quite earnest, as believing that most of my earlier sermons were constructed on a wrong principle. I would be plain, but O, I wish I had *fed* my hearers with more truth, and given them less harangue.[39]

In order for preaching to benefit its hearers in the long-run, Alexander believed it should be expositional and full of biblical content.[40] In his final decade of ministry, Alexander expressed his desire to give himself to "plainer, simpler, more instructive preaching."[41] The kind of preaching that instructs as well as exhorts is the kind of preaching that could transform whole communities over time.

Given his views on the value of preaching, Alexander was troubled by the fact that Presbyterian churches were by and large not preaching at all to the poor: "To the poor the gospel is *not* preached in our crack Presbyterian churches."[42] Alexander was troubled that the poor were not given much encouragement to enter a church and that little was being done about it:

One of the great Christian problems of the age seems to me to be how to carry the gospel to the thousands, in cities, who will not enter any church. Pews are high. Or they are not dressed well enough. ...When shall we come down from our stilts, and be in earnest with a perishing world? Decorum and conservatism do not rank as the most needed virtues just now... We have lost much by stiffness.[43]

One of the main reasons the poor were being kept out of the churches, Alexander believed, was in the way in which Presbyterian churches funded their infrastructure and ministries, namely, by selling or renting

---

[39] Alexander, *Forty Years' Letters*, 1:268.
[40] Alexander, *Thoughts on Preaching*, 228–253.
[41] Alexander, *Forty Years' Letters*, 2:179.
[42] Alexander, *Forty Years' Letters*, 1:345 (emphasis his).
[43] Alexander, *Forty Years' Letters*, 2:38.

the majority of the pews in any given church building.[44] While a pastor in New York City, Alexander strongly, yet quietly, opposed the system of annual pew-renting.[45] He wanted the seating in his church to be made equally free to all, but he chose not to make a public issue of it.[46] It became, however, a persistent source of frustration for him. In 1851, Alexander wrote to Hall, "I wish I could turn out about twenty pews of rich folks and fill them with poor. But this is one of those dreams not to be realized. I never was stronger in my opinion, that all church-sittings ought to be free. Yet we can't reach this without establishments, endowments, and all that."[47] In 1854, he again wrote:

> Daily do I grow more opposed to pews. I honour Popery and Puseyism for this point. Free churches are unanimously voted a nuisance by New York Christians; but my mind is unchanged. They have, with us, always been undertaken by poor preachers. If such Chrysostoms as you and I...were to open a free church, it would tell another story; and I am persuaded the only way to effect it will be for individual preachers to lead

[44] For the general acceptance of the pew-renting system among Protestants in nineteenth century America, see Sylvanus Stall, *How to Pay Church Debts and How to Keep the Church out of Debt* (New York: I. K. Funk, 1881), 108-111. Stall argues against the common practice of pew rental.

[45] Alexander, *Forty Years' Letters*, 2:95. Alexander was not the only one of his contemporaries who disagreed with the pew-renting system. In article published in the *Repertory* in 1862, Joshua Hall McIlvaine noted that the "American system of defraying the expenses of the church by renting the pews" was having a strong influence to "alienate the poor from the church." McIlvaine noted that this problem was becoming more widely felt, and a change was being more widely sought. Like Alexander, McIlvaine offered no clear solution to the problems involved in shifting away from this system. In this same article, McIlvaine also noted that the preaching of many is more oriented to the "intellectual and aesthetic tastes" of the wealthy and educated instead of on "reaching the lowest capacity" with "striking illustrations" (Joshua Hall McIlvaine, "The Church and the Poor," *Biblical Repertory and Princeton Review* 34 [1862]: 619-622).

[46] Alexander, *Forty Years' Letters*, 2:208.

[47] Alexander, *Forty Years' Letters*, 2:183.

the way. I have not the spirit of a reformer, or I know what I would do.[48]

Writing to Hall in 1856, Alexander again stated: "I utterly reject the entire pew-system—I speak of cities—as against the spirit of Christianity. But all my opinions are held too tremblingly for me ever to be a reformer. So I quietly and sorrowfully go on expounding those things I am sure about."[49] Not having the heart or the energy to take this on, Alexander declined to make an issue of it with his people.[50]

Instead of changing the pew-rental system, Alexander led his New York congregation to set up a "mission chapel" where the poor could come and sit freely to regularly hear the preaching of the Bible.[51] This was only one of such "mission" efforts Alexander led his congregation in to reach the poor. In December 25, 1855, Alexander reported on some of these efforts to Hall:

We had, notwithstanding the rain, 350 urchins and urchinesses at our cake-and-candy fete at the Mission Chapel. Our two Industrial schools promise well. The lower one, at Duane Street, (where we also have mission-preaching), already

---

[48] Alexander, *Forty Years' Letters*, 2:194.

[49] Alexander, *Forty Years' Letters*, 2:223.

[50] Writing to Hall in 1855, Alexander stated "If I were ten years younger, I would have a building erected to hold 2,000, and would preach to free seats..." (Alexander, *Forty Years' Letters*, 2:206).

[51] Alexander, *Forty Years' Letters*, 2:191. In 1845, Alexander stated to Hall that "I am not going to rest until, as a congregation, we have a preaching-place and missionary in regular operation (Alexander, *Forty Years' Letters*, 2:42). In 1853, Alexander again described his plan for setting up a mission church to Hall, noting: "I cannot get any other churches to agree with me" (Alexander, *Forty Years' Letters*, 2:187). Alexander was also discouraged by the lack of support he received from his presbytery in setting up a preaching station in New York (Alexander, *Forty Years' Letters*, 2:188). The mission chapel was finally finished in late 1854 or early 1855 (Alexander, *Forty Years' Letters*, 2:205).

numbers 200. We talk of going in largely toward the purchase of a building for a coloured congregation...[52]

Through these varied efforts, Alexander sought to bring preaching to the poor, and many were converted and received into communicant membership under this extension of a gospel-ministry to the poor.[53]

The idea of establishing mission chapels for the sake of preaching to the poor was not an idea original to Alexander. When he was a boy, his father, Archibald Alexander, had formed an "Evangelical Society" in Philadelphia, and the plans of this society for establishing mission chapels formed the model for Alexander's efforts.[54] Alexander also had as a model the work of David Nasmith of Glasgow. Nasmith was a zealous worker who founded the London City Mission in 1835, as well as other "City Missions" in Edinburgh, Glasgow, and Dublin.[55]

---

[52] Alexander, *Forty Years' Letters*, 2:217. See also Alexander, *Forty Years' Letters*, 2:193. It has already been noted how Alexander started a church for blacks in Princeton and regularly preached to blacks in Trenton and in Virginia. It is not clear whether this plan to build a black church was enacted, but one of Alexander's mission schools was involved in ministering to German immigrants (Alexander, *Forty Years' Letters*, 2:195).

[53] Alexander, *Forty Years' Letters*, 2:285. During the New York City Revival of 1857–1858, Alexander set up a nightly prayer-meeting in his mission chapel for the poor, following the lead of many others in New York City (Alexander, *Forty Years' Letters*, 2:277). A total of 157 new communicants were added in the years 1858 and 1859 to Alexander's church (Alexander, *Forty Years' Letters*, 2:279).

[54] In 1845, Alexander wrote of this to Hall, stating: "An effort is making to establish minor religious meetings, for such purposes, here and there, all over the city. It is a fine scheme, though not a new one, being that of the old Evangelical Society of our boyhood" (Alexander, *Forty Years' Letters*, 2:38). The Evangelical Society and its plans for the collaborative building of mission chapels are described in Alexander, *Life of Archibald Alexander*, 298–305.

[55] For more on Nasmith and the City Mission movement, see John Matthias Weylland, *These Fifty Years* (London: S. W. Partridge, 1884); and Irene Howat, *Streets Paved with Gold: The Story of the London City Mission* (Fearn, UK: Christian Focus, 2003). Alexander resonated with the London City Mission's opposition to socialism. See Committee of the London City Mission, *Lectures Against Socialism* (London: I. and G. Seeley, 1840).

Alexander first met Nasmith in 1831 and was "refreshed and awakened by [his] meeting with him."[56] Nasmith's "City Missions" were designed to provide evangelistic outreach in densely-populated urban areas, and Alexander eagerly approved of Nasmith's overall plan in bringing the gospel to the poor.[57]

In order to bring the preaching of the Bible to the masses, Alexander was also willing to support "many plans, yea many sorts of preachers, 'unlearned deacons' and all."[58] He recognized the significant role that lay-people could have in "saving the multitudes," and he was willing to support the lay-preaching labors of some who were not considered altogether satisfactory by others in his circles.[59] While viewing the regular preaching ministry of the clergy as having special importance, Alexander stated: "We are not of those who would have everything in the hands of the clergy. We have no morbid dread of lay-teaching."[60] Given the lack of gospel preaching among the poor and the importance

---

[56] Alexander, *Forty Years' Letters*, 1:160.

[57] Alexander appreciated Nasmith's work in evangelizing the poor, but believed that his plan of setting up mission outposts should be "modified upon the principle of [Thomas] Chalmers," who established a "territorial system" for systematically reaching each neighborhood with the gospel and Christian benevolence (James W. Alexander, "Poverty and Crime in Cities," *Biblical Repertory and Princeton Review* 17 [1845]: 623–624). Alexander faulted Nasmith for his "distrust of the regular ministry," an error which caused him to distance his mission organizations from local churches and clergymen. In spite of this, Alexander was wholly supportive of the City Mission work in New York City (Alexander, "Poverty and Crime in Cities," 624–625). For more on Alexander's appreciation for Thomas Chalmers' views on social reform, see James W. Alexander, "Chalmers on Education and Ecclesiastical Economy," *Biblical Repertory and Princeton Review* 14 (1842): 577–583.

[58] Alexander, *Forty Years' Letters*, 2:206.

[59] Alexander, *Forty Years' Letters*, 1:363; 2:188. Alexander expressed great appreciation for the lay-ministry of A. R. Wetmore of the City Tract Society (Alexander, *Forty Years' Letters*, 2:43, 56). He also noted the ministry of Dr. William A. Muhlenberg to the poor. Muhlenberg was an Episcopal clergyman, and his church was "a free-seat one" (Alexander, *Forty Years' Letters*, 2:188, 205–206, 217).

[60] Alexander, "Poverty and Crime in Cities," 625.

he placed on preaching, Alexander was eager to support "many sorts of preachers," who would function in a parachurch capacity.[61]

Sunday Schools and Social Reform

Alexander believed that the church must use every means possible to spread the truth of the Bible. In addition to preaching, he gave great importance to the religious education of children and youth, stating: "The Church of Christ has a duty to perform, to her own children, and to all within her reach; a duty which demands the concentrated energies of the highest minds, and which is second in its imperative claims to nothing but the preaching of the gospel by our authorized ministry."[62] If American society was to be transformed, efforts should be focused on children and youth, for the young are much more "susceptible of influence" than adults.[63] Preaching aside, Alexander held that "the religious education of youth is the most hopeful means of benefiting society."[64] While others might hold working with children in low esteem, Alexander encouraged Hall to consider that "what we do for infants [i.e. children], we do for the best interests of man, in the most hopeful way."[65]

As a vehicle for providing religious education to children, Alexander was an enthusiastic supporter of Sunday schools. The Sunday school movement originated with the work of Robert Raikes in England

---

[61] Samuel Miller appears to have had more concerns about lay-preaching than Alexander. See Calhoun, *Faith and Learning*, 298–299).

[62] [James Alexander], "Teaching a Science: the Teacher an Artist," *The Biblical Repertory and Princeton Review* 20 (1848): 554.

[63] Alexander, *Sunday School and Its Adjuncts*, 27. For more on the importance Alexander placed on ministry to children, see Alexander, *Sunday School and Its Adjuncts*, 27–81.

[64] Alexander, *Sunday School and Its Adjuncts*, 16.

[65] Alexander, *Forty Years' Letters*, 1:231. Given the importance he placed on the influencing of children for the good of society, Alexander was also a strong promoter of Christian nurture and instruction in the home. See the section entitled "The Influence of Family Worship on the Commonwealth" in Alexander, *Thoughts on Family Worship*, 162–173.

in the 1780s and quickly spread to America.[66] Sunday schools were originally established to offer basic religious instruction to children on Sunday, bringing literacy and fundamental Christian teaching to the large numbers of children whose families could not afford to send them to school during the week.[67] Sunday schools were not designed for children in the church but for children outside of it. Along with Packard and Hall, Alexander was heavily involved with the American Sunday School Union for a number of years. According to Alexander's own account, he was personally involved "in one of the earliest Sunday-schools set up in America."[68]

While family instruction and parochial schools were important means for training the children of Christian parents, Alexander believed that the Sunday schools were "the best means as yet devised for the rapid and successful instruction and salvation of the multitudes who are perishing for lack of knowledge."[69] According to him, "In neither of these methods [parochial and home training] do we reach that vast accumulation of want which confessedly lies without the limits of domestic and parochial faithfulness. What we require—what is indispensable to the thorough leavening of the corrupt mass—is a widely diffusive influence."[70] Sunday schools were able to reach into society far

---

[66] Rice, *Sunday-School Movement*, 14. For more on Robert Raikes, see J. Henry Harris, *Robert Raikes: The Man and His Work* (Bristol, UK: E. P. Dutton, 1899). For more on the history of Sunday schools in America, see Anne M. Boylan, *Sunday School: The Formation of an American Institution, 1790–1880* (New Haven: Yale University Press, 1990).

[67] Daniel Walker Howe, writing on the social impact of the Sunday school movement, states that Sunday schools "provided one day a week of instruction in basic literacy for 200,000 American children by 1827" (Howe, *What Hath God Wrought*, 449).

[68] Alexander, *Sunday School and Its Adjuncts*, 5. See James W. Alexander, *The Sunday-School Anniversary* (Philadelphia: American Sunday School Union, 1835), 5–13.

[69] Alexander, *Sunday School and Its Adjuncts*, 42–43. For an extended description of the state of "the multitudes who [were] perishing" in antebellum America, see Alexander, *Sunday School and Its Adjuncts*, 102–106.

[70] Alexander, *Sunday School and Its Adjuncts*, 40–41.

beyond the spheres of individual families and individual churches, and Alexander was very optimistic about the potential Sunday schools had for impacting society: "It is, as an engine, capable of [carrying Christian education to every corner of America], being, next to the preaching of the word, the most available instrument for evangelizing the country."[71]

Alexander's own connection with Sunday schools took on a variety of forms. While serving as a pastor in Trenton, he lectured regularly to the Sunday school teachers every Thursday evening. Regarding this weekly lecture, he told Hall that "I...bestow more preparatory labour upon this, than upon any of my services; it is by far the most delightful of my employments."[72] When he ministered in New York, Alexander opened Sunday schools in connection with his mission chapel.[73] He was also an outspoken advocate for the Sunday School movement in general and the American Sunday School Union in particular.[74] He wrote a large volume in 1856 entitled *The Sunday School and Its Adjuncts* to promote the spread of religious education through Sunday schools. In this volume, an extended section is devoted to a discussion of "the

---

[71] Alexander, *Sunday School and Its Adjuncts*, 99.

[72] Alexander, *Forty Years' Letters*, 1:124. It was common for local clergyman during this time to give a lecture to the Sunday school teachers on the upcoming week's Sunday school lesson. The Sunday school teachers of Philadelphia gathered for a weekly lecture, with Ashbel Green serving as the regular lecturer for a number of years. See Ashbel Green, *The Life of Ashbel Green*, ed. Joseph Huntington Jones (New York: Robert Carter and Brothers, 1849), 445, 598.

[73] Alexander, *Forty Years' Letters*, 2:186, 191, 193.

[74] Not all evangelicals supported the Sunday school movement in Alexander's day. Some viewed the role it gave to lay-people as undercutting the role of the clergy (see Alexander, *Forty Years' Letters*, 1:251). Others viewed all such voluntary societies as illegitimately usurping the place of the local church (see Alexander, *Forty Years' Letters*, 1:315). Others opposed it as a competitor to the parochial school movement (see Alexander, *Forty Years' Letters*, 1:244–245). Alexander supported the American Sunday School Union while also supporting denominational forms of religious education (Alexander, *Forty Years' Letters*, 2:52).

influence of Sunday Schools upon the social condition of the poor."[75] So in these many different ways, Alexander showed his enthusiastic belief in Christian education as a means of social reform.

Christian Literature and Social Reform

Closely connected to Alexander's work with Sunday schools was his activity in writing books and tracts. Part of the ministry of the American Sunday School Union was to publish a wide variety of tracts, books, booklets, and Bible reference materials for widespread use in Sunday schools and beyond.[76] Alexander wrote numerous books for the Sunday School Union, and he was very enthusiastic about the power and potential of the printed word for societal reform.

Alexander greatly enjoyed writing and laboring at what he called "a holy propagandism."[77] Whereas Alexander wrote other books and articles intended for a more scholarly audience, he believed that what American society needed most was not books of deep learning but books of widespread appeal. Writing to Hall in 1841, he stated: "I grow in my conviction, that in our day, when men have a thousand things to read, and won't read long at any thing, the books which reach the mass and colour its opinions, are not books of research, but books of feeling, of point, even of eccentricity; books written with a gush, *currente calamo* [with a flying pen]."[78] As a writer of this type of work, then, Alexander sought to popularize Christian truths so that they might reach and impact the popular mind.

While Alexander wrote articles and books for the working classes, he was most devoted to writing books for children.[79] While a pastor in Trenton, Alexander resolved himself to "devote much of my time to babes' books."[80] Shortly after this, Alexander wrote to Hall:

---

[75] Alexander, *Sunday School and Its Adjuncts*, 262–308.

[76] Alexander, *Sunday School and Its Adjuncts*, 143–145.

[77] Alexander, *Sunday School and Its Adjuncts*, 108.

[78] Alexander, *Forty Years' Letters*, 1:323.

[79] Alexander, *Forty Years' Letters*, 1:205, 219.

[80] Alexander, *Forty Years' Letters*, 1:195.

My aim is to do something before I die to reach the millions of
youth in our land. I have made up my mind to go for the
nursery practice. Let others take the fathers and grandfathers,
if I can only make an impression on the children. This I wish
to do by writing; and I am not sure ...that I will not do more
in this way, as a pastor, than if I were to set about it *ex professo*
[as a profession].[81]

He carried out his goal of writing for children, publishing over "thirty
trifles" with the American Sunday School Union over the course of his
life.[82] This was a work that he greatly enjoyed.[83] Writing in 1833, Alexander stated, "Next to preaching, there is no employment I should relish more, than writing books for the Union."[84] Even while Professor of
Rhetoric and *Belles Lettres* at Princeton College, he would tell Hall that
"some of my chief pleasures are in writing for and talking with children."[85] With Packard editing his books and with Hall editing his articles for the American Sunday School Journal, Alexander had kindred
spirits and partners with him in this publishing endeavour.[86] When Hall
was thus employed, Alexander encouraged him in his work by saying:

We are all of us in danger of undervaluing the importance of
our posts, and our means of usefulness. ... I should "deeply"
regret any change of an ordinary kind, which should remove
you from the S. S. U. You know very well that the publishing
crank is turned by yourself and P[ackard]; in a sort, therefore,
you have control of the juvenile literature of increasing thousands. ...I can conceive of no situation in which you could

---

[81] Alexander, *Forty Years' Letters*, 1:196.

[82] Alexander, *Sunday School and Its Adjuncts*, 5.

[83] Alexander, *Forty Years' Letters*, 1:205, 225.

[84] Alexander, *Forty Years' Letters*, 1:203.

[85] Alexander, *Forty Years' Letters*, 1:210.

[86] Alexander was offered a position of employment with the American
Sunday School Union in 1832. He turned down this offer and instead accepted
employment as editor of *The Presbyterian*, a position he held for one year (Alexander, *Forty Years' Letters*, 1:197).

possibly set so much truth a-running over our wicked nation as this.[87]

From his own experience in ministry, Alexander knew the power of Christian literature. In 1844, during a time of revival at Princeton, he remarked that "no one means of awakening has been so much blessed here [in Princeton], as the putting of books into people's hands."[88] When Alexander became a pastor in Virginia, one of the first things he did was to get "a reading room established in our little hamlet."[89] While a pastor in New York City, he served on the committee of the American Tract Society and was supportive of their efforts in literature distribution, writing many tracts for them as well.[90] His whole ministry and devotion to book-writing shows the value he placed upon the written word as a powerful means of spreading Christian truth and transforming society.

Conclusion

Alexander's vision of social reform revolved around the spread of Christian truth and Christian influence. In his words, "The true way...to benefit, and even remodel society, is to make it Christian."[91] He labored to spread Christian belief and Christian piety throughout all levels of American society by spreading and popularizing biblical truth. It was through the knowledge of the Bible, Alexander believed, that the

---

[87] Alexander, *Forty Years' Letters*, 1:293. See also, Alexander, *Forty Years' Letters*, 1:222.

[88] Alexander, *Forty Years' Letters*, 1:390.

[89] Alexander, *Forty Years' Letters*, 1:102.

[90] Alexander, *Forty Years' Letters*, 2:32. For a full sketch of Alexander's involvement with The American Tract Society, as well as a list of tracts Alexander wrote for this society, see Alexander, *Forty Years' Letters*, 2:236-237. Addresses and papers Alexander wrote during the New York City Revival of 1857-1858 were also collected and published by the American Tract Society as *The Revival and Its Lessons* (previously noted).

[91] Alexander, *Thoughts on Preaching*, 71.

supernatural working of God would remove the root cause of all societal ills, namely, the sinful corruption of man.

As a pastor and a writer, Alexander personally engaged in the spread of biblical truth through a wide variety of means. He believed that biblical preaching was God's special means of bringing his truth to man. As such, he often preached to the poor and started mission chapels of different types wherever he ministered. He also gave an important place to the religious education of America's youth, especially through the Sunday school movement. In connection with the American Sunday School Union especially, Alexander worked hard to "propagandize" the truths of the Bible, believing that popular literature was a powerful way to influence the mass of society. In all of these various ways, Alexander sought the reform of society through the gradual dissemination of biblical truth. The renovation of individual human souls through the spread of biblical truth was, for Alexander, the answer to the social ills he saw. Unlike the secular reforms then promoted, only this one could address the corrupt root of social ills—man's fallen nature.

In contrast with the secular social reformers of his day, Alexander believed that real social reform would come to antebellum America by Christianizing it. Other approaches to social reform, Alexander believed, were superficial, socially disruptive, "Jacobin" in nature, and linked to the secular ideology of social egalitarianism most clearly displayed in the French Revolution. Only Christianity could provide a remedy for the root cause of social ills, and the spread of Christian truth was the best answer for relieving human suffering. Alexander believed that the proliferation of biblical preaching, Sunday schools, and Christian literature was the best means for popularizing the transforming truth of God. In this vision of social reform, he agreed with the views of Charles Hodge, Frederick A. Packard, his brother Addison, and his father Archibald. He also expressed great appreciation for the work of evangelical social reformers in Great Britain, including Hannah More, William Wilberforce, Robert Raikes, Thomas Chalmers, David Nasmith, and the early Methodists. This more conservative and evangelical perspective on social reform was carried forward across the Atlantic by Alexander and others at Princeton.[92]

Alexander realized that the current of American culture was shifting away from the older mindset of his father's generation, embracing new social and political perspectives.[93] Underlying these trends was a deeper philosophical shift in America's broader intellectual culture—a shift away from divine revelation, propositional truth, and epistemological realism to man-centered secularism and the philosophical idealism of Europe. Alexander felt this shift, and noted that even Princeton was not immune to these new trends:

> Much talk in Princeton of the amazing genius of a young poet. He belongs to the set which may be said to constitute the "New America." They go for metaphysie, Coleridge, almost for Spinoza. They laugh at Locke, Reid, Stewart, &c. They undervalue Newton and Bacon. They applaud Plato. They care less, than they once did, for prayer-meetings, missions,

---

[92] A Princetonian who gave great attention to social reform after Alexander was Lyman Atwater. Atwater wrote numerous articles in the *Princeton Review* on social, political, and economic issues that carried forward the positions expressed by Alexander and Hodge (Smith, *Presbyterian Ministry in American Culture*, 237–245). Some of Atwater's articles include: "The True Progress of Society," *Biblical Repertory and Princeton Review* 24 (1852): 16–38; "The Nature and Effects of Money," *Biblical Repertory and Princeton Review* 34 (1862): 310–357; "The Labor Question in its Economic and Christian Aspects," *Presbyterian Quarterly and Princeton Review* 1 (1872): 468–495; "The Great Railroad Strike," *Presbyterian Quarterly and Princeton Review* 6 (1877): 719–744; "The State in Relation to Morality, Religion, and Education" *Princeton Review* 1 (1878): 395–422; "Political Economy a Science—Of What?" *Princeton Review* 1 (1880): 420–443. An article by William H. Lord in the *Princeton Review* also carried forward the thought of Alexander on social reform. See William H. Lord, "Liberal Christianity," *Biblical Repertory and Princeton Review* 40 (1868): 114–144.

[93] For the effect of these social and political trends upon American Christianity, see Nathan O. Hatch's classic work, *The Democratization of American Christianity* (New Haven: Yale University Press, 1989).

&c. Keep your eye on this. How much we need to stick by the plain declarations of the written word![94]

In spite of such trends in contemporary American thought, Alexander held to the older theological and philosophical outlook of the previous generation, along with many of its social and political views. His rejection of the social, political, and philosophical trends in American thought, then, can rightly be regarded as counter-cultural. He interacted with the issues facing his contemporary American society in a thoughtful and critical way, informed by voices from the past and from a wide range of evangelicals outside of America. In his views of society, in fact, he was much more in tune with the British evangelicals of a previous generation than with many of his contemporary Americans.

Alexander's Old School Presbyterianism and theological conservatism did not leave him unconcerned with the broader state of American society. In fact, it was this perspective that compelled him to engage society with the only adequate means of alleviating its social ills, namely, the spread of Christian truth and Christian virtue. This was at the heart of his efforts not only to prepare souls for eternity, but to transform society in the here and now as well.

---

[94] Alexander, *Forty Years' Letters*, 2:12.

Afterword

Alexander rightly understood that Christians need to be concerned with social ills and human suffering. Individual Christians are instructed to "do good to everyone" (Gal. 6:10), and they should each strive to be active within broader society with good works that commend the Saviour.[1] Whenever Christians engage in social or political issues, they enter into an arena of life that involves social and political philosophy. Most Christians are not trained in these disciplines, nor do they have a robust understanding of the past to provide context for addressing these issues. Instead, Christians, both those inclined to the right and to the left, are naturally prone to uncritically adopt the philosophical views of society and politics from their social circles and preferred media outlets.

Christians that wade into the arena of politics and social reform need to appreciate the powerful assumptions that people hold in these areas—assumptions about human nature, the ideal society, the nature of individual rights, the origin of political authority and legitimacy, the role of the family in society, the sources of inequality, and the meaning of justice. Added to these are assumptions about gender, ethnicity, and culture, assumptions that are sometimes formed in a context of brokenness and painful individual experience. These assumptions are often unstated and unquestioned, yet they shape the entire outlook that one brings to practical social questions.

---

[1] For a recent and helpful treatment of the "good-deeds mission of the church," see John A. Wind, *Do Good to All People as You Have the Opportunity: A Biblical Theology of the Good Deeds Mission of the New Covenant Community* (Phillipsburg, NJ: P&R, 2019).

Reading Alexander's thoughts on politics and social reform can be a jarring experience. Few American Christians today question the merits of democracy. Few have heard another Christian speak of nineteenth-century abolitionists with contempt or express empathy for slaveholders or question the prudence of pre-Civil War calls for immediate emancipation. Few have spoken in such dogmatic terms about labor unions. Rather than uncharitably rushing to pass judgment on a fellow believer who has no opportunity to defend himself, we should rather take to heart these words of Alexander's father: "It is a sound maxim, that men living at one time must not be judged by the opinions of an age in which all of the circumstances are greatly changed."[2] While God's truth never changes, our social and political perspectives certainly have changed. We live in a day when national governments dispense a wide variety of social services, and social egalitarianism has fundamentally changed how authority structures in society are viewed. Only a few would question whether the government should be involved in education, and even fewer would dare express empathy with a Christian slaveholder like Alexander did. Very few believers in the past held our modern notions of social equality, individual rights, liberty, and democracy. But should we condemn almost all believers of past ages for not holding to today's social and political views?

Popular views of social standards should not be the measure by which we evaluate the perspectives of others. Nor should we look to contemporary culture to provide the last word about today's problems and what needs to be done about them. Alexander challenges us to put the Bible at the very center of our thinking about social ills and social reform. His main point is that the best approach to social reform is one that emphasizes personal evangelism, Christian instruction, and discipleship in Christian truth. The gospel of personal salvation through faith in Christ has the power to transform society because it has the power to transform individuals. It produces new hearts of

---

[2] Archibald Alexander, *Address Delivered before the Alumni Association of Washington College* (Lexington, VA: R. H. Glass, 1843), 25.

righteousness and charity, and it alone brings about forgiveness and reconciliation, bringing oppressed and oppressor alike into one redeemed family.

There are biblical solutions to man's problems, and there are secular approaches as well. Some of these approaches are merely inadequate, and others are horribly destructive. Some secular approaches to social reform might bring about some good, but Christians should never settle for a social reform vision that is anything less than that of transforming society with the power of the gospel of Christ. This is truly the best approach and the one we should put into practice.

Appendix 1:
The *Newark Daily Advertiser* on Charles Quill

James W. Alexander wrote numerous letters to the working classes in the *Newark Daily Advertiser* under the penname of Charles Quill. Some of these letters were eventually published under Alexander's name in *The American Mechanic* (published in 1838) and *The Working Man* (published in 1839). The following article entitled "Charles Quill" appeared on page three of the Newark Daily Advertiser on May 25, 1838:

> We have published, from time to time, a number of essays which appear in the Newark (N. J.) Daily Advertiser, over the signature of "*Charles Quill*," and are addressed exclusively to the mechanics of our country. The signature is a fictitious name, and the name of the real author is unknown to us. To these essays every mechanic in America should give particular attention, for they are replete with practical wisdom, and are calculated to advance the prosperity of those for whose benefit they are written. There is much in his mode of thought and expression to remind one of Dr. Franklin, that great American mechanic, of whom it was greatly said that he "snatched the lightning from heaven and the scepter from tyrants." These essays, now appearing in the fugitive form of communications to a daily newspaper, are destined to a more elevated rank. Their merit, we think, must insure for them a publication in volumes, and the work will find an honored place in every library, and its instructions will sink into the heart, producing fruits of the very best quality.

Charles Quill, like poor Richard, comes into the dwellings of the humble and unlettered, but he comes to take away from poverty its meanness, and from humility its subserviency. He teaches the poor man how he can become rich in intellectual treasures, and exalts the humble, by implanting within them a nobility of thought without which there is no true independence. If the meed [sic] of a nations [sic] gratitude is due to him who renders productive, soil which had been barren, or, as the phrase is, "causes grass to grow where none would grow before," surely he lays his country under still greater obligations, who enters the house where ignorance and vice prevailed—roots out those noxious weeds—purifies the human temple, and sows broadcast the seeds of virtue and intelligence. *Charles Quill* is one of the latter class of benofactors, [sic] and long after his bones are mouldering [sic] in the dust there will be thousands rendered happy by his admonitions who will rise up and call him blessed. – *Frankfort Ky. Commonwealth of the 16th May.*

Appendix 2:
Alexander's Articles on Trade Unions for the *Newark Daily Advertiser*

In the summer of 1838, Alexander wrote a series of articles on trade unions for the *Newark Daily Advertiser*. Like many of his articles in this newspaper, he wrote all these under the penname "Charles Quill." Alexander clipped and pasted some (perhaps all) of these articles in a journal he entitled, "Papers on Trades Unions."[1] While eight articles altogether were printed in the *Advertiser*, Alexander's journal now contains only articles five through eight, with a partial clipping of article four as well.[2] In a slightly edited form, articles one and three were included in Alexander's *The Working Man*, published in 1839. This complete series of articles was never reprinted and is difficult to find. The series is included here below in its entirety.[3]

---

[1] James W. Alexander, "Papers on Trades Unions," 1838, The James Waddel Alexander Manuscript Collection, 2:1, Special Collections, Princeton Theological Seminary Library, Princeton, NJ.

[2] Some of the pages of this journal appear to have been cut out.

[3] Since these articles are extremely rare, I have printed the articles as they appear, preserving the formatting and appearance of the articles as much as possible. Punctuation, spelling, footnoting, and grammar that differ from modern usage have been preserved.

Article 1: June 30, 1838
For the Newark Daily Advertiser.
Trades' Unions.

Under this title I propose to communicate for your columns a few papers, addressed particularly to working men. The consciousness I fell of being unfeignedly devoted to their interests, makes me somewhat bolder than I might otherwise be, in going counter to opinions which are very prevalent among the younger members of the trades.

In what is to be offered, I shall make little effort to be original, but rather attempt to abridge and popularize important views of this subject, which have been given in works not very accessible to the persons for whom I write.

No. I.
Introductory Remarks—The Question stated.

Upon the question, *What shall be the wages of labour*, the world of enterprise is naturally divided into two parties. For it is obvious, that the employer will desire to give as little as he can, and the workman to receive as much he can. And in the great majority of instances, the advantage in this content has been on the side of the master-workmen, as being able to combine more easily, and to subsist longer without new receipts. This state of things, however, as will be shown, has received a very important disturbance from the expansion of the credit system; which, so far as this controversy is concerned, has brought the two parties more nearly upon a level.

In order to place themselves upon terms of some equality in the contest, it was necessary that operatives should in some way or other combine for mutual support; and in the case of those who are called "skilled workmen," the effect of such combinations has often been sudden and extensive. But in the progress of the feud, some dreadful evils have resulted, and it is the intention of these essays to draw the mind of the intelligent, moral, and patriotic workingman to the consideration of these evils, and of the question whether the dangers and losses occasioned by Trades' Unions do not overbalance all their supposed benefits.

In attempting to raise and keep up wages above their natural rate, various methods have been used. The most obvious is that of refusing to work for less than a certain sum agreed upon; and where the combination is universal or very extensive this is likely to have its effect in the case of skilled labour. Another method not much unlike this in its principle, is that of combining to lessen the hours of labour, the price remaining the same. A third is that of limiting the number of skilled workmen in any district, and this method has from time to time been embodied in the municipal customs and statutory provisions of many countries. To this source we owe all the guilds or trade corporations of England, the statues of apprenticeship, the tours of journeymen (*Wanderjahre*) in Germany, and similar expedients; the object being in every case the same, namely to make labour more costly, by making it more difficult to be procured. Upon the same principle, in some of the spice-islands, it has been customary to destroy part of the pepper crop in order to raise the price of the commodity.

The corporations of the middle ages were the basis of all our municipal privileges, as indeed they were the cradle of modern civic prosperity in general: they were, in these rude periods, a necessary safeguard for the peaceful burgher against the ruthless and ironhanded barons and their feudatories. But the state of this has greatly changed with the advancement of society.—As the feudal elements of our polity have, step by step, receded from view, and the defences of established law have formed themselves around the mechanic and the laborer, these irregular and extraordinary provisions should have been abandoned; and being no less antiquated and no less dangerous than the famous *Vehmgerichte*, or Secret Tribunals of the Dark Ages; which nevertheless were almost demanded in a state of things where society was in a perpetual conflict:

> For why? Because the good old rule
> Sufficed them; the simple plan,
> That they should take who have the power,
> And they should keep who can.
> WORDSWORTH

But we have lived to see a new growth springing up in the rank soil of modern civilization. In the unexampled increase and mighty influence of Trades' Unions there is every thing to awaken the interest of the political and the moral philosopher. Viewing what has occurred within a few years, we can only say, with Talleyrand, *It is the beginning of the end!* No man can examine the influence of this inceptive organization of the working classes, without perceiving that unless arrested, it must give origin to a texture of society totally different from any that the world has ever seen; whether better or worse than that which has preceded, events will prove.

The early dissensions of republican Rome gave occasion to Menenius Agrippa to rehearse the fable of the Belly and the Members; an apologue which is no less instructive and appropriate now, than it was then. Nothing can fail to be disorganizing and ruinous, which tends to set the rich against the poor, or marshals these two classes into conflicting hosts. And such is the tendency of that fearful system which is beginning to spread itself among our happy yeomanry. To examine the history and character of this system will not be without its use; and this I propose to do in a few subsequent papers.
CHARLES QUILL

156

Article 2: July 3, 1838
For the Newark Daily Advertiser.
Trades' Unions.

No II.
*Ancient and Modern Trade—Combinations—History of
Trades' Unions—Their object and demands*

There are many working-men who are so devoid of curiosity,
as never to have asked what might be the origin of the degrees
through which they have themselves been passing; namely
those of Apprentice, Journeyman, and Master-Workman. In
a more natural condition of society and trade, any man might
practice any trade, with or without preparation. But in order
to protect the rights and secure the profits of the different
handicrafts, the people of the middle ages at a very early period united into Guilds, Corporations, or Trade Companies;
some of the most venerable of which are still existing.[4] The
great object of these corporations was to provide support for
a certain number of skilled workmen, and to keep up the operations of art at a high degree of skill. In order to do this,
they limited the number of master-workmen, and the number
of pupils which each should have. They further originated
the distinction of subordinate bands into apprentices and
journeymen, or fellow crafts. The spirit of trade-monopoly,
derived from Gothic ancestry, reigned over all Europe until
the principle began to be admitted that freedom of trade was
the only safe policy for all parties. By degrees the rules with
regard to apprenticeships became less rigid. They are less so

---

[4] These Institutions were known by various names. In France they were
called *Corps de Metier*. In Germany, where they most of all flourished, such a
corporation was named *Gilde, Zunft, Innung, Gaffel, Amt, Bruderschaft*, &c.
The Latin names, common in the Civil Law, were *Collegia et corpora opificum*.

in Britain than in Germany, where every artizan is under the necessity of travelling for a certain term of months or years; and they are less so in America than in Britain. But that which was then sought in one method is now attempted in another.

The history of Trades' Unions has received a number of valuable contributions during the last two years. As I have no access to the original authorities, I shall abstract such facts as are necessary from the 135th number of the Edinburg Review, and from some other corroborative publications.[5]

By the 5th Geo. Iv. C. 95., and afterwards by the 6th Geo. Iv. C. 129., commonly called Mr. Hume's act, the former statutes against combination were repealed, and such combination was legalized, provided it were free from violence or intimidation.—When, in 1824, this act was passed, it was proved before the Committees, that these associations were almost universal over the kingdom, even before the laws were repealed. They existed in every trade, but were best organized among the tailors. A committee of five were supreme judges and rulers. "The whisper (say the committee) is spread among the dbody that there is to be a strike; and, without discussing the subject, *they strike whenever they are ordered to do so.*" In many places, the object of these combinations was not so much to raise wages, as to exclude from a given district such as had not served their time within it.

There was this great difference between the ancient Guilds and the modern Unions; the Guilds arrayed masters and operatives in one hand against the world; the Unions arrayed journeymen against their employers. Trades' Unions, where fully organized, are active, not merely (as too many imagine) when a sudden rise of wages is needed, but at all times; being permanent institutions. They are founded on the principle of universal suffrage; though, in some trades, there are

---

[5] Ed. Review for April 1838, Art. ix.

certain modifications of this principle. The grand agent, however, is the central or executive Committee. To this formidable body each workman is bound to yield implicit obedience. It is a principle agreed upon, that no person shall work with them in any establishment who does not belong to the association; and if such a one strays into their number, and the employer declines to dismiss him, the whole combined workmen immediately *strike*. Till this stranger's excluded, no one of the association is permitted [unreadable] employer, unable to proceed without those skilled workmen, who are thus combined against him, ceases to resist and accedes to their demands.

In Great Britain the oppression of the common hands by the *skilled workmen* has become a regular part of the system. To keep up the monopoly of the former, the Executive Committees usually rule, that no master shall employ more than a small proportion of apprentices to skilled workmen. The proportion varies in different trades: one to three, one to four, and even one to five. The least neglect or transgression here also produces a strike.—The same is true as to the foreman, overseer, or manager, who must be agreeable to the workmen.

The number of *hours*, which the men are to labour, and the *wages* they are to receive, are also fixed by these dictators. The power of their tyranny is amazing. In 1835 and 1836, the colliers of Lanarkshire were ordered not to work more than four days in the week, or more than five hours in the day. This was implicitly obeyed by more than two thousand colliers, in three counties. The prices of coals was consequently raised one hundred per centum, and stood at that price for eighteen months. The last nine of these, viz, from January to October 1837, was a period of unexampled commercial and manufacturing distress. "Notwithstanding that circumstances, the workmen stood out for the old rate of wages; the greater part of them struck work, to the number of nearly two thousand,

and continued idle for about five months, till at length they were compelled to give in, and commence working at the rates which the ironmasters had offered; which was, eight hours a day for five days a week, at which even the inferior hands could earn five shillings, and the better, six shillings a day.

Another principle is that the master-workman shall not choose his hands. We have not yet fully adopted this in America, but with every fresh cargo of English steerage passengers, we gain new advancement. The master-workman must go to a certain office, called "a house of call," and hire the man whose name stands first upon a list for employment. This principle is adopted among tailors and other trades, in London, Edinburgh, Glasgow and Dublin.

In order to guard against the influx of new hands into the trade several methods are used. One of these is a tedious apprenticeship, before the expectant can become a skilled workman. All this time the apprentice pays a stated tax to the funds. Entry-money is demanded of every stranger, sometimes as much as five pounds. And as an encouragement to American readers, and lest they should fear that we may not proceed fast enough in these great improvements, let me say, that the associated cotton-spinners in the West of Scotland have a permanent bounty of £10, which is given to every member of the trade who will emigrate to America. They also pay £5 for every skilled hand who is *unshopped*, or induced to leave his employment.—Such are some of the principles of the Trades' Unions of Great Britain

CHARLES QUILL

Article 3: July 7, 1838
For the Newark Daily Advertiser.
Trades' Unions.

No III.
The sufferings of the Working Classes real—Resort to Combination very natural—Yet unavailing—Error in the principle of Trades' Unions.

The true way to judge of Trades' Unions is to see them at home, to examine their working in the place of their origin, and where their influence is most extensive. In this country, they are still in their infancy, and we can scarcely see their ultimate tendencies; but in Great Britain and Ireland they have existed for a long period, and we may sit in fair judgment upon their results. Every year brings us nearer and nearer to the transatlantic pattern: we borrow their organization, their methods, their "slang-terms," and their men. Here, as there, we have our weekly contributions, our forms of initiation, our committees of vigilance, our flags and mottos and processions. Perhaps in due course of time we may have our burnings, maimings, and assassinations. But before we allow things to get to this pass, it becomes us to sit down and count the cost. Let us look into some of the reasons *pro* and *contre*.

If a contest were necessary between the rich and the poor, (which we heartily believe it is not, but on the contrary that, in the long run, their interests are identical,) if it were necessary that capital and labor should be placed in conflict— we should be ready to concede that every facility and aid should be allowed to the working man, because he is under all sorts of disadvantage. This is less true in America where, for the most part, labor and capital go together; but in Great Britain mechanics and other laborers need every species of lawful union to bear them up against the weight of capital and easy concert which is marshalled on the other side. No man who has a heart can become acquainted with the distresses which exist in the thronged manufactories of Britain, without being tempted to pray that this unnatural system may never become paramount in our own beloved country, where millions of un-titled acres still invite the pallid and starving artizans. No wonder the working-classes desire to increase the rewards of labor; no wonder they take pity on their own flesh and blood, and combine to relieve them. And if wages, by any such expe-dient, could be made to rise and stand at an elevated point, we should say that the benefit had almost had almost indemnified society for the dreadful losses sustained in the process. If, as has been held by distinguished economical philosophers, the average rate of wages is an exponent of national prosperity, the Trades' Unions which should effect this, would be public benefactors. And it was in the expectation that the laborer by coping with his employers would in some degree effect this, that the British Parliament removed the restrictions from trade combinations. But to the astonishment of many, and the sorrow of all who know the facts, the chief effect of this repeal has been to increase the misery of the very class which it sought to benefit, by subjecting laboring men to a despotism almost incredible in its power, and fruitless as to its grand in-tention.

How far does combination tend to produce a permanent ele-vation of wages? This is a proper question for seasons of tran-quility, such as the present. In the midst of a panic or a strike it would be vain to agitate it, because the present or proximate advantage—the rise of wages however temporary—would dazzle the excited workman, and blind him to future evils. But in this time of contentment we ought to establish *principles*, which may stand us in stead when the struggle comes. Let us take a case in which the immediate effect of combination is that which was desired; and this is very common, where the strike has been well-timed, at seasons when great bills are running against employers, and where credit is low, and especially if the establishment is in some degree separate and single-handed. Here the triumph of the working-man seems to common observers to be complete. But let us look a little deeper.

Take the case of journeymen tailors. Suppose this class of operatives, in Newark, to strike for higher wages, and to succeed. Journeymen tailors will be at once tempted to flow in from N. York; and this influx will be in proportion first to the general distress, and secondly to the amount of increased remuneration. Of course it will be less than it would be in the case of unskilled labor, such as that of the piecers and pickers of cotton factories; where the vacuum would be filled up almost immediately. The consequence of this transfer of labor is that wages rise elsewhere, and by degrees fall here: after a short time the proportion is much what it had been, and the general rise of level is scarcely appreciable.

But put the case that all the journeymen tailors throughout all the country, combine to raise the rate of wages. Here the transfer of labor is more slow, but not less certain. It is now a transfer, not from city to city, but from trade to trade. The man who is apprenticing his boy, chooses that trade whose wages are the highest: if the state of things continue the current will change its bed, and find channels in new sorts of business. The case is extreme; one so favorable never occurs; as the struggle is commonly terminated long before any such results can be matured.

But imagine the case, that all the Unions, of all the trades thus combined in all the country, agree to force up the wages of labor. Unless they can simultaneously augment the productive power of the country, there is of necessity a fall in profits, or in other words a decrease in the accumulation of capital. Let us hear Dr. Vethake upon this point. "Every retardation of the rate in which capital accumulates will be accompanied by the two effects of a less rapid increase of population, and of a diminished rate of wages. Moreover, but for the enjoyment *for a time* by the laboring classes of a higher rate of wages, which will render them less disposed to content themselves with the wages they were before accustomed to, the diminution of wages will proceed until they are reduced once more to their former rate. The tendency of them, however, to be for this rason at a somewhat higher rate than formerly would in all probability be more than counteracted by the sum total of production, when compared with the augmented population, having, from the necessity of applying capital and labor to the land under more disadvantageous circumstances than before, become diminished; a condition of things, it will be recollected implying a rise of rents, and a fall of profits and *wages.*"[6] The same learned man guards us against the selfish rejoinder that this effect may not take place until years shall have passed away; by showing that *from the very moment* a rise of wages takes place, the rate of profits will be reduced, capital accumulate slowly, and wages will fall. Besides this, the *real* wages of the workingman will not increase by any means as his *pecuniary* wages. He will find it harder to get work, and the commodities he needs will be higher in price.

The voice of political philosophy is therefore unequivocal. "*Even setting aside wholly* (says Dr. Vethake) *the permanently injurious affects to result.*—I think that an unprejudiced person can scarcely avoid concluding against every system of the kind: not only in respect to the interests of the community regarded as a whole, but also in respect to those of the very parties to benefit whom in the object proposed."

CHARLES QUILL

---

[6] Principles of Political Economy, 329.

Article 4: July 10, 1838
For the Newark Daily Advertiser.
Trades' Unions.

No IV.
Distinction of labor into skilled and unskilled — Undeniable
success of combination — This success, however, temporary
and illusory.

In this paper, I shall endeavor, still further, to correct the opinion that the working-man is really benefited by combination. And I find it necessary to say a word or two with regard to different kinds of labor. All manual work admits of being classified with reference to the degree of education or skill required in performing it. Hence in the same establishment, some are apprentices, and some ore journeymen, and the division might be carried further. The Germans call the journeymen *Gesellen*, ('comrades' or 'fellows') and the foreman *Meister-gesell*. They distinguish also between *Knechte*, or journeymen who labour under others, as bakers, butchers, shoemakers, &c., and *Knappen* or journeymen who work independently, as the weaver at his separate loom. In all great manufactories, there is one class of duties requiring great experience, and another which anyone can learn in a few hours. The former fall to the lot of *skilled trades*. Thus in the cotton manufacture the skilled hands are the spinners; in building, the masons and joiners; in mining, the miners; in iron-works, the moulders &c. And these are the classes which always take the lead in strikes: for the obvious reason that their places cannot be readily supplied.

It is the predominant influence of this class of laborers which with other causes has changed the whole aspect of the question since the time of Adam Smith, who seems to have thought that in the long run the workman could not hold out against the employer. It cannot be denied, that the temporary success of combination has been a glittering bait to multitudes. The demagogues in the Trades' Union interest confidently maintain that they have succeeded in raising their wages. In many of the skilled trades, this must be admitted to be true for a time: as for instance among the Lanarkshire colliers already mentioned. While these colliers, during a term of eighteen months were receiving thirty-five shillings a week, for working three days a week, and four or five hours a day, and while spinners and moulders were earning thirty shillings, the labour of hand loom weavers and agricultural hands was standing at about seven and twelve shillings respectively. Whence this difference? We grant it is due to the monopoly and conspiracy which has been pointed out; but then it is a case of high disease, a congestion in the body-politic, in which free circulation of labour is obstructed, and the productive power is forcibly and unnaturally accumulated about particular points.

Dr. Smith could not have anticipated such a state of things when he wrote as follows: "It is not however difficult to foresee which of the two parties must upon all ordinary occasions, have the advantage in the dispute, and force the other into a compliance with their terms. The masters being fewer in number, can combine much more easily." * * * * "A landlord, a farmer, a master manufacturer, or merchant, though they did not employ a single workman, could generally live a year or two upon the stocks which they have acquired. Many workmen could not subsist a week, and few could subsist a month, and scarce any a year without employment."[7] These remarks are far less applicable to our own times, when trade combinations have become permanent bodies, levying immense revenues in times of peace for the support of their

---

[7] Wealth of Nations, Book I. chap. 8.

members in times of war. The expansion of the credit system has also thrown great trammels around manufacturers and merchants, who in many cases are less able to suspend operations than their journeymen. Upon a sudden strike, the master-workman is forced to pay off what he owes, even though [unreadable] sells: for his resources are in proportion to the work done, and his disbursements only equal to the wages. The workman is as independent, in many cases:[8] and far more so where Trades' Union flourishes. For while the operatives are supported by weekly allowance, the manufacturer is left alone. His fellows in trade are not prepared to advance him ten or twenty thousand dollars: his wheels are stopped, his capital is unproductive, and his bills are running against him in a tide. The time is chosen for a strike with a view to all this, when the embarrassments of the employer are very great. To use the language of one of their own papers (the Liberator, Feb. 1, 1834) "They (the work-men) merely abstain, when their funds are sufficient, from going to work for one week, or one month, throughout the three kingdoms. And what happens in consequence? Bills are dishonored, the Gazette teems with Bankruptcies, capital is destroyed, the revenue fails, the system of government falls into confusion, and every link in the chain which binds society together is broken in a moment by the inert *conspiracy of the poor against the rich.*" This was actually exemplified in a terrible manner among the skilled trades in the west of Scotland in 1834.

Yet we return to our former position, and maintain, that notwithstanding all this seeming success, the voice of stubborn facts settles it indisputably, that the whole plan fails of its object. "They go on expecting a succession of victories," says an able writer in the Edinburgh Review, until either by the extravagant height to which they have continued to force

---

[8] Ib. note 10.

up wages, or the vexatious restrictions they have imposed on their masters, they produce a universal conviction of the necessity of a combined resistance; and when that takes place, capital, after a protracted and ruinous struggle, generally proves victorious; and after several months of agony, and the loss of some hundreds of thousands of pounds to the community, the workmen are driven, in sullen despair, into their masters' terms."

CHARLES QUILL

Article 5: July 14, 1838
For the Newark Daily Advertiser.
Trades' Unions.

No V.
Evils of Trades' Unions—all the evils of secret societies—their expense—their oaths—their tendency to produce poverty, disease and crime—

It is possible to buy a momentary gain at the price of lasting injury. If this should prove to be true of Trades' Unions, the young mechanic ought, in the exercise of common prudence, to shun them as great evils. To make them in any degree effective, they must be costly, permanent, secret and absolute; every one of these characteristics is fraught with disaster.

It has been already stated, that no combination of operatives can expect to hold out against capitalists or thriving employers, unless there is a fund to suppor them during this pause of labour. Now the quota of the journeyman toward this fund, and the loss ensuing upon this pause, more than overbalance the gain in the rate of wages. Few persons out of their immediate influence, suspect the expensiveness of Trades' Unions. The contribution of the Glasgow Cotton Spinners was proved by the books of the Union at the late trial for conspiracy in Glasgow, to have been half a crown a week, and in extreme cases, five shillings from each man.—The sum expended by the Trade Committee in the latter part of 1836 and beginning of 1837, was no less than eleven thousand eight hundred and eighty one pounds! As manufactures increase in America, these expenses must necessarily increase. The expenses of management often eats up all the profits, and is therefore a grand preventive of the object sought.

The Trades' Unions in order to raise these sums must be permanent bodies; and there are many other obvious reasons for the same character of permanency. A thousand evils, some of which shall be hinted at, grow out of this perpetuity of combination. In order to secure all the objects of concert, they necessarily become secret societies, and have the disadvantages inherent in all such bodies. This is well understood in Great Britain, and is becoming more and more familiar here. The formalities of imitation, the watch words, the espionage, and the solemn oaths of these associations are such as to threaten the safety of the social compact. It was fully proved in the late trial, that oaths of the most revolting and immoral character were enjoined.[9]

In 1825, Mr. Huskisson proved by the testimony of the Sheriff of Lanarkshire, that the following oath was used; — 'I, A. B., do voluntarily swear, in the awful presence of Almighty God, and before these witnesses, that I will execute with zeal and alacrity, as far as in me lies, every task or injunction which the majority of my brethren shall impose upon me

---

[9] The case to which I refer to often, is the Trial of Thomas Hunter, and others, operative cotton-spinners in Glasgow, before the High Court of Justiciary, at Edinburgh, on Wednesday, Jan. 3d, 1838 and the days following, for the crimes of Illegal Conspiracy and Murder. See the Edinburg Review for April, and Blackwood's Magazine for March: or the Report of the Trial, by Archibald Swinton, Advocate.

in furtherance of our common welfare; as the chastisement of nobs, the assassination of oppressive and tyrannical masters, or the demolition of shops that shall be deemed incorrigible' – &c &c. This oath was never to be divulged, and took precedence of all the subsequent ones, in courts of justice. Let the American journeyman, who is soon to become himself a master workman (a point which makes a great difference between himself and the majority of British operatives) pause and ask himself, whether for a trifling gain, or even a real temporary relief, he is willing to entail upon his children the evils manifestly flowing from such a secret fraternity as this.

It would be easy to show how vast is the loss of productive power to the country, and how certain the eventual fall in the real price of labor, from the aggregate amount of the hours of idleness in any extensive strike. The fatal error of the workingman is that he imagines it possible to abstract large quantities from the reservoir of labor and still keep up the level of wages; an absurdity as great as if one were to stop off the water from the Fairmount works, and yet expect to maintain a stream through the city. It would be easy, further, to show that these hours of idleness inevitably induce habits of conviviality, intemperance, and crime.—This was remarkably evinced in the last year's strike of the cotton spinners of Glasgow. When they had held out with zeal worthy the best cause, until each man was living on the pittance of 18d a week—immortality increased in a frightful manner. Dr. Cowan in his work entitled 'Vital Statistics of Glasgow,' has furnished data showing the effects of combination on the physical & moral health of the working classes. And let me once more, and with all earnestness, remind the young American mechanic that the true way to judge of this whole matter, is to examine its tendencies in the old country, on large masses, where the system is carried out to the full: for it will be too late to make the discovery when we shall have grown to the same enormities ourselves. From these statistics then, it appears,—and figures cannot lie—that the number of criminal convictions, and the number of mortal diseases, have been vastly the greatest in those years which have been signalized by the strikes among the operatives. The consumption of spirits, in Scotland, which have paid duty during the last fifteen years, has tripled. There are 2,200 spirit shops in Glasgow proper—being a tenth part of the houses it contains. Within the same period crime has increased about 400 per cent. Fever has increased about 1600 per cent; consumption of spirits has increased about 500 pr. ct.; and *the chance of life has decreased* from 1 in 40 to 1 in 24, or about forty-four percent. During all this period, the salubrity, situation, and climate of Glasgow have been the same. Precisely similar results are obtained from statistical calculations, concerning England and Ireland.

Nor are these the only forms in which crime is multiplied. In communities where many females are employed, a protracted strike is a sacrifice of virtue to hundreds—a hecatomb of virginity. Painful as the theme is, it must be touched, that fathers, brothers, and virtuous lovers may be on their guard. It is but a day or two since I was informed by a gentleman of the highest respectability, that the number of street prostitutes in Glasgow and vicinity, as they came under his immediate observation during the late strike, was such as to fill him with astonishment and consternation. The high-sheriff of Lanarkshire, in his address to the judges and jurymen last winger, says: "At the Christmas jail delivery last year only seven prisoners remained in custody for trials in this city; by the schedule I hold in my hand, there are at this moment *sixty-eight*, almost all committed during the last two months! Nor is this result surprising. During the disastrous strikes of the last summer, twenty or thirty thousand young persons of both sexes were thrown idel for many months in this city and its immediate neighborhood, almost all accustomed to high wages, and too often to habitual intemperance." — "Often they openly ascribe in their declarations the origin of their crime to the idleness, drunkenness, and suffering consequent on the strikes of the trade to which they belonged, or on which they depend.["] This is the testimony of one of the most eminent scholars and soundest politicions of Scotland; it merits the profound consideration of every American mechanic. Our danger is that we may admit the tiger's whelp, in its season of playfulness or seeming innocence, and at length become the victim of its fangs and claws. Prevention is possible; resistance, amidst our democratic population, may be fruitless.

CHARLES QUILL

Article 6: July 17, 1838
For the Newark Daily Advertiser.
Trades' Unions.
No 6.

The Tyranny of Committees—Real object of the leaders is tumult—Oppression on the humbler operatives—Total subjugation of free opinion

It would be well if every working-man in our country could be made acquainted with the character and progress of Trades' Unions in the United Kingdom. Such knowledge would serve to put us on our guard against those tremendous evils which follow in the train of these combinations, but which do not become manifest until matters have risen to such a height as to baffle all opposition.

Even among our ourselves, the moral affects of the system are deplorable. Some hundreds of men, young and old, cease from work. Now, even supposing that there is no open violence, this concert of idleness cannot fail to produce evil. There is a gathering of multitudes, all in an excited state, all prepared to receive the mighty stimulation which acts and re-acts in the fluctuations of a tumultuous crowd, and the yet more maddening impulses of strong drink. Here is the nursery for our destructive mobs. Here is the influence which makes the mechanic lose his relish for the quietude of home and seek the excitements of the tavern and the public meeting. And be it observed, that human nature no where deteriorates so rapidly, as in an exclusively *male* society.

Under the guise of freedom, the modern combination system imposes a galling yoke on the working-man. Look at the state of things in England or Scotland, and it will appear that these thousands who parade the streets with badges and colors are led by a few agitators and demagogues. The latter direct the tumult, indulge their malignant ambition, and divide the spoil: their real object is confusion and misrule. Their grand scheme is to array numbers against property; a scheme which has never failed to be popular, from the days of the Gracchi to those of Marat. Let the common mind be poisoned with this intention, and we shall witness once more the scenes of the French capital, where even Robespierre is said to have perished, because he would not utter the shibboleth *Equality of Property*. In order to accomplish the design, there must be disturbance; there must be a rising of the poor against the rich: there must be, against all fact and experience, a persuasion in the populace that numbers can go forward to success without capital; in fine there must be an incipient civil war. There is less concealment of these designs in Britain than among ourselves. In January last, an address was made to a great assembly of Glasgow operatives by the *Reverend* Mr. Stephens of Ashton, in England; in which he said— "If they will not reform this, ay, uproot it all, they shall have the revolution they so much dread; we shall destroy these abodes of guilt which they have reared to violate all law and God's book; if they will not learn to act as law prescribes and God ordains, so that every man shall by his labor find comfortable food and clothing, not only for himself, but also his wife and babes; then we swear by our love of our brothers: by our God, who made us all for happiness; by the Earth he gave for our support, and by the Heaven he designs for those who loved each other; and by the hell which is the portion of those, who, by violating his book, have consigned their fellow-men, the image of their God, to hunger, nakedness, and death. We have sworn by our God, by heaven, earth, and hell, that from the East, the West, the North, and the South, WE SHALL WRAP IN ONE AWFUL SHEET OF DEVOURING FLAME, which no army can resist, the manufactories of the cotton-tyrants, and the palaces of those who raised them by rapine and murder." And this was received with "tremendous cheers."

God forbid that we should cloak the injustice which provokes such rage; it cries to heaven for vengeance; yet we grieve for the blindness of those who seek redress in a method so suicidal. The mass of those who follow such leaders are reduced to still greater misery, by their self-appointed rulers. The tyranny to which the humbler operatives are subjected is almost incredible. Even when wages are raised by one of these spasmodic efforts, the average of domestic and personal comfort is not raised; the surplus gains are often wholly spent in drink; and it has been repeatedly declared, that there is generally more real comfort in the family of a hand-loom weaver, with wages of only nine or ten shillings a week, than in that of a spinner with from thirty to forty.

Even when wages are raised, let it be further noted, it is the wages of *skilled labor*. But how fare the *unskilled operatives*, all the while? The latter are in the proportion, at least, of four to one. They are scattered and unorganized, and never combine, except as "hewers of wood and drawers of water" to fill the train of the regular trades. The Trades Unions do them no good, but on the contrary are "monopolies of skilled against unskilled labour." If employers raise the wages of the former, they are at the same moment forced to depress that of the latter, besides throwing thousands of regular artisans back into the unskilled host. Indeed many of the scattered trades, which cannot combine, have been kept working at the starving point, in consequence of that tyranny which has forcibly prevented the current of labour from flowing over from those channels which were overcharged.

The leaders in these combinations seem to have taken their cue from the Egyptian taskmasters.—Their most unreasonable mandates are law. During the Glasgow strike of last summer, the edict of a few committees threw out of work, at one moment, twenty thousand laborers, or reduced to destitution sixty thousand individuals. Here is a despotism which no one can resist. The *nob* or stray mechanic is at once an outlaw. It is in evidence, that the 'idle men' receive five pounds for every spinner they unshop; that is, whom they get removed anyhow from his place. The following is an entry in one of the Trades' Union minute books: "June 5, 1837. At all events the names of all who remain nobs at the termination of the strike shall be printed, and sent to all the spinning districts in Scotland, England, and Ireland; and that they *remain nobs forever*; and a persecuting Committee be appointed to persecute them to the utmost."[10]

If any reader will look into the Edinburgh Revew as above cited, he will find the testimony which proves that 4 men were hired by the Trades Union Committee to shoot a *nob*, by way of striking terror into the rest; that the persons engaged in the murder were four in number; that they were to get £100 for it; that the money was accordingly paid from the funds of the association; that the expenses of defending the assassins at

---

[10] Blackwood's Mag. March, 1838, p. 235

their trial was borne by that body, and that the one who was sentenced to Bridewell was sent after his liberation to *America*; where he is probably engaged at this moment in introducing the latest improvements among the natives.

C. Q.

Article 7: July 21, 1838
For the Newark Daily Advertiser.
Trades' Unions.

No VII.

Means of enforcing the tyranny—Extent of disastrous consequences on multitudes at once—History of Preston and Glasgow strikes--Intimidation

Are American Mechanics prepared to subject themselves to a tyranny so ruthless as that which was the theme of my last essay? If not, let them nip the bud; let them crush the cockatrice's egg. No Sultan, no Czar, no piratical commander ever lorded it over his creatures with a more arbitrary sway than the petty despots of the trades. And their mode of vengeance is as diabolical as it is new. Let the American Journeyman read the certificates produced before the Commons' Committee in 1825.[11] These statements, from competent medical authorities, detail cases where men have had their eyes put out, or have been otherwise injured in a hopeless manner, by having oil-of-vitriol dashed in their faces by fellow-workmen employed for that purpose.—By such terrors, the oligarchy forces the thousands beneath them into any measures it may choose. In the Glasgow strike, so often alluded to, this is remarkably exemplified. "The aliment allowed each man during the latter part of the strike was only *eighteenpence* a week.

---

[11] Ed. Review, p. 121.

Such was the deplorable pittance to which the deluded was reduced, who refused, or was compelled by the committee to refuse during the whole time from thirty to thirty-five shillings a week! The condition of the female operatives—the piecers, pickers, carders and reelers—was infinitely worse, for these was no fund whatever provided for *their* maintenance, and from the commencement they were thrown upon the streets without either asylum, employment or subsistence. It may readily be conceived what must have been the consequence of six or seven thousand women being kept in a state of destitution and idleness for four months; especially when in close proximity to equal numbers of the other sex, always trained to disorderly habits by the habitual recept of high wages, and by frequent intemperance."

Consider further what multitudes are affected by these calamities at one and the same moment. In the three months' strike at Preston, which I have already mentioned, there were 8500 persons out of work. At the end of the first month, the streets began to be full of beggars; and the workhouse overflowed. At the end of six weeks the funds of the Union began to run very low, and at the end of the second month, the distress was universal and intense. During the turn-out, the operatives generally filled the streets; about twenty young women became prostitutes; three persons died of starvation, and no less than 5000 must have suffered long and severely from hunger and cold. The total loss to the town and trade of Preston in this unavailing struggle has been calculated at £107,196.[12]

Now be this system of combination successful or unsuccessful, one thing is certain, namely, that it is eminently anti-social and disorganizing; engendering a malign and scowling opposition between the two classes of society which are thus

---

[12] Statistical Journal, No. 2, Vol. 1. p. 88.

placed in hostile array.—The warfare that is excited is more than civil—more than savage—it is a warfare of secret malice and with poisoned weapons. "The recent trial at Edinburg," says an able writer, proves that in the latter stages of a strike, the conspirators sometimes are brought to think no more of shooting a new hand, or "*nob*," as he is called, than they would of shooting a wild duck." All power of combination is brought to bear on these measures. In the cotton-spinners' case, a placard against the sheriff of Lanarkshire was posted, *in one day*, (Aug. 26, 1837,) in every manufacturing town in Great Britain and Ireland. Of this conspiracy, Sir Edward Sugden said in the House of Commons, in February last: "A more atrocious case he could not conceive; and it showed most clearly that there was no crime to which combination leading into conspiracy could not lead."

Happy will it be for American working-men, if they will be content to *borrow* the experience of their European brethren without insisting on a repetition of the same experiment here. The day may come when we may need to remember the history of Preston and Glasgow in relation to Pittsburgh or Lynn, or Lowell, or Paterson, or Newark. It is good policy to look at the working of a system on the large scale. Take the case of the Glasgow turn-out of last spring and summer, as recorded by the Sheriff of Lanarkshire. It lasted 17 weeks, and gave in because the committee was arrested in consequence of the crimes perpetrated. More than 20,000 persons were thrown idle by the spinners' strike. The poor unskilled operatives, dupes of their tyrannical associates, had no provision made for them. Six or seven thousand women and children were thrown into idleness, temptation, and misery for four months, at the decree of *fifteen men!* The cost of this strike to the operatives concerned in it was alone £50,000. While not a shilling was gained by any one, the loss to Glasgow was £200,000. This wound was inflicted by the working classes on themselves; if a tyrant had inflicted it, he would have been strangled on his throne. This is the precise point to which I earnestly desire to attract the attention of the American working-man; the system of combination is a system of destruction to the interests of its misguided originators. It must be evident to every impartial examiner, that its whole tendency is agrarian, levelling, and revolutionary. It is idle to speak of *peaceable combinations* for any length of time, among great numbers. The whole force of the method lies in one word INTIMIDATION. The workingman who upholds it, says, 'I hereby yield my neck to the yoke of terror.' Every member must strike when he is bidden; and if he do not, he may be persecuted by the 'persecuting committee,' or burned with sulphuric acid, or shot at in the streets. The system, according to the work above cited, has two parts: "In the first place, the cajoling, molesting, threatening, and assaulting the new hands, or *nobs*, who are in any manner acting contrary to the mandates of the committee,—then getting up mobs to terrify the refractory hands, and strike a general terror into the whole community; and if all these methods fail of success, the resource remains of appointing by secret ballot, '*a secret select committee*,' to organize the means of assassinating the refractory hands, and masters, and setting fire to the mills of such employers as hold out against the desire of the association."

In order to gain these ends, every means is taken to secure impunity to crime. The oath first taken, in the union, is considered more binding than any which can follow before magistrates. A number of persons are always in readiness to prove an *alibi*, however false. If the culprit, however, is committed, he is immediately defended at the expense of the Union. Witnesses are placed under such intimidation, that at the late trial at Edinburgh, none of them would come to the

Sheriff's office, but would at first consent to meet him, only in a vault under one of the public buildings in Glasgow.

Shall such a domination be allowed to gain place in our land of freedom? Better far never to have attempted self-government! The consequence of every measure of this sort is to familiarize our people to violence, intolerance, persecution, terror, and crime. Already we are beginning to have our 'Committees of Vigilance' among Abolitionists, against the rights of slave owners; and our Lynch law and mobs against the rights of Abolitionists. But all that we have yet seen will be forgotten, if ever, in this land of popular power, our increasing body of mechanics and manufacturers become insane enough to hoist the flag of INTIMIDATION.

CHARLES QUILL

Article 8: July 24, 1838
For the Newark Daily Advertiser.
Trades' Unions.

No VIII.
Is there any danger at home? Importation of European villany—Loco foco terrorism—Levellere—Testimony of O'Connell to the effects of the Unions.

Before bringing these papers to a close, it seems desirable to anticipate a suggestion which may be ready to arise in certain minds. After all the authentic and appalling details of crime and misery, which have been given, as the result of combination, it will be natural for some to rejoin: How can this be? We have seen Trades' Unions, and watched their progress; but we have seen no such enormities. The reply is easy, and ought to be conclusive: Combination is here in its infancy; to judge of the leopard's claws, we must examine not the whelp but he beat full grown. The manufacturing class in America, though rapidly increasing, is small and scattered, as compared with that of Great Britain. But if the system, which I have tried to expose, gain a footing among us while we are few in number, and become a sort of 'State within the State,' it will be by this means all the more formidable, when our manufacturers and our population shall have increased twenty-fold.

If these and other evils attendant on the manufacturing system were to go on increasing by their mere native energies, with the growth of our people and the play of inventive discontent, the result would be sufficiently bad; Americans are competent of themselves to work out a fair amount of mischief. But we have more than this to dread. Who can number the British artisans and laborers that come over every year? These are likely to be poor, discontented, and sometimes depraved. There are, I rejoice to know, thousands who are just the reverse; yet, it is obvious, that among these there is every inducement to be vicious, to those who have fallen into crime, yea, to ringleaders, to those who have taken the highest degrees in the school of agitation and incendiarism. The fact of our having a common origin and common language with the British, affords us untold advantages, but at the same time some great evils. The same vessel which brings treasure and food, may also bring rats and vermin. The English radical is not the same man as the American Democrat; and we are receiving the most degraded and malignant of the former class. These are they, whose hoarse provincial utterance often makes itself heard above the clamors of the popular meeting; these are they who swell the lists of agrarian, infidel, and abolition societies, and who pour their illegal votes *into both sides of the great political balance.* I am no party politician. In speaking of the Loco-focos or Agrarian faction, I do not mean to characterize any political party, certainly not that of the

Administration, with whom rather than with its opponents I am disposed to agree in one of the points incidentally involved in this discussion. But every *American* feeling boils within me, when I find a few English demagogues, ignorant of our polity, and hating our institutions, engaged and countenanced by treasonable and fanatical editors, lecturers and preachers, in laying the train, which, under pretence of philanthropy, has no tendency but to dissolve the Union, if not the social compact itself. And I regard the anti-property, anti-wealth, and anti-colonization aspects, as so many vizards for the same Jacobinical and anti-social face.

Young men! Beware of those connexions which are destined to embitter your days when you are old. Buy not a momentary elevation or doubtful gain, at the price of what all good men hold dear. For the petty satisfaction of levelling the quarter-deck with the forecastle—do not scuttle the ship. But if you persist in borrowing the practices of the old-country, take notice, that these practices, when carried out to the full, produce more direful evils than the worst they seek to remedy, while they familiarize our people to persecution, terrorism, and crime.

It would be to me a very painful result, and as unmerited as undesirable, if a single reader of these paragraphs should imagine that I am pleading the cause of the rich against the poor. It is not so. I am pleading against a system of measures, which, if they are carried out, will, (I do solemnly declare it to be my settled conviction) draw rich and poor together into one destructive vortex. It is only ignorance or treason which can soberly maintain the reverse. In the old world, men of all political parties are united in this opinion. Hear, not merely the Whigs of the Edinburgh Review, but the great Agitator himself. The following are some of the remarks of Daniel O'Connell respecting the Irish Trades Unions: he said—'Combination was driving trade out of Dublin and other placed in Ireland.' 'With respect to the city of Dublin, he was sure he did not overstate the matter when he said that wages to the amount of £500,000 a year were withdrawn from it, in the manufacture of almost every article of consumption.' 'Mr. Sheridan, a master manufacturer, stated at one meeting, that his workmen were his masters.' Now though this sounds well in the ears of idle journeymen, what was the consequence? The effect of this system was, that much of the capital which otherwise would have been employed in Ireland was withdrawn. The articles of hats, boots and shoes were imported into Dublin instead of being manufactured there.' 'To such an extent did the combination among the tailors go that it was found expedient to bring tailors over from Germany. Some branches of trade have been removed altogether from Dublin. Not very long ago there were four ship-builders in extensive business in Dublin: there was at present not one. What was the cause of this? It was that, when there was any employment, the hands at once turned out for higher wages. One man, who had resisted the turnout, and had agreed to work for a lower rate of wages, was assassinated in the open day in the presence of twenty persons.' After the repeal of the combination laws, continues Mr. O'Connell, 'for murders were committed, not by the clubs, but by person whom they paid for that purpose.'

'Many who belonged to the body would not sanction such atrocious proceedings, but they assented as a body to acts from which they would have shrunk as individuals. In Cork, within the last two or three years, *no fewer than thirty-seven individuals have been burned with vitriol, many of whom were deprived of sight.* — These were the results of the acts of the Trades' Clubs. In Dublin four murders had been committed by similar agents. The Clubs did not themselves act openly, but they paid agents, whom they called *Welters.*

These Welters attacked any man who was pointed out to them, and murdered him when the opportunity offered. The number of these is about 6000! On Thursday last the premises of a timber merchant were set on fire immediately after his having been served with a notice. These men were ready to execute any vengeance according to order, and although the trade combinatators did not commit actual offences themselves, they had always a standing army in the Welters. It as thus that employers were controlled. A fortnight previous to this last distasteful crime, a man and his wife having died of cholera, the master in whose employment they had been, took two helpless orphans, the children of these two as apprentices. The Combinators revolted at this, and insisted on their immediate discharge.[13]

Let American mechanics ponder this. Open wide our ports to the foreigner, rich or poor. I am one of the last to lay a straw in his way. But, for virtue's sake, for our children's sake, for our country's sake, for God's sake, throw not the determination of our destiny into the hands of an organized conspiracy.

CHARLES QUILL

---

[13] Mirror of Parliament, Feb. 14, 1838, ap. Ed. Rev. No. 135.

Bibliography

Adams, Henry, ed. *Documents Relating to New-England Federalism.* Cambridge: John Wilson and Sons, 1887.

Addis, Cameron. *Jefferson's Vision for Education, 1760-1845.* New York: Peter Lang Publishing, 2003.

Ahlstrom, Sydney E. *A Religious History of the American People.* 2nd ed. New Haven: Yale University Press, 2004.

Alexander, Archibald. *Biographical Sketches of the Founder and Principal Alumni of the Log College.* Philadelphia: Presbyterian Board of Publication, 1851.

_____. *A History of Colonization on the Western Coast of Africa.* Philadelphia: William S. Martien, 1846.

Alexander Family Collection. Department of Rare Books and Special Collections. Princeton University Library, Princeton, NJ.

Alexander, Henry Carrington. *The Life of Joseph Addison Alexander, D.D.* 2 vols. New York: Charles Scribner, 1870.

[Alexander, James W.]. *The American Mechanic.* Philadelphia: Henry Perkins, 1838.

_____. *The American Mechanic and Working-Man.* 2 vols. New York: William S. Martien, 1847.

_____. *Carl, The Young Emigrant.* Philadelphia: American Sunday School Union, 1851.

_____. "Chalmers on Education and Ecclesiastical Economy." *Biblical Repertory and Princeton Review* 14 (1842): 577–583.

_____. *Charles Clifford.* Philadelphia: American Sunday School Union, 1834.

_____. *Discourses on Common Topics of Christian Faith and Practice.* New York: Charles Scribner, 1858. Reprint, *A Shepherd's*

Heart: Sermons from the Pastoral Ministry of J. W. Alexander. Birmingham, AL: Solid Ground Christian Books, 2004.

_____. "The Evils of an Unsanctified Literature." *Biblical Repertory and Princeton Review* 15 (1843): 65-77.

_____. *Faith: Treated in a Series of Discourses.* New York: Charles Scribner, 1863.

_____. *Forty Years' Familiar Letters of James W. Alexander, D. D.* Edited by John Hall. 2 vols. New York: Charles Scribner, 1860.

_____. *Good, Better, Best; or, The Three Ways of Making a Happy World.* Philadelphia: American Sunday School Union, 1844. Reprint, Birmingham, AL: Solid Ground Christian Books, 2009.

_____. *Letters to a Very Young Lady.* Philadelphia: American Sunday School Union, 1843.

_____. *The Life of Archibald Alexander, D. D.* New York: Charles Scribner, 1854. Reprint, Harrisonburg, VA: Sprinkle Publications, 1991.

_____. "The Life of William Wilberforce." *Biblical Repertory and Princeton Review* 10 (1838): 560-602.

_____. *Memoir of the Rev. James Waddel, D.D.* N.p., 1880.

_____. *The Merchant's Clerk Cheered and Counselled.* New York: Anson D. F. Randolph, 1856.

_____. *My Brother's Keeper: Letters to a Younger Brother on the Virtues and Vices, Duties and Dangers of Youth.* Philadelphia: American Sunday School Union, 1838.

_____. "Necessity of Popular Education." *Biblical Repertory and Princeton Review* 7 (1835): 41-56.

_____. "On the Use and Abuse of Systematic Theology." *Biblical Repertory and Theological Review* 4 (1832): 171-190.

_____. "Pastoral Records of my Connexion with the Duane Street Church, New York." 1844-1848. Fifth Avenue Presbyterian Church Archives, 21:B2-3-1. Fifth Avenue Presbyterian Church, New York.

_____. "Poverty and Crime in Cities." *Biblical Repertory and Princeton Review* 17 (1845): 606-625.

[_____]. "The Prospects of the Mechanic." *Princeton Magazine* 1 (1850): 77-81.

_____. "Religious Instruction of Negroes." *Biblical Repertory and Princeton Review* 17 (1845): 590-606.

_____. *The Revival and its Lessons: A Collection of Fugitive Papers, Having Reference to the Great Awakening, 1858.* New York: American Tract Society, 1858.

_____. *School-Boy Heroes: The Story of Maurice Gray and Carl Adler.* London: T. Nelson and Sons, 1872.

_____. *The Scripture Guide: A Familiar Introduction to the Study of the Bible.* Philadelphia: American Sunday School Union, 1838.

_____. "Speech for the Theological Society." February 1823. The James Waddel Alexander Manuscript Collection, 1:11. Special Collections. Princeton Theological Seminary Library, Princeton, NJ.

_____. "Suggestions in Vindication of the Temperance Society." *Biblical Repertory and Theological Review* 3 (1831): 44-60.

_____. *Suggestions in Vindication of the Temperance Society.* Philadelphia: Russell and Martin, 1831.

_____. *The Sunday-School Anniversary.* Philadelphia: American Sunday School Union, 1835.

_____. "Teaching a Science." *Biblical Repertory and Princeton Review* 20 (1848): 47-56.

_____. *Thoughts on Family Worship.* Philadelphia: Presbyterian Board of Education, 1847.

[_____]. "Trades Unions." Articles 1-8. *Newark Daily Advertiser.* June 30, 1838 - July 24, 1838.

[_____]. *The Working Man.* Philadelphia: Perkins, 1839.

Alexander, James W., and Albert Dod. "Transcendentalism." *Biblical Repertory and Princeton Review* 11 (1839): 37-101.

Alexander, James W., and Joseph A. Alexander. *A Geography of the Bible*. Philadelphia: American Sunday School Union, 1830.

Alexander, Joseph Addison. *Sermons*. 2 vols. New York: Charles Scribner, 1862.

_____. "Theories of Education." *Biblical Repertory and Theological Review* 5 (1833): 165-179.

Alexander, Samuel Davies. *Princeton College During the Eighteenth Century*. New York: Anson D. F. Randolph, 1872.

Allibone, Samuel Austin. *New Themes Condemned: Or, Thirty Opinions upon "New Themes," and its "Reviewer."* Philadelphia: Lippincott, Grambo, 1853.

[_____]. *A Review by a Layman, of a Work Entitled, "New Themes for the Protestant Clergy: Creeds without Charity, Theology without Humanity, and Protestantism without Christianity."* Philadelphia: Lippincott, Grambo, 1852.

Anderson, Gregory Martin. "The Religious Rhetoric of James W. Alexander: Texts and Contexts of an Antebellum Rhetorical Tradition." PhD diss., University of Minnesota, 1994.

Atwater, Lyman H. "The Great Railroad Strike." *Presbyterian Quarterly and Princeton Review* 6 (1877): 719-744.

_____. "The Labor Question in its Economic and Christian Aspects." *Presbyterian Quarterly and Princeton Review* 1 (1872): 468-495.

_____. "The Nature and Effects of Money." *Biblical Repertory and Princeton Review* 34 (1862): 310-357.

_____. "Political Economy a Science—Of What?" *Princeton Review* 1 (1880): 420-443.

_____. "The State in Relation to Morality, Religion, and Education." *Princeton Review* 1 (1878): 395-422.

_____. "The True Progress of Society." *Biblical Repertory and Princeton Review* 24 (1852): 16-38.

Bache, Alexander Dallas. *Report on Education in Europe*. Philadelphia: Lydia R. Bailey, 1839.

Backhouse, James. *A Narrative of a Visit to the Mauritius and South Africa*. London: Hamilton, Adams, 1844.

"Backhouse's *Visit to the Mauritius and South Africa.*" *North British Review* 2 (November 1844): 105-135.

Baird, Robert. "The American Sunday School Union." *Biblical Repertory and Theological Review* 2 (1830): 210-242.

_____. *Religion in America*. New York: Harper & Brothers, 1856.

Baker, Carlos. "Parke Godwin: Pathfinder in Politics and Journalism." In *The Lives of Eighteen from Princeton*, edited by William Thorp, 212-231. Princeton: Princeton University Press, 1946.

Barker, William S. "The Social Views of Charles Hodge (1797-1878): A Study in 19th-Century Calvinism and Conservatism." *Presbyterian* 1 (Spring 1975): 1-22.

Bennett, William J. *America: The Last Best Hope*. 2 vols. Nashville: Nelson Current, 2006.

The Biblical Repertory and Princeton Review: The Index Volume, 1825-1868. Philadelphia: Peter Walker, 1871.

Binder, Frederick M. *The Age of the Common School, 1830-1865*. New York: John Wiley & Sons, 1974.

Boardman, Henry A. "Gall's Lesson System of Education." *Biblical Repertory and Theological Review* 5 (1833): 113-141.

Boardman, Henry A., and James W. Alexander. *The Bible in the Family; and Thoughts on Family Worship*. London: T. Nelson, 1858.

Boylan, Anne M. *Sunday School: The Formation of an American Institution, 1790-1880*. New Haven: Yale University Press, 1990.

Breckinridge, Robert. J. "Denominational Education." *Southern Presbyterian Review* 4 (July 1849): 1-19.

_____. "Hints on Colonization and Abolition." *Biblical Repertory and Theological Review* 5 (1833): 281-305.

A Brief History of the Theological Seminary of the Presbyterian Church at Princeton, New Jersey. Princeton: John Bogart, 1838.

A Brief Outline of the Rise, Progress, and Failure of the Revolutionary Scheme of the Nineteen Van Buren Electors. Baltimore: Sands & Neilson, 1837.

Brisbane, Albert. *Social Destiny of Man*. Philadelphia: C. F. Stollmeyer, 1840.

Broadus, John A. *Memoir of James Petigru Boyce, D. D., LL.D.* New York: A. C. Armstrong and Son, 1893. Reprint, *A Gentleman and a Scholar: A Memoir of James Petigru Boyce*. Vestavia Hills, AL: Solid Ground Christian Books, 2004.

Brownson, Orestes. *Charles Ellwood*. London: Chapman Brothers, 1845.

Burke, Edmund. *Reflections on the Revolution in France*. Edited by Frank M. Turner. London: J. Dodsley, 1790. Reprint, New Haven: Yale University Press, 2003.

_____. *Vindication of Natural Society*. In *The Works of the Right Honourable Edmund Burke*. Vol. 1. Boston: Wells and Lilly, 1826.

Calhoun, David B. *Faith and Learning, 1812-1868*. Vol. 1 of *Princeton Seminary*. Edinburgh: Banner of Truth, 1994.

_____. *The Majestic Testimony, 1869-1929*. Vol. 2 of *Princeton Seminary*. Edinburgh: Banner of Truth, 1996.

Carey, Henry Charles. *A Memoir of Stephen Colwell*. Philadelphia: Henry Carey Baird, 1872.

Carus, William, ed. *Memorials of the Right Reverend Charles Pettit McIlvaine, D. D., D.C.L.* New York: Thomas Whittaker, 1882.

Carwardine, Richard J. *Evangelicals and Politics in Antebellum America*. New Haven: Yale University Press, 1993.

_____. "The Politics of Charles Hodge." In Stewart and Morehead, 247-297.

Chambers, T. W. *The Noon Prayer Meeting*. New York: Board of Publication of the Protestant Dutch Church, 1858.

"Charles Quill." *Trenton State Gazette*. January 16, 1847.

Cheever, George B. *Right of the Bible in our Public Schools*. New York: Robert Carter & Brothers, 1859.

Cleves, Rachel Hope. *The Reign of Terror in America: Visions of Violence from Anti-Jacobinism to Antislavery*. New York: Cambridge University Press, 2009.

Colwell, Stephen. *New Themes for the Protestant Clergy: Creeds without Charity, Theology without Humanity, and Protestantism without Christianity*. Philadelphia: Lippincott, Grambo, 1852.

_____. "The Poor and Poor Laws of Great Britain." *Biblical Repertory and Princeton Review* 13 (1841): 99-131.

_____. *The Position of Christianity in the United States, in Its Relations with our Political Institutions, and Specially with Reference to Religious Instruction in the Public Schools*. Philadelphia: Lippincott, Grambo, 1854.

_____. *The South: A Letter from a Friend in the North, with Special Reference to the Effects of Disunion upon Slavery*. Philadelphia: C. Sherman & Son, 1856.

Committee of the London City Mission, ed. *Lectures Against Socialism*. London: L. and G. Seeley, 1840.

Culver, Raymond B. *Horace Mann and Religion in the Massachusetts Public Schools*. New York: Arno Press, 1969.

Cuyler, Theodore L. "Address on James Waddell Alexander, D.D." In *The Alexander Memorial*, 19-27. New York: Anson D. F. Randolph, 1879.

Dabney, Robert Lewis. *Discussions*. 5 vols. Harrisonburg, VA: Sprinkle Publications, 1994-1999.

De Lubac, Henri. *The un-Marxian Socialist: A Study of Proudhon*. Translated by R. E. Scantlebury. New York: Sheed and Ward, 1948.

Elkins, Stanley, and Eric McKitrick. *The Age of Federalism*. New York: Oxford University Press, 1993.

Engels, Frederick. *Socialism: Utopian and Scientific*. Chicago: Charles H. Kerr, 1914.

Fischer, David Hackett. *The Revolution of American Conservatism: The Federalist Party in the Era of Jeffersonian Democracy*. New York: Harper and Row, 1965.

Foner, Philip S. *History of the Labor Movement in the United States*. 10 vols. New York: International Publishers, 1947-1994.

Forsyth, John. "Alison's History of Europe." *Biblical Repertory and Princeton Review* 15 (1843): 250-270.

Foster, Lawrence. "Free Love and Community: John Humphrey Noyes and the Oneida Perfectionists." In Pitzer, *America's Communal Utopias*, 253-278.

Frohnen, Bruce. *Virtue and the Promise of Conservatism: The Legacy of Burke and Tocqueville*. Lawrence, KS: University Press of Kansas, 1993.

Galloway, Charles B. *Christianity and the American Commonweath*. Nashville: Methodist Episcopal Church, 1898.

Garretson, James M. *An Able and Faithful Ministry: Samuel Miller and the Pastoral Office*. Grand Rapids: Reformation Heritage, 2014.

_____. *Thoughts on Preaching & Pastoral Ministry: Lessons from the Life and Writings of James W. Alexander*. Grand Rapids: Reformation Heritage, 2015.

_____. *Pastor-Teachers of Old Princeton*. Edinburgh: Banner of Truth, 2012.

_____. *Princeton and Preaching: Archibald Alexander and the Christian Ministry*. Edinburgh: Banner of Truth, 2005.

_____. *Princeton and the Work of the Christian Ministry*. 2 vols. Edinburgh: Banner of Truth, 2012.

Gentz, Friedrich von. *The Origin and Principles of the American Revolution, Compared with the Origin and Principles of the French Revolution*. Philadelphia: Asbury Dickins, 1800.

Green, Ashbel. *The Life of Ashbel Green*. Edited by Joseph Huntington Jones. New York: Robert Carter and Brothers, 1849.

Guarneri, Carl J. "Brook Farm and the Fourierist Phalanxes." In
Pitzer, *America's Communal Utopias*, 159-180.

_____. *The Utopian Alternative: Fourierism in Nineteenth-Century
America*. Ithaca, NY: Cornell University Press, 1991.

Guelzo, Allen C. "Charles Hodge's Antislavery Moment." In Stewart and Morehead, 299-325.

Gutek, Gerald L. *Historical and Philosophical Foundations of Education:
A Biographical Introduction*. 3rd ed. Upper Saddle River, NJ:
Prentice Hall, 2001.

Hageman, John Frelinghuysen. *History of Princeton and Its Institutions*.
2 vols. Philadelphia: J. B. Lippincott, 1878.

Hague, William. *William Wilberforce: The Life of the Great Anti-Slave
Trade Campaigner*. London: Harper Collins, 2007.

Hall, Mark David. *Did America Have a Christian Founding?: Separating Modern Myth from Historical Truth*. Nashville: Thomas
Nelson, 2019.

Hall, John. "The Duty of the Church in Relation to Sunday Schools."
Biblical Repertory and Theological Review 4 (1832): 377-393.

_____. "Education in Europe." *Biblical Repertory and Princeton
Review* 12 (1840): 244-268.

_____. "[Memorial] Sermon." In Hodge and Hall, 39-96.

_____. "Mental Cultivation." *Biblical Repertory and Princeton Review* 16 (1844): 463-477.

_____. "The Religious Obligations of Parents." *Biblical Repertory
and Theological Review* 6 (1834): 172-181.

Hall, Robert. *Modern Infidelity Considered with Respect to Its Influence
upon Society*. Charlestown, SC: Samuel Etheridge, 1801.

Harris, J. Henry. *Robert Raikes: The Man and His Work*. Bristol, UK:
E. P. Dutton, 1899.

Harrison, J. F. C. *Robert Owen and the Owenites in Britain and America:
The Quest for the New Moral World*. London: Routledge and
Kegan Paul, 1969.

Hart, D. G., and John R. Muether. *Seeking a Better Country: 300 Years of American Presbyterianism*. Phillipsburg, NJ: Presbyterian and Reformed Publishing, 2007.

Hart, Daryl G. *Defending the Faith: J. Gresham Machen and the Crisis of Conservative Protestantism in Modern America*. Philipsburg, NJ: Presbyterian and Reformed, 2003.

Hatch, Nathan O. *The Democratization of American Christianity*. New Haven: Yale University Press, 1989.

Hayes, William. *Horace Mann's Vision of the Public Schools: Is It Still Relevant?* Lanham, MD: Rowman and Littlefield, 2006.

Helseth, Paul Kjoss. *"Right Reason" and the Princeton Mind: An Unorthodox Proposal*. Phillipsburg, NJ: Presbyterian and Reformed, 2010.

Hillquit, Morris. *History of Socialism in the United States*. New York: Funk and Wagnalls, 1903.

Hodge, Archibald A. *The Life of Charles Hodge, D.D., LL.D.* London: T. Nelson and Sons, 1881.

Hodge, Charles. "Abolitionism." *Biblical Repertory and Princeton Review* 16 (1844): 545-581.

_____. "The Church and the Country." *Biblical Repertory and Princeton Review* 33 (1861): 322-376.

_____. "Civil Government." *Biblical Repertory and Princeton Review* 23 (1851): 125-158.

_____. *A Commentary on the Epistle to the Ephesians*. New York: Carter & Brothers, 1856. Reprint, Edinburgh: Banner of Truth, 1991.

_____. "Diversity of Species in the Human Race." *Biblical Repertory and Princeton Review* 34 (1862): 435-464.

_____. "The Education Question." *Biblical Repertory and Princeton Review* 26 (1854): 535-536.

_____. "Emancipation." *Biblical Repertory and Princeton Review* 21 (1849): 582-607.

_____. "The General Assembly." *Biblical Repertory and Princeton Review* 17 (1845): 437-441.

_____. "The General Assembly." *Biblical Repertory and Princeton Review* 18 (1846): 418-456.

_____. "The General Assembly." *Biblical Repertory and Princeton Review* 19 (1847): 396-444.

_____. *Memorial of Cortlandt Van Rensselaer*. Philadelphia: C. Sherman & Son, 1860.

_____. "[Memorial] Sermon." In Hodge and Hall, 15-35.

_____. "The Princeton Review on the State of the Country and of the Church." *Biblical Repertory and Princeton Review* 37 (1865): 627-657.

_____. "Public Education." *Biblical Repertory* 5 (1829): 370-410.

_____. "Public Religious Education Enforced in a Discussion of Different Plans." In *Home, the School, and the Church; or The Presbyterian Education Repository, Volume 1*, edited by Cortlandt Van Rensselaer, 95-107. Philadelphia: William S. Martien, 1850.

[_____]. "Retrospect of the History of the Princeton Review." In *The Biblical Repertory and Princeton Review: The Index Volume, 1825-1868*, 1-39.

_____. "Slavery." *Biblical Repertory and Princeton Review* 8 (1836): 268-305.

_____. "The State of the Country." *Biblical Repertory and Princeton Review* 33 (1861): 1-36.

_____. "The Unity of Mankind." *Biblical Repertory and Princeton Review* 31 (1859): 103-149.

_____. "The War." *Biblical Repertory and Princeton Review* 35 (1863): 140-169.

_____. "West India Emancipation." *Biblical Repertory and Princeton Review* 10 (1838): 602-644.

Hodge, Charles, and John Hall. *Sermons Preached Before the Congregation of the Presbyterian Church, Corner of Fifth Avenue and Nineteenth Street, at the "Memorial Services," October 9, 1859.*

Appointed in Reference to the Death of their Late Pastor, James Waddel Alexander, D. D. New York: Anson D. F. Randolph, 1859. Reprint, *Mourning a Beloved Shepherd: Memorial Sermons for James W. Alexander.* Birmingham, AL: Solid Ground Christian Books, 2004.

Hoffecker, W. Andrew. "Princeton Theology." In *Dictionary of Christianity in America*, edited by Daniel G. Reid, 941-942. Downers Grove, IL: InterVarsity Press, 1990.

Holifield, E. Brooks. "Republican Dialect or European Accent? The Sound of American Theology." *Church History* 72 (2003): 624-630.

_____. *Theology in America: Christian Thought from the Age of the Puritans to the Civil War.* New Haven: Yale University Press, 2003.

Holt, Michael F. *The Rise and Fall of the American Whig Party: Jacksonian Politics and the Onset of the Civil War.* New York: Oxford University Press, 1999.

Hopkins, Charles Howard. *The Rise of the Social Gospel in American Protestantism, 1865-1915.* New Haven: Yale University Press, 1940.

Howat, Irene. *Streets Paved with Gold: The Story of the London City Mission.* Fearn, UK: Christian Focus, 2003.

Howe, Daniel Walker. "Religion and Politics in the Antebellum North." In *Religion and American Politics: From the Colonial Period to the 1980s*, edited by Mark A. Noll, 121-145. New York: Oxford University Press, 1990.

_____. *What Hath God Wrought: The Transformation of America, 1815-1848.* New York: Oxford University Press, 2007.

Howse, Ernest Marshall. *Saints in Politics: "Clapham Sect" and the Growth of Freedom.* London: Allen & Unwin, 1953.

The James Waddel Alexander Manuscript Collection. Special Collections. Princeton Theological Seminary Library, Princeton, NJ.

Johnson, Gary L. W., ed. *B. B. Warfield: Essays on His Life and Thought*. Phillipsburg, NJ: Presbyterian and Reformed, 2007.

Johnson, Paul. *A History of the American People*. New York: Harper Collins, 1997.

Kirkup, Thomas. *A History of Socialism*. 3rd ed. London: Adam and Charles Black, 1906.

Kliebard, Herbert M., ed. *Religion and Education in America: A Documentary History*. Scranton, PA: International Textbook Company, 1969.

Lochemes, Mary Frederick. *Robert Walsh: His Story*. New York: American-Irish Historical Society, 1941.

Loetscher, Lefferts A. *Facing the Enlightenment and Pietism: Archibald Alexander and the Founding of Princeton Theological Seminary*. Westport, CN: Greenwood Press, 1983.

Lord, William H. "Liberal Christianity." *Biblical Repertory and Princeton Review* 40 (1868): 114-144.

Maclean, John. "Common Schools." *Biblical Repertory and Theological Review* 5 (1833): 217-229.

_____. *A Lecture on a School System for New Jersey*. Princeton: Princeton Press, 1829.

Magness, Phillip W., and Sebastian N. Page. *Colonization after Emancipation: Lincoln and the Movement for Black Resettlement*. Columbia, MO: University of Missouri, 2018.

Mann, Horace. *The Republic and the School*. Edited by Lawrence A. Cremin. New York: Teachers College Press, 1957.

Marshall, Peter. *The Anarchist Writings of William Godwin*. London: Freedom Press, 1986.

Mathews, James McFarlane. *The Bible and Civil Government*. New York: Robert Carter & Brothers, 1851.

Matthews, John. *The Influence of the Bible in Improving the Understanding and Moral Character*. Philadelphia: Presbyterian Board of Education, 1864.

May, Henry F. *Protestant Churches and the Industrial Revolution*. New York: Octagon Books, 1963.

Mayer, Henry. *All on Fire: William Lloyd Garrison and the Abolition of Slavery*. New York: W. W. Norton, 1998.

McDougall, Walter A. *Throes of Democracy: The American Civil War Era*. New York: Harper Collins, 2008.

McIlvaine, Joshua Hall. "The Church and the Poor." *Biblical Repertory and Princeton Review* 34 (1862): 601-634.

_____. "Covenant Education." *Biblical Repertory and Princeton Review* 33 (1861): 238-261.

_____. "Mathusianism." *Biblical Repertory and Princeton Review* 39 (1867): 103-128.

_____. "A Nation's Right to Worship God." *Biblical Repertory and Princeton Review* 31 (1859): 664-697.

McMahon, Darrin M. "Edmund Burke and the Literary Cabal: A Tale of Two Enlightenments." Afterward to Burke, *Reflections on the Revolution in France*, 233-247.

McVickar, John. *Outlines of Political Economy*. New York: Wilder & Campbell, 1825.

Miller, Samuel. *The Christian Education of the Children and Youth in the Presbyterian Church*. Philadelphia: Presbyterian Board of Publication, 1840.

_____. *Memoir of Rev. Charles Nisbet, D.D.* New York: Robert Carter, 1840.

Miller, Jr., Samuel. *The Life of Samuel Miller, D.D., LL.D.* 2 vols. Philadelphia: Claxton, Remsen, and Haffelfinger, 1869.

Minutes of the General Assembly of the Presbyterian Church in the United States of America, Volume 11. Philadelphia: William S. Martien, 1846.

Moffat, James C. "Popular Education." *Biblical Repertory and Princeton Review* 29 (1857): 609-635.

Morgan, Bruce. "Stephen Colwell (1800-1871): Social Prophet Before the Social Gospel." In *Sons of the Prophets: Leaders in*

Protestantism from Princeton Seminary, edited by Hugh T. Kerr, 123-147. Princeton: Princeton University Press, 1963.

More, Hannah. *The Shepherd of Salisbury Plain, and Other Tales*. New York: Derby & Jackson, 1857.

[_____]. *Village Politics: Addresses to All the Mechanics, Journeymen, and Day-Labourers in Great Britain*. York: G. Walker, 1793.

Morris, Celia. *Fanny Wright: Rebel in America*. Harvard: Harvard University Press, 1984.

Morton, A. L. *The Life and Ideas of Robert Owen*. New York: International Publishers, 1962.

Murray, Iain H. *Heroes*. Edinburgh: Banner of Truth, 2009.

_____. *Revival and Revivalism: The Making and Marring of American Evangelicalism, 1750-1858*. Edinburgh: Banner of Truth, 1994.

Myers, Robert Manson, ed. *The Children of Pride: A True Story of Georgia and the Civil War*. New Haven: Yale University Press, 1972.

_____, ed. *A Georgian and Princeton*. New York: Harcourt Brace Jovanovich, 1976.

National Reform Association. *Proceedings of the National Convention to Secure the Religious Amendment of the Constitution of the United States*. Philadelphia: James B. Rogers, 1872.

Noll, Mark A. *America's God: From Jonathan Edwards to Abraham Lincoln*. New York: Oxford University Press, 2000.

_____. "The Founding of Princeton Seminary." *Westminster Theological Journal* 42 (1979): 72-110.

_____. *Princeton and the Republic, 1768-1822*. Vancouver: Regent College Publishing, 1989.

_____. "The *Princeton Review*." *Westminster Theological Journal* 50 (1988): 283-304.

_____, ed. *The Princeton Theology, 1812-1921*. Grand Rapids: Baker Book House, 1983.

_____, ed. *Religion and American Politics: From the Colonial Period to the 1980s.* (New York: Oxford University Press, 1990.

"Notices of Books." *New Englander and Yale Review* 18 (August 1860): 794-850.

"Notices of Recent Publications." *Biblical Repertory and Princeton Review* 42 (1870): 326-340.

Owen, Robert. *A New View of Society and Other Writings.* Edited by Gregory Claeys. London: Penguin Books, 1991.

Owen, Robert, and Alexander Campbell. *Debate on the Evidences of Christianity.* Bethany, VA: Alexander Campbell, 1829.

Owen, Robert Dale. *An Outline of the System of Education at New Lanark.* Glasgow: University Press, 1824.

_____. *The Wrong of Slavery, The Right of Emancipation, and the Future of the African Race in the United States.* Philadelphia: J. B. Lippincott, 1864.

Packard, Frederick A. *The Daily Public School in the United States.* Philadelphia: J. B. Lippincott, 1866.

_____. "English School Systems." *Biblical Repertory and Princeton Review* 15 (1843): 1-22.

_____. "Horace Mann." *Biblical Repertory and Princeton Review* 38 (1866): 74-94.

_____. "Irish School System." *Biblical Repertory and Princeton Review* 14 (1842): 87-119.

_____. *Life of Robert Owen.* Philadelphia: Ashmead & Evans, 1866.

_____. "Religious Instruction in Common Schools." *Biblical Repertory and Princeton Review* 13 (1841): 315-368.

_____. *Teacher Taught: An Humble Attempt to Make the Path of the Sunday-School Teacher Straight and Plain.* Philadelphia: American Sunday School Union, 1839.

_____. *The Teacher Teaching: A Practical View of the Relations and Duties of the Sunday-School Teacher.* Philadelphia: American Sunday School Union, 1861.

[_____]. *Thoughts on the Condition and Prospects of Popular Education in the United States.* Philadelphia: A Waldie, 1836.

Paine, Thomas. *The Rights of Man.* London: J. S. Jordan, 1791.

Perlman, Selig. *A History of Trade Unionism in the United States.* New York: Macmillan, 1923.

Pitzer, Donald E., ed. *America's Communal Utopias.* Chapel Hill, NC: University of North Carolina Press, 1997.

_____. "The New Moral World of Robert Owen and New Harmony." In Pitzer, *America's Communal Utopias,* 88-134.

Potter, Alonzo. *Political Economy.* New York: Harper & Brothers, 1840.

Prime, Samuel. *The Power of Prayer: Illustrated in the Wonderful Displays of Divine Grace at the Fulton Street and Other Meetings in New York.* Halifax: Milner, 1860.

Pulliam, John. *History of Education in America.* 2nd ed. Columbus, OH: Charles Merrill Publishing, 1976.

Rice, Edwin Wilbur. *The Sunday-School Movement, 1780-1917, and the American Sunday School Union, 1818-1917.* Philadelphia: American Sunday School Union, 1917.

Ruffner, William Henry. *Charity and the Clergy: Being a Review by a Protestant Clergyman of the "New Themes Controversy."* Philadelphia: Lippincott, Grambo, 1853.

Rush, Benjamin. "A Defence of the Use of the Bible as a School Book." In *Essays: Literary, Moral, and Philosophical,* 93-113. 2nd ed. Philadelphia: Thomas and William Bradford, 1806.

Scheuermann, Mona. *In Praise of Poverty.* Lexington, KY: University Press of Kentucky, 2002

Schlesinger, Jr., Arthur M. *The Age of Jackson.* Boston: Little, Brown, 1945.

Sherrill, Lewis Joseph. *Presbyterian Parochial Schools, 1846-1870.* New Haven: Yale University Press, 1932.

Simpson, Stephen. *The Working Man's Manual: A New Theory of Political Economy.* Philadelphia: Thomas L. Bonsal, 1831.

Singer, C. Gregg. *A Theological Interpretation of American History.* 3rd ed. Greenville, SC: A Press, 1994.

Skidmore, Thomas. *The Rights of Man to Property!* New York: Alexander Ming, 1829.

Smith, Elwyn Allen. *The Presbyterian Ministry in American Culture: A Study in Changing Concepts, 1700-1900.* Philadelphia: Westminster Press, 1962.

Sprague, William Buell. *Annals of the American Pulpit.* 9 vols. New York: Robert Carter and Brothers, 1857-1869.

Stall, Sylvanus. *How to Pay Church Debts and How to Keep the Church out of Debt.* New York: I. K. Funk, 1881.

Steinfeld, Robert J. "Property and Suffrage in the Early American Republic." *Stanford Law Review* 41 (1989): 335-376.

Steward, Gary. *Princeton Seminary (1812-1929): Its Leaders' Lives and Works.* Phillipsburg, NJ: P&R, 2014.

Stewart, John W. "Introducing Charles Hodge to Postmoderns." In Stewart and Morehead, 1-39.

_____. *Mediating the Center: Charles Hodge on American Science, Language, Literature, and Politics.* Princeton: Princeton Theological Seminary, 1995.

Stewart, John W., and James H. Moorehead, eds. *Charles Hodge Revisited: A Critical Appraisal of His Life and Work.* Grand Rapids: William B. Eerdmans, 2002.

Stott, Anne. *Hannah More: The First Victorian.* Oxford: Oxford University Press, 2003.

Stuart, Moses. *Essay on the Prize-Question, Whether the Use of Distilled Liquors, or Traffic of them, is Compatible at the Present Time, with Making a Profession of Christianity?* New York: John P. Haven, 1830.

Sutton, Robert P. "An American Elysium: The Icarian Communities." In Pitzer, *America's Communal Utopias,* 279-294.

Thompson, Joseph P. *The Workman: His False Friends and His True Friends.* New York: American Tract Society, 1879.

Thornwell, James Henley. "The Christian Doctrine of Slavery." In *The Collected Writings of James Henley Thornwell*, edited by John B. Adger and John L. Girardeau, 4:398-436. Richmond: Presbyterian Committee of Publication, 1873.

Torbett, David. *Theology and Slavery: Charles Hodge and Horace Bushnell*. Macon, GA: Mercer University Press, 2006.

Turner, Frank M. "Edmund Burke: The Political Actor Thinking." Introduction to Burke, *Reflections on the Revolution in France*, xi-xliii.

Tyler, Ransom Hebbard. *The Bible and Social Reform, or, The Scriptures as a Means of Civilization*. Philadelphia: James Challen & Son, 1860.

United States. "Treaty of Peace and Friendship between the United States and the Bey and Subjects of Tripoli, of Barbury." November 4, 1796. *United States Statutes at Large* 8, 155.

Van Rensselaer, Cortlandt, ed. *Home, the School, and the Church; or The Presbyterian Education Repository, Volume 2*. Philadelphia: C. Sherman, 1852.

_____. *Miscellaneous Sermons, Essays, and Addresses*. Philadelphia: J. B. Lippincott, 1861.

Vethake, Henry. *Principles of Political Economy*. Philadelphia: P. H. Nicklin & T. Johnson, 1838.

Walsh, Jr., Robert. *An Appeal from the Judgments of Great Britain respecting the United States of America*. Philadelphia: Mitchell, Ames, and White, 1819.

_____. *Didactics: Social, Literary, Political*. 2 vols. Philadelphia: Carey, Lea, & Blanchard, 1836.

_____. *A Letter on the Genius and Dispositions of the French Government*. Baltimore: P. H. Nicklin, 1810.

Ward, John William. *Andrew Jackson: Symbol for an Age*. New York: Oxford University Press, 1955.

Wayland, Franics. *The Elements of Political Economy*. 4th ed. Boston: Gould & Lincoln, 1841.

Webb, Sidney, and Beatrice Webb. *The History of Trade Unionism.* London: Longmans, Green, 1894.

Webster, Daniel. *Defence of the Christian Religion and the Religious Instruction of the Young.* New York: Mark H. Newman, 1844.

Wells, David F. *Reformed Theology in America: A History of Its Modern Development.* Grand Rapids: Baker Books, 1997.

Weylland, John Matthias. *The Man with the Book; or, The Bible among the People.* London: William Hunt, 1872.

_____. *These Fifty Years.* London: S. W. Partridge, 1884.

Wind, John A. *Do Good to All People as You Have the Opportunity: A Biblical Theology of the Good Deeds Mission of the New Covenant Community.* Phillipsburg, NJ: P&R, 2019.

Wood, Gordon S. *Empire of Liberty: A History of the Early Republic, 1789-1815.* New York: Oxford University Press, 2009.

Zaspel, Fred G. *The Theology of B. B. Warfield.* Wheaton: Crossway, 2010.

About the author

Dr. Gary Steward (B.A., M.Div., Th.M, Ph.D) is an Assistant Professor of History at Colorado Christian University in Lakewood, Colorado. Prior to this, he served as the pastor of Calvary Baptist Church in St. John's, Newfoundland. He holds a Ph.D in Church History and Historical Theology from the Southern Baptist Theological Seminary in Louisville, Kentucky, and currently lives in the Denver area with his wife and three children.

Subject Index

A

Abolitionism, 10, 31, 50, 66, 87, 90, 91, 92, 93, 94, 95, 96, 97, 99, 103, 104, 109, 129, 154
Absolutism, 56
Adams, Henry, 46
Adams, John, 45, 46, 49, 58
Adams, John Quincy, 40, 41, 42, 43, 45, 46, 65
Alcohol, 35, 36, 80
Alexander, Archibald, 11, 12, 15, 16, 18, 26, 58, 102, 119, 126, 142, 154
Alexander, Henry Carrington, 19, 30, 47
Alexander, James W.
  as Charles Quill, 76, 77, 78, 81, 82, 111
  as preacher, 14, 16
  as professor, 21, 22, 37, 107, 132, 148
  as scholar, 11, 21
  as tutor, 17, 18, 40
  birth, 14
  call to ministry, 18
  calvinism, 24, 25, 28, 37
  catholicity, 28, 29, 37
  Charlotte Court House, 18
  concern for the poor, 32, 37, 63, 111, 139, 141, 143
  conversion, 16
  death, 12, 14, 23, 87
  depression, 17
  disapproval of slavery, 88, 89
  Duane Street Church, 21

  education, 15, 17, 30
  family, 14, 19, 30, 44, 47
  Fifth Avenue Church, 22
  First Presbyterian Church in Trenton, 19
  letters, 12, 13, 39, 76, 78
  marriage, 19
  on social reform, 130, 137, 144, 147, 154
  politics, 39, 40, 43, 45, 58, 154
  rejection of abolitionism, 87, 91, 93, 97
  rejection of secular education, 111
  religious education of children, 144
  sickness, 18, 20, 22, 23
  temperance movement, 35, 36
  trade unionism, 74
  utopian socialism, 68, 74, 82
Alexander, James Waddell, Jr., 19
Alexander, Joseph Addison, 11, 47, 48, 119, 129, 134
Alexander, William Cowper, 44, 47
Allibone, Samuel Austen, 34
American Sunday School Union, 12, 19, 20, 29, 32, 33, 69, 115, 116, 135, 145, 146, 147, 148, 150
Antebellum America, 7, 8, 9, 10, 12, 13, 30, 37, 39, 40, 60, 63, 65, 66, 67, 70, 74, 75, 87, 107, 111
Atheism, 52, 54, 55, 60, 135
Atwater, Lyman, 150
Augustine, 26
Authority of Scripture, 96

207

B

Baptists, 27
Belgian Revolution, 52
Biblical Inerrancy, 8
Bonaparte, Napoleon, 51
Breckinridge, Robert J., 99, 120
Brisbane, Arthur, 66
Brownson, Orestes, 57, 67
Burke, Edmund, 48, 49, 51, 125
Burr, Sr., Aaron, 7

C

Cabell, Elizabeth, 19
Calvin, John, 136
Campbell, Alexander, 65
Candlish, Robert S., 132
Capitalism, 63
Carnahan, James, 119
Carrington, Edward C., 41, 42
Channing, William Henry, 66
Cholera Outbreak, 55
Church Membership, 36
Civil War, 9, 40, 58, 64, 67, 100, 105, 129
Clapham Sect, 49
Clay, Henry, 41
Colwell, Stephen, 33, 34, 35, 36, 37, 126, 129
Cuyler, Theodore, 13

D

Davies, Samuel, 7, 8, 24
de Lafayette, Marquis, 66
de Saint-Simon, Henri, 72
De Tocqueville, Alexis, 125
Declaration of Independence, 102, 127
Democracy, 39, 45, 46, 52, 53, 54, 56, 59, 60, 63, 71, 93, 129, 154

Democratic, 39, 40, 44, 45, 60, 128
Dickinson, Jonathan, 7
Divorce, 71

E

Economic Collectivism, 63, 85
Edwards, Jonathan, 7, 8, 24
Egalitarian, 39, 44, 58, 59, 60, 63, 66, 68, 71, 74, 84, 93, 95, 109, 125, 128, 129, 150, 154
Erasmus, Desiderius, 80
Evans, George Henry, 76, 79
Expositional Preaching, 139

F

Fatalism, 24
Federalist Party, 45, 46, 58, 59
Forsyth, John, 51
Fourier, Charles, 66, 68, 69, 72, 75
Franklin, Benjamin, 80
French Revolution, 45, 48, 50, 51, 52, 58, 69, 70, 75, 94, 150

G

Garrison, William Lloyd, 87, 96
Gladden, Washington, 36
Godwin, Parke, 66, 68
Gould, James, 46
Greeley, Horace, 66, 68

H

Hageman, John Frelinghuysen, 44
Hall, Basil, 53
Hall, John, 12, 14, 15, 16, 17, 39, 87, 114, 115, 132
Hamilton, Alexander, 45

Hodge, Charles, 11, 13, 14, 16, 19, 25, 27, 42, 45, 58, 60, 88, 93, 98, 99, 100, 114, 119, 121, 126, 150
House of Representatives, 41
Humanism, 64, 67, 70, 82, 84, 94, 109
Hyper-Calvinism, 24, 26

I

Infidel Politics, 57

J

Jackson, Andrew, 39, 40, 41, 42, 43, 45, 47, 52, 55, 58, 60, 63, 66, 71, 84, 94, 109, 129
Jefferson, Thomas, 46, 52, 58, 60, 65, 66, 112
Jones, Charles Colcock, 105
July Revolution, 51

L

Liberalism, 56
Lincoln, Abraham, 8, 33, 102
Linnaeus, Carl, 80
Locke, John, 48
Lord, William H., 151
Luther, Martin, 26

M

M'Cheyne, Robert Murray, 24
Madison, James, 65, 66
Mann, Horace, 113, 114, 116, 117
Martyn, Henry, 24
Miller, Samuel, 11, 16, 21, 36, 52, 58, 119, 126, 144
Mobs, 52, 53, 54, 57
Monroe, James, 65
More, Hannah, 49, 50, 76, 83, 150

N

Nasmith, David, 142, 143, 150
Newton, John, 24
Nisbet, Charles, 52, 59
Noyes, John Humphrey, 64

O

Old Princeton, 4, 5, 8, 9, 11, 13, 35, 58, 68, 129
Old School-New School, 27
Owen, John, 5, 24
Owen, Robert, 63, 64, 65, 69, 117, 133
Owen, Robert Dale, 66, 72, 93

P

Packard, Frederick Adolphus, 69, 74, 114, 115, 116, 117, 118, 127, 128, 135, 138, 145, 148, 150
Paine, Thomas, 48, 50, 52, 53, 96
Parochial Schools, 118, 120, 121, 122, 145
Pascal, Blaise, 35
Patriotism, 42, 47, 113
Polygamy, 71
Populism, 39, 40, 45, 52, 58, 60
Princeton Seminary, 4, 5, 7, 8, 15, 16, 21, 22, 33, 37, 60, 87, 105, 126
Public Schools, 116, 117, 118, 121, 122, 123

Q

Quakers, 27

R

Radicalism, 83, 84, 92, 93, 94, 109, 133

Raikes, Robert, 144, 150
Randolph, John, 96
Randolph, Richard, 96
Rape, 89
Rauschenbusch, Walter, 36
Roman Catholicism, 24, 29, 57, 114
Ruffner, William Henry, 34
Russell, David, 25

S

Scholasticism, 25
Scott, Thomas, 24
Second Party Era, 39, 40
Secularism, 54, 57, 69, 123, 124, 125, 127, 128, 129, 133, 151
Separatists, 27
Slavery, 34, 42, 66, 87, 88, 89, 90, 91, 93, 94, 96, 97, 98, 99, 100, 101, 102, 104, 105, 106, 107, 108, 109
Social Gospel, 33, 34, 36, 37
Social Justice, 5, 7
Socialism, 10, 35, 63, 64, 67, 68, 69, 70, 71, 72, 73, 74, 76, 82, 83, 84, 85, 93, 129, 133, 135, 142
Society of Free Inquirers, 53
Stuart, Moses, 36
Sunday Schools, 144, 145, 146, 147, 150
Synod of Dort, 27
Systematic Theology, 137

T

Tariffs, 41, 42, 43
Thornwell, James Henley, 99, 121

Trade Unionism, 10, 63, 74, 76, 77, 78, 82, 83, 84, 85, 93, 129
Turretin, Francis, 24
Tyranny, 51, 56, 92

U

Ultra-Democracy, 57
United States Constitution, 45, 92, 126
Utopian Socialism, 63

V

Van Buren, Martin, 59
Van Rensselaer, Cortlandt, 99, 121, 122
Venn, Henry, 49
Vethake, Henry, 78
von Bismarck, Otto, 56
von Gerlach, Ernst Ludwig, 56

W

Walsh Jr., Robert, 46, 47, 48, 51, 83
Washington, George, 45, 58
Wesley, Charles, 28
Westminster Confession of Faith, 24
Wetmore, A. R., 143
White House, 65
Wilberforce, William, 49, 92, 94, 133, 150
Witherspoon, John, 7
Witsius, Herman, 24
Women's Rights, 66, 93
Wright, Frances, 66, 93, 133

CPSIA information can be obtained
at www.ICGtesting.com
Printed in the USA
FSHW011311030122
87356FS